NASKAPI

The Savage Hunters of the Labrador Peninsula

THE CIVILIZATION OF THE AMERICAN INDIAN SERIES

NASKAPI
The Savage Hunters of the Labrador Peninsula

Frank G. Speck

Foreword by J. E. Michael Kew

NORMAN
UNIVERSITY OF OKLAHOMA PRESS

TO MY WIFE

FLORENCE INSLEY SPECK

Copyright 1935, 1963 by the University of Oklahoma Press. New edition
copyright 1977 by the University of Oklahoma Press, Publishing Division of
the University. Manufactured in the U.S.A.

Naskapi: The Savage Hunters of the Labrador Peninsula is Volume 10 in *The
Civilization of the American Indian Series.*

ISBN: 0-8061-1412-6

LC # 77-365978

TABLE OF CONTENTS

LIST OF ILLUSTRATIONS

Foreword to the New Edition

NASKAPI has long been one of my favorite ethnographic works on Canadian Indians. Speck's unassuming account of Naskapi religious thought has a perennially fresh sense of discovery which is a joy to share with students, and our dog-eared library copy of the 1935 edition long ago announced this new edition to be overdue.

The Naskapi Indians are one of several Algonquian-speaking groups occupying interior Labrador and northern Quebec. Along with Montagnais and Cree they form a series of contiguous regional groups whose dialects constitute a language continuum stretching across the Canadian sub-arctic from Labrador to central Alberta. The multiplicity of names on our maps for local bands, and groups of bands, is consistent with Indian usage but confusing to outsiders. From a linguistic and cultural perspective there is relatively little to distinguish one band from another. The term Cree could appropriately be extended to include the people Speck describes, for the main cultural differences between various groups arise from slight variations in subsistence activities, which are related to regional variance in abundance of different species of game and fish. Differences certainly existed in styles of decorative work on clothing, forms of canoes and snowshoes, minor elements of mythology, and the like, but basic similarities overshadow differences. *Naskapi* is a work which stands well as a representative account of the religious life of Cree and related tribes.

The culture of these people as we know it from historical records and works of anthropologists, is the culture of the fur trade era. Trading posts have operated in the region more or less continuously since the late seventeenth century. Indian life at the time of initial White contact was not fully described and changes effected by the fur trade have made reconstruction problematic. However, the traders' influences were limited and relatively stable over a long period of time. Paramount changes in Indian culture seem most likely to have centered on realignment of social units and hunting efforts in response to policies and persuasions of traders. There was an increase in geographic mobility among Indians, and an overall expansion of Cree territory at the expense of other tribes less closely connected with traders. It is also certain that total populations decreased with the advent of smallpox and other new diseases.

Characteristically, trading posts became centers of annual congregations of families and bands during the slack summer season. Guns, axes, knives, needles, and cloth enhanced technical efficiency and became essentials of everyday life, and most important, solidly established the traders who controlled such wealth as the local bosses of a sociopolitical structure extending down through band leaders to heads of families and multi-family lodge groups. Finally, the family hunting territory, which Speck identified and mapped extensively among many Algonquian speaking tribes, emerged as a pivotal unit of land use or resource management. Though it now appears that family hunting territories may not have been an indigenous feature of this area, as Speck believed, it is clear they were an integral part of the long enduring fur trade era.

Fur traders brought a new technology and created a new economy of sorts, but they did not change basic subsistence patterns or dependence of Indians on the natural resources of their land. Hunting and fishing remained the mainstay of life, and the vital religious and philosophical foundations of Indian culture persisted too. Proprietary rights over land have been regarded as a major mechanism which enabled rational, controlled harvesting of game resources by these hunters and trappers. However, it seems to me that the Indian idea of reciprocity between man and nature was equally important. Game gives itself to man, man must give in return. It is this relationship between man and nature, the widely spread and certainly ancient ideological foundation of sub-arctic cultures, which Speck reveals in *Naskapi*.

Speck began his career in anthropology just after the turn of the century, studying under Franz Boas at Columbia University, undertaking original linguistic and ethnographic fieldwork from the start. His earliest published articles were on the Algonquian Pequot and Mohegan Indians. Throughout a long career at the University of Pennsylvania he maintained interest in fieldwork and museum collecting, devoting the bulk of his efforts to recording accounts of the rapidly disappearing Algonquian and Iroquoian peoples of the Eastern United States and Canada. His work among northern Algonquians apparently began in 1909 and continued well on into the 1920's, mainly through a series of visits to trading posts and settlements of Quebec during both winter and summer seasons. It was from notes assembled through these efforts and from his careful reading of historical records that Speck compiled *Naskapi*.

When his northern fieldwork began, Naskapi territory was wilderness and the fur trade was in full sway. Highways and railroads were tentatively reaching northwards but development of gigantic mines and electrical power installations were a long way off. Though they now number nearly 13,000, in 1915 the Cree-Montagnais-Naskapi of Quebec were only slightly more than 5,000 in number, and were scattered over an immense tract of territory. Considering distances, lack of modern means of transportation, and no doubt lack of funds, Speck's work was a notable achievement.

The people he met were hunters and fishermen, supplementing their diet with a few imported groceries obtained in exchange for furs, but living mainly off the country. Meat of caribou, moose, bear, beaver, and hare along with fish were staple foods. Christian missionaries were at work and a little schooling was available, but the indigenous language and religious beliefs flourished. The Indian culture encountered here was far from the elusive "memory culture" of the developed and civilized regions to the south. It was a vibrant, living culture and Speck did justice to what he found. His work touched on almost all aspects of life and was reported in a long series of articles and monographs.

Naskapi is frankly and squarely about religious beliefs and practices. When Speck mentions animals or hunting, decorative work on baskets, or clothing, it is to get at the underlying ideological connections between these and the supernatural. However, the book is not tightly organized, having almost the character of a collection of separate essays. While such discursive sections and some of the terminology are old fashioned, Speck's basic approach is completely up-to-date. He gets at the subject through the minds of his informants, letting them tell the readers about their life. He gives us rich illustrations from his field notes and enlarges on issues with references to the work of earlier scholars. Speck's was not the speculative approach. He did not presume to learn the messages of the diviner or the dreamer by direct personal experience, nor did he attempt to guess what the messages were. Instead he asked questions and told plainly what the answers were.

Although it is the Naskapi who reveal for us their world, Speck has given to their accounts an integration which is that of the scholar and outside observer, not the actor. As with most small scale societies lacking full-time religious specialists or philosophers, Naskapi cosmology and religion are implicit and pervasive in all aspects of life. There was no codification, no analytic dismemberment of one part of life from another. To set out to study and write a book about their religious life was, therefore, to violate from the start the native view of things. This is the old and thorny dilemma which the ethnographer can never completely escape. There is a good deal of Speck in this account, but how unobtrusive he must have been in his dealing with the people, how careful he was to listen to them and to resist the temptation to oversimplify. It was from long experience and with great regard for his informants' views that he leads us to the central, informative perception that ". . . hunting is a holy occupation."

Descendants of Speck's Naskapi friends are now experiencing a series of catastrophic disruptions which threaten to extinguish forever their traditional way of life and the remarkable balance with nature their ancestors achieved. In 1967 the start of work on the massive Churchill Falls hydroelectric complex in Labrador began the destruction of the northeastern Naskapi territory. In 1972 bulldozers started on the even larger James Bay development which will ultimately transform and destroy the rivers flowing westward from the heartland of Naskapi territory into James Bay. Those few Crees of Misstassini, Rupert House, and Fort George, holding precariously to a life of hunting and trapping, struggling for a few brief months each winter to maintain the balance through hunting, dreaming and propitiating the souls of bear and beaver, will become fewer and fewer. Soon their world, the world Speck tells us about, will be gone forever.

It would be too much to suggest that had we read Speck's account forty years ago and taken its lesson to heart, that the course of history would have been different. But there is still a lesson and a warning for all of us in this revelation of the Naskapi's certain grasp of the reciprocity between man and nature, and their equally certain, unequivocal acceptance of man's heavy responsibility to make return for what he gets.

Vancouver, B.C.   J. E. Michael Kew
December, 1976

Naskapi Indian chief of Northern Labrador. (From R. J. and F. H. Flaherty, *My Eskimo Friends,* New York, 1924)

NASKAPI

The Savage Hunters of the Labrador Peninsula

INTRODUCTION

Chapter One

Outline of the Ethnology of the Region

AMONG the host of thoughts that sometimes impress themselves upon the mind are those bringing before the imagination the peopling of vast areas in North America before the arrival of Europeans. And there follows a vision of the era of first contact with the old world. Among the various parts of America which can so be conjured up in vision, there are some for which we have abundant material in published sources upon which to draw, notably the Carolinas, the Virginia and the northern New England coasts. But these scenes of wild life, of uncivilized tribes and barbarous events—barbarity marking the behavior of whites as well as of natives—are mostly of the past, and so they have become tinted with the soft light of distance and romance. It is largely in the more northern latitudes that we come within the borderline of the life of the past merging with that of the present, where those conditions survive under which native man in northeastern North America still lives in the environment which has continued to be his normal one from many prehistoric generations to the present. Here, as one proceeds farther from the frontiers of civilization, step by step the native cultures unfold themselves as though in retrospect, terminating among the Eskimo, whose contemporary existence represents in act and thought the behavior of man of an early new-stone age Short of the Eskimo sphere—entirely a coastal one, however, which has long engaged the attention of many intrepid and careful explorers—there remains that of the most northerly Indian tribes whose life, for its part, is a partition of existence in the forests of the interior plateau and on the coasts of the Labradorean peninsula.

Since the middle of the century before the last, the interior of the plateau region geographically known as the Labrador peninsula, lying north of the Gulf of St. Lawrence and east of Hudson Bay, has been inhabited by a score of closely related bands of Algonkian-speaking Indians, estimated to number approximately between three and four thousand, whose names and locations are shown in figure 1

FIGURE 1

Map of Labrador Peninsula from author's survey showing approximate distribution since 1850 of local groups or bands of Montagnais-Naskapi and Eskimo. The blank areas on the northern and eastern coasts are, or were, occupied by Eskimo. As late as the eighteenth century the latter existed on the north shore of the Gulf of St. Lawrence west at least to the longitude of Anticosti Island (from *American Anthropologist*, Vol. XXXIII, 1931).

as determined through a survey made over some years and published in a separate report from which the chart is reproduced. The local bands form loose geographical and, to an extent, dialectical units recognized and named by the Indians themselves. [1]

The older tribal titles, Montagnais and Naskapi, assigned to these bands collectively, have, on account of misleading political inferences, been changed to the form *Montagnais-Naskapi*. [2] The published ethnology of the entire region is comprised within the covers of a single monograph [3] which treats at first hand solely the populations adjacent to Ungava Bay almost fifty years ago. Only a few pages are devoted in this report to the engrossing subject of the spiritual beliefs and practices of the same people; and we look in vain for other original sources of descriptions of their religion. Since the Jesuit fathers, laboring among the savages of the vast peninsula during the seventeenth and eighteenth centuries, ceased to write their impressions of native life of the region, no attention worth mentioning has been given to this lacuna of ethnology. It seems appropriate, therefore, to mention these circumstances in introducing the first study of religious life to be made among these people whose phase of culture, marginally isolated, is characteristic of an area covering nearly one-twelfth of the continent of North America. The writers of theoretical treatises have in their turn suffered from the lack of information from an area so important: accordingly, we look in vain for treatment of the Labradorean types of spiritual belief in the generalized studies of religion of races living primitively.

Though the Montagnais-Naskapi are found to be an exceptionally crude and simple people, they possess an essentially religious nature. Obtaining subsistence solely by the chase, they have worked out a spiritualistic system as complete and as artificial for gaining control over animal spirits as their hunting devices and weapons are effective in accomplishing the physical slaughter of game.

A glance at the culture history of these seminomadic bands shows strikingly their lack of material progress since some period of culture history coincident with the mesolithic age. Sheltered only in draughty caribou-skin or bark tents, clad in caribou-skin raiment, using mostly bone and wooden implements, and professing neither political institutions nor government, they follow no occupation or industry

1. Results of the first survey of the history and distribution of these bands, with bibliographical reference, are given in an article by F. G. Speck, "Montagnais-Naskapi Bands and Early Eskimo Distribution in the Labrador Peninsula," *American Anthropologist*, Vol. XXXIII (1931), No. 4.
2. A. I. Hallowell, "The Physical Characteristics of the Indians of Labrador," *Journal de la Société des Américanistes de Paris*, XXI (1929), 338, n. 1.
3. L. M. Turner, "Ethnology of the Ungava District," *11th Annual Report, Bureau American Ethnology* (Washington, 1889-90).

other than hunting wild animals and fishing amid the most physically exacting and rigorous climatic environments of the continent.
One may account for lack of government and other social institutions by visualizing the sparsity of population and its scattered
manner of living in family groups. The culture province is typical
of the "snowshoe stage" described by Birket-Smith. Compared with
the agricultural and socially complex native populations everywhere
to the south of them, they stand comparable in cultural low-relief
with the backward Athapascan of northwestern Canada and the
northern tribes of California and the Rocky Mountain plateau area.
In general, we may imagine, as Goldenweiser concludes for the
Eskimo, that progress has stopped because their civilization was
completed ages ago, and the urge toward further mastery of conditions of the country and development of its resources has ceased
through their accomplishing a state of culture balance, to which
bodies and mental dispositions have achieved an adjustment. (Pl. 1.)

But in how far this condition is true of their religious life, I
propose to show in this study. We shall survey varied aspects of
their religious life which appear in native cosmology, in quasi-
scientific superstitions, in theories of animal-spirit conquest and self-
or soul-mastery, in control by thought, wish-force, miracle performance, and finally in lyric composition and symbolic art, which
form no small part of the religious system. We shall then be in a
position to observe something of what achievement in the non-
material sphere has been attained in respect to emotional qualities
of religious behavior and intellectual insight. The Montagnais-
Naskapi, by comparison with those more advanced types of civilization having abundant social dissipations and materialistic distractions,
appear to be dominated by religious associations. [4]

The impression of the primitiveness of these people is even so
strong at the present day as to lead an eminent contemporary writer

4. The conditions of life here and the fate in hardship of these natives of the cold-forest and steppes zones of
Canada have evoked much commiseration among writers on the North, which they fully deserve; but it is chiefly
because of their singular adaptation and fitness to the places where they are found that they claim our attention
and evoke interest in the principles underlying the processes rather than pity for their lot. Said one of the habitués
of the country over a century ago: "The country of which I have been drawing the limits is perhaps the part the
least favored by nature, in point of climate and soil, of the inhabited Globe. Men placed here have no other resource
but to prey upon the inferior animals around them, for the soil, composed of moss, sand and rock, is too sterile and
the climate too cold to produce a substitute for satisfying the cravings of hunger; often does the poor miserable
sinner retire to his hard cold bed without a supper and leave it next morning without a prospect of procuring for
himself and his family a breakfast or a dinner.

"Very few sights, I believe, can be more distressing to the feelings of humanity than a Labrador savage, surrounded by his wife and five or six small children, half famished with cold and hunger, in a hole dug out of the snow
and screened from the inclemency of the weather with the branches of trees. Their whole furniture is a kettle, hung
over the fire, not for the purpose of cooking victuals, but melting snow." James McKenzie, The King's Posts (1808),
as quoted in L. R. Masson, Les Bourgeois de la Compagnie du Nord-ouest (Quebec, 1890) p. 407.

to characterize them as "the most degraded of all Algonquians,"[5] possibly relying for his estimate upon the declaration of the Jesuit author, Gabriel Sagard (1636), who described the Montagnais in like terms, and a later officer of the Northwest Company, James McKenzie (1808), who paints a melancholy picture of Montagnais and Naskapi intelligence and conduct.[6]

A few remarks upon the character of religious feeling among these bands may serve to define conditions now prevailing in the field. It is not the habit of these Indians to seek information concerning what they do not know. Matters of knowledge pertaining to their own religious beliefs are passed by with no concern in many cases, even when a single question would supply the missing facts.[7] To cite an example: When I spent several days interrogating various elderly men on the character of *Tce''mɔntu*, Great [[Real]] Spirit, and when none of them seemed sure as to whether the ancients knew of the concept, I was deeply interested in what would be the testimony of the centenarian, Étienne, a notorious individual of the Lake St. John band. But after getting his opinion not an individual among the others evinced enough interest in the mooted question to show a spark of curiosity over Étienne's recollections. I might add that Étienne himself showed a similar apathy, for when questioned about the belief in dwarfs he was unable to discuss it, because even he had not heard much particularly concerning them. Yet he proved valuable in other topics which were closer to his experiences.

The same is true of the details of Christian belief. I do not believe, from my observation of them, that these people ever voluntarily ask a single question respecting creed. Not one that I have questioned cares a whit about the character of deity, the nature of retribution, the problem of trinity, the virgin birth. They accept without scepticism; they perform without systematic reasoning when once creed has become a part of tradition. The mention of these qualities is intended to aid in understanding the tenor of mind of these savages as applied to their own religious developments. To illustrate further,

5. A. C. Haddon, *The Races of Man* (1925), p. 130

6. James McKenzie (1808), in Masson, op. cit. With somewhat tempered prejudice he says: "Free from their infancy, however, from restraint, and forced, early, to think and act for themselves, they acquire much cunning and sagacity in whatever may concern their own manner of life, and if we can find among them none who can please the eye by their own cleanliness, yet, we meet with some who are endowed with sufficient natural sense to puzzle the savant" (p. 419). McKenzie's opinion of the so-called Montagnais or the Shore Indians is even lower; although being Christians, he says they possess "indolence, ingratitude, malice, stubbornness and a propensity to drinking, stealing, lying and trickery" (ibid., p. 421).

7. McKenzie, op. cit., p. 410, accuses them of the same trait of mind in response to his inquiry of their traditional origin; he received a vacant stare from many that he questioned. They were, he adds, "the only tribes of savages I found who live in such perfect ignorance and indifference about their origin."

the frame and log houses occupied by some of them who have settled down to a semicivilized existence are decorated inside with framed chromos and prints of the Virgin Mary and of Jesus in agony carrying the cross, on the cross, before the scribes, before Pilate, and similar themes utterly beyond the comprehension of their native owners. Ask a few questions as to their meaning and you get a "don't know" in a tone implying that you ought at least to know that much yourself. Indeed, I do not believe that one of them would of his own volition buy one of these pictures since they are trafficked to them by the priests at prices by no means cheap, reaching amounts that I am convinced no Indian of this region has been known to spend voluntarily for anything except tobacco, liquor, food, or clothing and equipment. For the white metal crucifixes four or five inches long, worn by the women on a ribbon hanging from the neck, they pay the priests two dollars and a half. And as fast as the savages are learning to pray to the European God, the Europeans are learning to scoff, as one of the missionary priests has been heard to lament!

The Montagnais-Naskapi have no formal religion any more than they have a nationality. They lack consciousness of religion as an objective property of life. Nevertheless, it is just as true to say that every individual male hunter of this nomadic race holds to a doctrine and a system of practices by which he maintains and propagates his existence in the flesh. Every successful hunter is more or less of a conjuror adjusting himself to a realm of the Unknown which he senses about him, and of which he thinks he sees everywhere evidences as convincing as those he can grasp with his hands. This theory— an intensely practical one to him—is an individual concern, not some- thing brought to his attention by any school of sages, nor controlled by a long-evolved heritage of standardized teaching, but by a process of independent experience interpreted out of the background of sug- gestion leveled upon the mind of the native by the tribally inherited pattern. He imitates the practices; he profits by the sayings and doings of his elders through association with them in their wander- ings as he grows from boyhood to maturity.

In short, he learns two things as the requirements of existence: "to work," that is, to hunt, trap, fish, to make and use the articles employed therein; and to "operate mantu' (Manitu)," a native term the meaning of which we can scarcely grasp, but which represents something near our notion of unseen force. The two are equally important and inseparable, according to his notion. This means that a spiritual factor in human industrial activity is as important a mechanical process as a physical. This, then, for the sake of dealing with these aspects of life under an arbitrary term in our language, we may call religion. All phases of native life in the region under consideration are pervaded by it. The ethnologist cannot escape it in looking over any trait in their culture except social organization, which is rather peculiar. Accordingly, in my study, I have touched upon many topics which, as Europeans think of them, would appear to be concerned solely with practical industry such as hunting equipment, dress, and ornamentation. The reason has been that these crafts, as they are actually regarded in native belief, are as spiritual as they are practical in their power to function; the sum total of which is that supernatural agencies reign in the life of hunters who manifest themselves to be at heart confirmed mystics in their peculiar attitude toward existence. Indeed, the internal life of the people comprises a system of belief and practices, without an understanding of which it would be hopeless to deal with the ethnology of the area, so thoroughly does it permeate every act in life. The business of creative ethnology being to interpret it, not merely to describe it, the implications of a study of this character are sufficiently eloquent; to fulfill the requirements in an ideal sense would call for a complete mastery of the material. In the course of a single lifetime this opportunity hardly comes to the student of preliterate people.

It may seem that the tendency to dematerialize nature, as these tribes have done in their system of thought, has been overstressed in my study. But it is against the artificial interpretation of native practices that I have long been on guard. Therefore, I have followed the plan of presenting the comments and explanations of native informants by transcribing as literally as possible the notes taken down by rapid notation during the discussions with them. This accounts for the first-person style of many passages which may seem didactic. Many of the explanations offered are paraphrased from native texts to be published later, while some have been entered here in phrases with translations.

The generalized interpretations, where such were made in accordance with our system of religious study, were carried back into the field time and again, being read and translated to selected informants for their approval and criticism. Such a process is expensive and protracted, yet it has a great advantage over taking notes and finally preparing them away from the sources. The likelihood of intrusion of the author's subjective reasoning on the material is thereby much reduced.

In accordance with the idea that hunting is a holy occupation and that game animals are holy as well, we see how the entire aboriginal life and being of this people is held in a holy light. This simple statement explains the whole economic and social doctrinal program of the natives. The distinction between the meat of wild and domestic animals is wide. The diet consisting of wild game was to the ancients a sanctified medicinal one. A similar feeling seems widespread among Algonkian-speaking peoples, though the subject has attracted little attention among ethnologists. I would strongly commend it for research as a trait in primitive belief of much significance among the hunting cultures.

Another matter of concern in treating the topic is that Montagnais-Naskapi religion, being an unorganized mode of thought, evinces some ideas which are firmly established and which amount almost to a creed, and others which are most indefinite and perplexing. The classification and arrangement of the latter depends, then, entirely upon the subjective judgment of the essayist.

The unelaborated natural philosophy of the Northeast seems to have consisted of scarcely more cosmology than we find among the Eskimo. The earth appears always to have existed in about the same form. The great changes in nature seem to have been brought about in the transformations of men and animals. In general, the animals have evolved from human beings through the operation of magic or the machination of conjurors. And among them, as the mythical heroes, there is the pre-eminent figure of *Tsəka'bec*, whose rôle assumes the prominence of that of a culture-hero. These statements apply to all the band divisions of the peninsula that have been so far consulted.

The Algonkian-speaking populations of the extreme northeast do not show those communal developments of belief and religious performance that mark the tribes of the central regions. Medicine societies and image masks are lacking. The vastness of the country, the sparsity of the population, and the necessity of their separating into family groups remaining out of contact with each other for long periods of time during the winter, might in themselves be sufficient to account for the absence of community celebrations. Social gatherings for worship or religious performances in general would be quite impossible except for the short period of summer rendezvous at the seacoast. [8] And even here, amidst the abundance of purchasable food and the excitement of trade, not to mention the distractions provided by the Roman missions, which for a century have claimed their attention, little opportunity is left for the carrying out of prolonged rites of assembly. We observe only the semireligious social round dances and games at such times. And it is quite probable that this condition may have held likewise in the past. The professional conjuror is said to have displayed his power at these times, but we miss completely the feature of religious congregation and organized worship that so strongly stands forth among the tribes of similar speech affinity in the central and Great Lakes regions, where a more genial climate, a more abundant game supply, and especially the economic blessings of cereal cultivation made possible a more numerous and less nomadic population, at the same time providing both leisure time and the means of subsistence for those who gathered to participate. The horizons of several other common central Algonkian traits disappear suddenly when, turning northward, we reach the Montagnais frontier. Due consideration, of course, must be given to the possibility that traits being diffused failed to reach them. Perhaps, even under their pauperized circumstances, the Naskapi could have acquired the spirit of carrying on religious activity in congregated bodies if they had experienced sufficient contact with tribes possessing group festivals to have learned and imitated from them. For some such thing is true in respect to their acquisition of Catholicism. The fact, however, that no religious organizations exist, whether because of isolation or poverty of environment, is in itself a forceful argument for the oft-repeated assumption that the Labradorean culture area is a strikingly backward one.

The Algonkian of more temperate regions, by contrast, pursues existence amid the plenitude of an environment where the fruit of

8. It is during the winter that the Montagnais inhabit the interior. The summer they spend near water, either on the shores of the larger lakes or on the Gulf coasts for periods of time varying according to the distance to be traveled. The change in locations and environment between the summer and winter cycles has been discussed in a previous short article, "Culture Problems in Northeastern North America," *Proceedings of the American Philosophical Society* (Philadelphia, 1926), Vol. LXV, No. 4. The two phases of life in the animal cycle seem to be of early origin and are referred to in the Jesuit narratives.

the soil insures his family against the perpetual menace of starvation. He lives in communities which rely on a constant source of food supply in which the uncertainty of the chase becomes a side issue instead of the sole one; where the winter, even in its more intense form, is but a short-lived inconvenience, not a deadly continuous blast. His dangers lie more in the presence of human enemies and disease. He is surrounded with steadily evolving organization in the social and political life of his tribe, and chiefly in the tribal religious creed to whose ceremonies in the period festivals he is a witness, but in which he is forbidden to participate until his period of spiritual maturity arrives. The basis of spiritual experience is entirely different in the two regions. The central Algonkian individual sees and hears the performances and recitations of the school of elders for years before he feels the call to assume their enactment himself. He gradually adjusts himself to a religious system maintained and interpreted for him by a self-selected group of religious men—self-appointed priests in short. And among their ranks we discover the expounders of monotheism. [9]

Montagnais-Naskapi religion has a deep bearing on the general problem of monotheism among Algonkian peoples. It has no priest-hood, no theological creed, naturally no ethical code. Its doctrine is individual, yet determined by a traditional tribal pattern widely common, it seems, to the northern area. In it every individual finds himself to be a partaker of the common system of thought and practice through the necessity of having to maintain his subsistence through his own adjustments to the spiritual realm where the agents are animals, plants, demons and nature forces upon the earth and in the sky. Thus we may state it by saying that the individuals of the group, collectively the masses, have held their religion to their own plane. It has not been advanced by the philosophical meditations of a priestly group nor has its level been raised to a formal cult through the formulation or code of religious reasoning produced by exceptionally gifted thinkers of a type encountered in every group of beings, as might be pointed out, for instance, in the case of another division of the same linguistic family, the Delawares. The Montagnais-Naskapi finds his religious experience within himself as a

9. An arrangement of evidence pointing to a general belief in implicit monotheism, in parts of North America, has been attempted by Paul Radin in *Monotheism among Primitive Peoples* (London, 1924), p. 64, who discusses the scheme of classification of worship and dulia proposed by C. Buchanan Gray, *Hebrew Monotheism* (Oxford Society of Historical Theology, 1922-23).

growing one beginning with his earliest attempts to overcome the animal-spirit realm about him; and by so overcoming it to secure his living. As he develops physical strength and mental cunning, he formulates his individual systems of procedure, keeping, however, within the bounds of traditional knowledge acquired through imitation of the older men, whose systems appear to him as having virtue in proportion to the length of life and prosperity of their advocates. He cannot avoid being himself responsible for his own spiritual any more than for his physical welfare. Nothing that the others perform will render him aid in his religious hunting or trapping any more than would an organized military government be his protection against invading enemies in his remote and lonely camp.

My earlier interpretation of culture conditions here, as being archaic Algonkian and thoroughly accommodated to a very early subarctic interior forest environment, seems to be supported by evidences in the religious manifestations of these tribes. In this perspective, there are some noteworthy and fundamental correspondences: first, with the Eskimo; and second, with the Athapascan. And no one conversant with Siberian ethnology can ignore the evidence of intercontinental similarity reported for the rudiments of religious custom.

Informants and Sources

My preceptors and informants among the native bands include those whose names are widely known among the traders and administrators of the North. Year after year many of them, giving their time and knowledge in building up our common study, deserve to be entered by name upon the list of those who have contributed to the preservation of records of native cultures developed through the ages, now passing away. (Frontispiece and pls. II, III, IV.)

Their names are: Joseph Kurtness (Ka'kwa), headman at Lake St. John, David Basil, Thoma Ka'kwa, Simon Rafaël, Tsibish Rafaël, Étienne, Sylvestre Mackenzie, headman of the Michikamau band, André Mackenzie, Francis St. Onge, Tcibas St. Onge, Jos. Tcelnic, Jos. and Peter Hester, Nabe'oco, Peta'banu, Batiste Picard, Gregwenic, Mattheo Kabec, Pien Wapistan, Charley Metowe'cic, Johnny Miantckam, Old Paul Ross, Alex Denis, Gabriel Nataskwanic, Napani, and their families. These, my teachers and counselors! Among the factors of the Hudson's Bay Company, for whom I have acquired great respect, as well as the independent traders, the following merit acknowledgment: Richard White, Jr., Richard Joncas, Robert Ross, W. R. Hamilton.

Aside from the names of these gentlemen of nature to whom if living I doff my hat in respect—if not, I cast a sigh of regret—there are certain gentlefolk of the intellectual world to whom I also owe acknowledgments for their counsel and help in various forms: My colleagues Dr. A. I. Hallowell, Dr. John M. Cooper, Dr. Dorothy K. Hallowell, Mr. E. A. Golomshtok; Dr. William John Phillips and Dr. Mac Edward Leach of the University of Pennsylvania; and Mr. Frederick Johnson of Harvard University have rendered aid in the task; and also to Miss Edna F. Myers, Miss Carolyn D. Harbaugh, Miss Dorothy M. Spencer, and Mr. L. C. Eiseley, of the University of Pennsylvania, are my acknowledgments due for secretarial aid.

The exploration, begun in 1908 among the Montagnais-Naskapi, was continued through 1932. The field work and research have been carried on chiefly through funds provided by the Director of the Museum of the American Indian (Heye Foundation), New York; the American Museum of Natural History, New York; the National Museum of Canada, Ottawa; the National Museum of Denmark; and the University Museum, University of Pennsylvania, for all of which ethnological collections have subsequently been made. From these collections the sketches and photographs of specimens have been made and acknowledged in their titles. To the Faculty Research Fund of the University of Pennsylvania (Grant No. 50), I am also indebted for financial aid in 1932, enabling me to return to the field and make some refinements in the material through consultations with native informants.

As for previous studies, there is remarkably little to say. The religious beliefs of the Indians of the Labrador peninsula do not comprise more than a few pages of notes by any of the writers dealing with the region. Except for the observations preserved for us in the *Jesuit Relations*, which have been largely quoted in these pages, we have only the scattered remarks of Hind and Turner, and some from Cartwright to incorporate with certain topics in the present volume. [10] Consequently the generalized studies of native

10. H. Y. Hind, *Explorations in the Labrador Peninsula*, 2 vols.; L. M. Turner, "Ethnology of the Ungava District," *11th Annual Report, Bureau of American Ethnology* (Washington, 1894); C. W. Townsend, *Captain Cartwright and His Labrador Journal* (Boston, 1911).

religion in North America have been deprived of occasion to refer to the peculiarities of spiritual beliefs and magic practices in this important region. [11]

In short, the northeastern Algonkian-speaking peoples have come in for only a meager share of attention from writers on the general topics embraced in the history of religion. [12]

Other writers, among whom may be mentioned Low, [13] Cabot, [14] Wallace, [15] the Hubbards, [16] and Grenfell, [17] have abstracted largely from Turner as a primary source, contributing practically nothing original to our knowledge of the religious life of these peoples, even to the general ethnology of the region, although in several cases the explorations, we are naïvely told, were undertaken with the intention of studying the natives. The virtues of these books lie in other lines.

The Contact with Christianity and Decline of the Natives

And now we shall see what occurs when the priests enter upon the scene, the self-denying emissaries of ecclesiastical orders commissioned by royalty and by private religious enterprise. Jesuits: Paul le Jeune (1632); Gabriel Sagard (1636), who served the Montagnais between Quebec and Tadoussac; Charles Albanel (1650-54); Ménard, a Jesuit (1660) whose knowledge extended as far east as Seven Islands, where also the [Récollet], Hierosme Lalemant, knew them in 1660; Henri Nouvel (1664), who penetrated the Manikuagan region; and the Jesuit, Laure, who in 1731 first made mention of les Cuneskapi (the Naskapi) as dwelling north of Lake Ashuanipi.

Most missionaries of the period thought that effort and time would banish the difficulties of conversion and habilitation of the savages; that by taking the young and educating them at the missions some latent capabilities for civilization would be brought out. In 1808 no

11. To what extent these meager references have been turned to account by Dr. P. W. Schmidt, among European writers, has already been witnessed, while other students (besides J. Lowenthal, whose paper entitled *Die Religionen der Ostalgonkin*, Inaugural Dissertation, Berlin, 1913, I have not been able to secure) in America and Europe seem to have been obliged to ignore the area.

12. In this grouping appear P. W. Schmidt, *Die Ursprung der Gottesidee* (Munster, 1929); and C. Kirkpatrick, *Religion in Human Affairs* (New York, 1929), who has exploited some aspects of Montagnais-Naskapi religion in his discussion. Father Schmidt has more recently reviewed his ideas in *The Origin and Growth of Religion, Facts and Theories*, trans. by H. J. Rose (New York, 1931), and again in his *High Gods in North America* (Oxford, 1933).

13. A. P. Low, *Report on Explorations in the Labrador Peninsula, 1892-5* (Ottawa: Geological Survey of Canada, 1896).

14. W. B. Cabot, *In Northern Labrador* (Boston, 1902).

15. Dillon Wallace, *The Long Labrador Trail* (New York, 1907).

16. Mrs. Leonidas Hubbard, Jr., *A Woman's Way Through Unknown Labrador* (New York, 1908).

17. W. T. Grenfell, *Labrador, the Country and the People* (New York, 1912).

striking results had been produced by the effort, according to the impressions received by McKenzie, who wrote as follows: "Attempts have been made by missionaries to convert such as have come within their reach, but it is hard to teach tricks to an old dog, and no less so is it to convince a Nascapee that our notions of religion are preferable to his own, which have been taught him by his parents and instilled into him by long habits. However absurd these may appear to us, it is certain ours seem no less so to them." [18] Another century has seemingly rendered its answer to their zealous hopes, the situation being summed up in a memorandum published by a civil agent who visited the St. Lawrence coast in 1926 and reported what has so generally impressed the social observer in regard to the natives of the region.

"Au point de vue intellectuel, le sauvage est absolument borné. Il est radicalement incapable de tout développement..... Les missionnaires ont souvent essayé de faire instruire des petits garcons et des petites filles indiennes avec l'idée d'en faire des prêtres et des religieuses, mais ce fut peine perdue. Ils ne parviennent pas à raisonner plus qu'un enfant en bas âge; ils demeurent naïfs, crédules et ignorants.

"Voilà jusqu'où la décadence peut atteindre une race. On se console en constatant que ces dégénérés paraissent heureux. S'ils meurent, individuellement ou collectivement, la mort est édifiante.

"Et quand la mort viendra, le Ciel devra être la juste récompense de ces chrétiens fervents si dociles à suivres les enseignements de Dieu et de l'Église. Heureux mortels tout de même dans leur déchéance!" [19]

Evangelization rests very lightly upon their moral conscience. The case of the Waswanipi Lake Indians affords a good example. They are both Catholic and Protestant. When a priest comes to administer his service, the people take their prayerbook and attend; when the Protestant minister comes to hold service, they take their books and assemble for him—for they have both.

The naïve declarations of Father Peter Laure (1720-30), one of the writers most concerned with native behavior, originally describe the Mistassini as being such "sweet-tempered and simple people that you can form no idea of their goodness [sic!], having no liking for

18. James McKenzie in Masson, *op. cit.,* p. 420.
19. Edgar Rochette, Avocat et Conseil du Roi, *Notes sur la Côte Nord du Bas St. Laurent et le Labrador Canadien* (Quebec, 1926), pp. 103-4.

fire water; and if the French, who are more eager to plunder them of their peltries than to help them save their souls, did not. . . . force it on them, they would never take it." [20] He speaks of their admirable docility. Of the Montagnais he observes them as "kind, gentle and peaceable, who readily do what you ask, provided you keep your eye on them, credulous, never answering back, timid, obedient and poor." Although confessing to great admiration myself for these amiable and simple people, I see in these sanctifications some optimistic exaggeration.

After the prolonged siege of Roman influence to which the Indians were subjected, although they were at first bewildered, one may imagine them later captivated with the unaccustomed splendor of the Roman ritual with its woodland chapels and decorations of "pictures and new stuffs. . . .hung here and there on the walls." [21] We may wonder why the doctrine and ritual of the Mass, the Lenten fastings, the holy-water rite, the distribution of the *pain béni*, the reciting of beads, even the conception of Trinity, [22] have none of them become assimilated into native devotional procedure as we learn of it nowadays. Can it be that the Indians simply forgot and dismissed it when far away in the bush beyond the importunate coercions of the unflagging priests? Buteux, Le Jeune, Albanel, Laure, De Crespieul, whose aggregate of time together in pressing the Christian rites upon them, rites with the appeal of novelty and display to savage eyes, would cover the latter half of the eighteenth century. Another instance of the quickness with which the natives relapse or, may we say, return to their original ancestral practices, is shown at Tadoussac, where after twenty years during which missionaries were absent there, the supply priest, Father Laure, who went there in 1720, found some old Indians who could mumble some of the prayers, but the younger growing up with "all the vices of pa-

20. "Mission du Saguenay," *Relation Inédite du R. P. Pierre Laure, S. J., 1720 à 1730*, par P. Arthur E. Jones (Montreal, 1889), Archives du Collège Ste. Marie.

21. J. Buteux (1651), Jesuit, missionary to the Attikameg (White Fish Indians) on St. Maurice river, quoted by T. J. Campbell, *Pioneer Priests of North America, 1642-1716* (New York, 1910), II, 60.

22. That such a concept is not above the grasp of the Naskapi mind is shown in the following anecdote by an observer who allowed the savages of the region no premium either on their character or intelligence.

"Some years ago, a priest wishing to explain to one of those Indians the principles of religion, among other important tenets, told him that in God there were different persons, the Father, the Son and the Holy-Ghost, and, yet, that these three different Persons were in reality the same and made but one. The Indian, struck with this seeming paradox, begged the Reverend Father to explain his meaning more clearly, for he could not conceive how the Son could be as old as the Father. The priest, taken off his guard by the unexpected objection, said it was a mystery in his religion which he was bound to believe without thoroughly understanding it. 'Well,' said the man of Nature, 'since you have not sense enough to explain the doctrine you advance, I shall offer you my opinion on it,' on which folding the skirt of his *capot* in three, he said: 'Look Patriache'—so they called the priest—'these folds of caribou are different in number but the same in size, quality and age, yet, you see,' pulling them asunder, 'they make in reality but one.' " James McKenzie, in Masson, *op. cit.*, pp. 419-20.

— 17 —

ganism." [23] Thereupon, Laure himself added the weight of ten years' service among them (until 1730), but they still after two hundred years remember the aboriginal rites. And who but an ecclesiast would not smile at the statement of one of the zealots, mentioning the baptism of Algonquin babies, "two hundred of whom went straight to heaven." [24]

The holy church, this time not assuming the symbolical guise of the bride but that of the father, tried for a century or more to fecundate the age-old body of savage superstition to produce devotees and acolytes if not saints. But after the prolonged effort, after a magnificent incision had been made, one beholds emerge, what? A handful of miserable, unhappy, and dwindling bands of errant hunters galvanized with an ill-becoming sheen on feast days, but sick and corroded at heart.

The gradual decline of their numbers is fully recognized by the natives themselves and is much discussed in their gatherings. The condition is commonly attributed to their change of diet from wild fruits and the flesh of game to the food of the Europeans, which they regard as not fitted to their constitutions. Wild game to them is "pure" and conducive to health, while European food, like alcohol, they believe to be detrimental to their health and vitality. Yet, in their inconsistency of action, they succumb to temptation along these lines like children. Other writers have emphasized the food question in considering the causes of extinction among northern savages.

Jenness (1921) gives it weight as applying to Eskimo health. [25] Hind, writing in 1861, refers to the Montagnais as being conscious of their own decline and attributing it to the forest fires denuding their territories and destroying the game and ultimately leading to starvation and disease. [26] An interesting opinion concerning the causes of decline of the Siberian natives, whose cultural problems facing civilization are similar to those existing in Labrador, is expressed by Anoutchine. [27] He lays it to the effects of nervous debility.

23. Campbell, op. cit., p. 219. An amusing example of savage sophistry is a remark on the opinions of the Cree by Thompson. "They do not believe in hell for they do not think it possible that anything can resist the continuous action of fire." David Thompson's Narrative of His Explorations in Western America, 1784-1812, (ed. J. B. Tyrrell; Toronto: Champlain Society, 1916), p. 83. Those outside the church being, in the esteem of the clergy, the personal vassals of Satan, it follows that their heretical doctrines were believed to derive from the blowing of Beelzebub's bellows into the ears of humanity—an actual belief of the medieval church which with other interesting legends of the age are given in an article by M. J. Rudwin, The Open Court, Vol. XLIII (1929), No. 883.
24. Campbell, op. cit., p. 135.
25. D. Jenness, "The Cultural Transformation of the Copper Eskimo," Geographical Review, Vol. XI (1921), No. 4, pp. 549-50.
26. H. Y. Hind, op. cit., II, 115.
27. V. Anoutchine, Les Causes de l'extinction des indigènes dans la Sibérie septentrionale, Anthropological Institute of University of Prague, Vol. IV (1926), No. 1, pp. 12, 23.

Laure (1720-30) says further that pestilence broke out at Chicou-timi and that they lost twenty-four adults, though he was consoled by their "beautiful deaths."[28] The Indians used vapor baths against sickness. Many pagan Indians fled, with muskets pointed toward the village to prevent evil spirits from following them. The Indians believed that they were poisoned by merchandise from a ship. Indeed, the only ones who caught the fever were those who bought goods from the ship, and the clerk and others who opened the goods were the first victims. The cargo had been shipped from Marseilles, where pestilence was raging. This was shortly after 1721. The event referred to here is, I believe, the same one remembered by the Mon-tagnais of Escoumains as having taken place at a site now known as Pointe Sauvage, about twelve miles east of Tadoussac, which evidence I have incorporated in notes given in an article on the family terri-tories of the Montagnais.[29]

Father Laure (1720-30) says, at Tadoussac in former days, three thousand people gathered then under three Jesuit Fathers, but now (1720-30) there are at the most only twenty-five families.[30] Decima-tion of the same wretched populations is noted as early as 1650 by the missionary Father Charles Albanel, who wintered with the Montagnais at Tadoussac. He records them as dying of a loathsome fever. He stayed through with them until 1664. In 1669 he was again at Tadoussac and the pestilence was there. In 1760 he visited the Oumamiois, Papinachois and Godbout Indians (130 persons were at the latter place then), and found them fast disappearing, he said, on account of continual famines.[31]

Albanel, again starting out from Tadoussac for the north, expres-sed his grief (1670) at seeing scarcely a hundred people at Tadoussac where he once saw ten or twenty hundred. He also remarked of the Oumamiois, whom he encountered on his journey to the interior northward, that they were fast disappearing on account of the con-tinual famines. Again in 1672, on his way to find a route to Hudson Bay, under a commission from the Intendant Talon, he met the Indians of Lake St. John, known then, as now, by the name Pikoua-gami, whom he called Kakouchaes or Porcupines, because of the

28. Campbell, op. cit., p. 236.
29. "Family Hunting Territories of the Lake St. John Montagnais and Neighboring Bands," Anthropos, Vienna, XXII (1927), 397.
30. Campbell, op. cit., p. 237.
31. This term signifies in Montagnais-Naskapi a "northeasterner," according to Lemoine and McKenzie, though its precise significance is "down-river (person)." For further discussion of local and group names see p. 559 of my article referred to in n. 1, p. 15.

abundance of that animal there; and he says of the people that in former times twenty nations assembled there for trade, but that war and pestilence had made sad havoc among them.

A question naturally presents itself in turning attention to the ethnology of the Montagnais-Naskapi as to how far present religious characteristics are typical of the original native practices of these tribes. The answer must necessarily be conjectural, for the Jesuit narratives to the era of first contact do not offer a systematic description for comparison. There has been, however, little alteration in the *spirit* of Montagnais-Naskapi culture, despite the many material innovations which have been acquired from Europeans. Their culture has continued largely in its original pattern—hunting and wandering. And the elementary religious associations of this phase of existence cannot be conceived of as being likely to change, as long as the culture-pattern holds firm. Radical change would only ensue upon change of their culture base, *e.g.*, from hunting-nomadism to agriculture, to pastoral life, or to civilized employment. Nothing of such a nature has occurred. The introduction of Christianity to these hunting hordes would not supplant their ancient beliefs and practices if it did not change their economic life. Their superstitions were generated by life in the northern "bush" and centered for ages about the control of spirits of wild animals and fish, of a cold barren wilderness; they were designed to protect man from freezing, starvation, and drowning—the three nemeses of the Naskapi. Christianity has not even competed with them. For Christianity is essentially adapted to the life of a people following a civilized mode of life in a densely populated pastoral or agricultural (if not an industrial) culture sphere. When we learn from these Indians that ritual obligations, fees, prohibitions, and mission services which the Roman church has lured them into are matters of concern only when they are at the coasts, the situation becomes clearer. There the performances and demands of the priest hold their attention for a duration of two to six weeks, according to the band and locality. [32]

The Rupert's House and the other groups on the Hudson and James Bay coasts are served by the Anglican missionaries, while all the rest on the St. Lawrence coast, so far as they have been converted, are met by the Roman priests. When the hunters have returned to

32. The Mistassini Indians who come out at Pointe Bleue seldom remain for more than two weeks; the same being true of most of those at Seven Islands, while those of the Lake St. John band are in contact with the church for varying periods, some as much as three months.

the interior, they are again under the thrall of the spiritual forces of the forest; and, except for some acquired rules of conduct, and an attempt, always too vague for their theological comprehension, to imitate the services of the far-off "prayer-house," their orthodoxy becomes an exotic memory. One might observe that their conversion is, actually, equivalent to baptism, submission to tithing demands and the monogamous regulation. Among some of the interior bands on the north and northeast of the peninsula the effect of these influences is still nothing. Subordination to sacerdotal authority—which means only the abolishment of polygyny, conjuring and the performance of individual "pagan" rites of divination, dream control, drumming and dancing—holds sway only for limited periods.[33]

This situation may be summed up within the declaration of Peta'-banu (Ungava Band), who discussed the superstitious life of himself and his comrades while in the interior. Said he with finality and a mien of impatience, "You speak about singing for game; about using the rattle and drum before and after dreaming about the caribou! Yes, I have a song and I dream songs, and read the shoulder-blade divination. They all do, he (indicating Mictaben, sitting near at hand), he (indicating Nabe's), in fact all! That's how we kill the animals and live!" On the whole, however, there was and is little that is immoral, perverted or vicious in the native religious behavior of these lonely tribes, and so, should these remarks seem discouraging to the minds of any who read them, there is little more to lament in their case than in that of many civilized Christian communities lying the whole year round within hearing of church bells and under the shadow of church spires.

In short, the one yearning of the Naskapi mind is for subsistence while living and postponement of death. As regards the latter, unlike the Indians in other parts of America, there is not even the glamor of war to alleviate it; no compensating glory of battle in which death may be risked. In the main, the Montagnais-Naskapi faces the prospect of losing his life directly by accident or mishap resulting in starvation or freezing; next, by the contraction of bronchial and pulmonary inflammation and disease through malnutrition or exposure. The latter is the cause of the high mortality of the children. Year after year, I have seen the summer gatherings of these Indians

<hr />

33. Hind, *op. cit.*, II, 116, writing in 1861, says in effect that most of the Naskapi are still heathen, though many Montagnais have become Christians.

numbering some hundreds of individuals, not a single one of whom was free from the cough. The consequence of this is that the minds of the people are open to any suggestion, whether by doctrine or experience, which may come to them as a remedial measure to their physical and spiritual condition. And since Christianity does not pretend definitely to help them kill animals nor increase the supply of caribou, seals, fur-bearers, and fish, their reason induces them to rely upon the old traditional agencies which have served so well the generations of their ancestors whom they revere as stronger, greater men than themselves. But, since Christianity does teach regulation of the immortal spiritual element, promising definite compensation for its obligations in the glories portrayed as belonging to the Christian heaven, its system is accepted. I have included these remarks to account for the liberal acceptance of Catholicism so widely throughout the peninsula. No coercion of the natives is necessary to accomplish it. The same was noted with surprise by several of the early missionaries who served these tribes.

In consideration of the tone of respectability given to studies of contemporary primitive peoples by reference to their circumstances of life in earlier accounts, especially when they happen to be from ecclesiastical pens, we may borrow the expressions of several illustrious missionaries writing in the seventeenth century, to introduce and summarize the conditions which mark the life of the Montagnais and Naskapi nomadic bands to this very day:

"It is a wandering life of people scattered here and there according as hunting and fishing lead them, now upon the rocks or in the islands in the midst of some great lakes, now upon the banks of rivers, without shelter, without houses, without any fixed abode, without collecting anything from the land except what it gives in an unfruitful country to those who have never cultivated it." [34]

"The inhabitants of this country are really savages in name and nature," as Father Jean d'Olbeau, the Récollet, wrote from Quebec on July 20, 1615. "They have no settled place of abode, and they live in tents here and there, where they know they will find game and fish, which is their ordinary food." [35] "The savage tribe with whom we are now," as Father Charles Lalemant wrote from Quebec in 1626, "wanders about six months in the year, that is, the six months

34. Father Vimont in *Jesuit Relations*, 1642.
35. Father Jean d'Olbeau, letter, 1615.

— 22 —

PLATE I   UPPER PHOTOGRAPH BY LIVERNOIS OF QUEBEC

Upper photograph: Birch bark wigwam, Montagnais. Lower photograph: Skin and canvas wigwam, Naskapi, probably of Northwest River band, Hamilton Inlet.

PLATE II

Montagnais-Naskapi hunters: Left, Malek Bejin (Lake St. John); center, Joseph Kurtness (Mistassini); right, Gregwenic (Michikamau).

of winter, wandering here and there according as they find hunting, and they pitch their tents only two or three families together in a place, two or three in one place, and two or three in another. During the other six months of the year, twenty or thirty gather on the banks of the St. Lawrence near our settlement [[of Quebec]], and as many forty leagues above us, and as many at Tadoussac; and there they live upon the proceeds of their hunting during the winter; that is to say, upon smoked moose and upon provisions which they have got by barter with the French." [36]

In the preceding pages, I have attempted to sketch in rough form an outline of the framework of culture of the Mongoloid hunter-nomads of the far Northeast; the indigenes of a region so harsh in its natural aspects as to affright the sensibilities of some who feel its desolation, yet exerting an almost irresistible allurement upon the wandering-instincts of others—the awe of a wilderness of snowy mountains, the glory of sunrise on the shores of the great gulf, the star-studded night on limitless barrens.

The Religious Categories

The logical mind invariably thinks of manifestations in terms of categories. Where no ready-made categories exist we strive to create them. This may be done by an arrangement determined through the classification implied in terms of language, for vocabulary seems to imply classification of ideas whether or not the speakers are conscious of it. While the procedure is apt to develop an aspect of artificiality, there is reason for making an attempt provided there is sufficient material to utilize. Much depends upon the quality of data employed and the intellectual personality of the author of the arrangement. Accordingly, as concerns the Montagnais-Naskapi, since no objective classification of religious conceptions exists in the native mind, it does not follow that the terminology for religious ideas is wanting in the language. For a system is scarcely to be expected to appear on the surface as covering the aggregation of metaphysical ideas so rudimentary as those exhibited in Montagnais-Naskapi thought.

The analysis of ideas through the medium of native terms and their classification, however, is one procedure possible in this case. That any conception of categories is alien to the thought of the people

---

36. Father Charles Lalemant, letter, 1626. (See *Jesuit Relations*, IV, 203.)

must be apparent to anyone who has viewed their undisciplined life. The results of an attempt at schematization are accordingly offered for consideration, with full consciousness that until touched by the hand of a master, they can lay little claim to conclusiveness.

The trivium of cosmology, religious practice, and ethics is the groundwork of the arrangement proposed.

1. *Məntu'* (*Ma'nitu*):*The universe,* natural law, the unknown, spirit-forces, supreme power.
2. *Məntoci·'win:* "Practice based upon *mantu'*." *Man's relationship with nature,* magical practice, shamanism (spirit-control, magic power in art, in economic operation), divination, soul, or "great-man," control.
3. *Minoto'tak:* "Proper conduct, behavior." *Human interrelationships,* ethical principles, social usages, customs in general.

The above system represents the order in which the topics, subdivided into three parts, are dealt with in the study to follow. The last subdivision, however, forms the field of treatment of a separate report which has already appeared. [37]

37. F. G. Speck, "Ethical Attributes of the Labrador Indians," *American Anthropologist,* Vol. XXXV (1933), No. 4, pp. 559-94.

THE SPIRITUAL FORCES

Chapter Two

The Məntu' Concept

THE background upon which rest the supernatural relationships of the Montagnais-Naskapi must be understood in the term *məntu'*, variants being *manətu'* (Lake St. John), *mantu'* (Mistassini). The term cannot be adequately translated, since it is an abstraction having no definite compass in the genius of a vague philosophy. To the native it is not as difficult a thought to grasp as it seems to us, for we use the term "power" to think of transcendental qualities, whereas he does not. Everything not understood is implied in it. [1] He intends the term to have no definite application. One informant will try to illustrate the meaning of the term by comparing it to natural physical force observable in electricity, gravity, heat, steam, while another will liken it to psychic principles operating in thought, invention, memory, co-ordination, in animal generation and human procreation, in heredity, and especially in supernatural control. While *məntu'* cannot be lexically defined, we can glean some little idea of its purport from the extensive use to which it is put in the spiritual vocabulary of the people. In the sense of "spiritual being" or "deity" we have glanced at its adaptation to Christian theism. In the sense of "power" we find it in common use in the translations given by thoughtful Indians in explaining the miracles of the shaman or conjuror. It often appears, moreover, in terms expressing mental states which result in producing physical effects. Not a few attempts have been seriously made by ethnologists to discuss its cognates in various Algonkian tongues, such as those of William Jones, Michelson, Skinner, Dixon,

---

1. In this connection *Wah'Kon-Tah*, by John Joseph Mathews, appearing in this series, may be cited as the Osage analogy.

and others; but at present, lest we assume too much correspondence in meanings given to the term between related dialects in rather widely differing culture subareas, I have decided to present only the evidence of its meaning in the region under discussion. Even here, despite our best effort to define the idea, we fail to strike soundings.

Etymological terms containing the root show certain animal names, some of which have been mentioned: Məntu'c, meaning "snake," "worm," and "insect"; məntume'kuc, "smelt," "spirit fish" (diminutives);[2] and again some manufactured articles coming from the hands of the wonder-making Europeans such as məntu'wian, "məntu-skin," "cloth";[3] and məntu'minəs'it', "məntu-berries" (diminutive), mantu'c, "little spirits, powers," (Mistassini), meaning "beads" or "beadwork." We shall see this belief brought out later in the discussion of decorative art. Besides, the term enters into verbal compositions designating certain mental states which imply accomplishment by concentration, a condition most natural in view of the conjuror's practices in which cloth and beads are employed as accessories.

The connotation of supernatural force denoted by the element is shown in such terms as məntu' eltc'ltək', "spirit-power thinking," the process by which the hunter can concentrate his thought upon a desire and bring it to realization.

Great Spirit (High God) Concept

To the influence of the missionary priests, I am now inclined to believe, may be attributed the concept of an anthropomorphic supreme deity—the historic and often-discussed Tcetciməntu', "Great Power," commonly interpreted as "Great Spirit." A synonym for the same deity is Tipe'ltak (Montagnais), Tipe'ntak (Naskapi), "Governor, Owner." There having been some inclination among ethnologists to attribute the belief in a supreme deity having human form to all the early Algonkian groups, I had originally confessed some skepticism as to its antiquity among the natives of Labrador. Whether other Algonkian-speaking tribes originally had the concept is not the concern of the present discussion, but I believe it is correct to arrange the Wabanaki peoples south of the St.

2. *Mallotus villosus* (Müller).
3. The fabric designated is fine black or red cloth, a textile so mysterious in construction as to evoke this feeling. The related term for beads expresses a similar attitude of mind toward such wonderful particles of glass.

Lawrence in the same category with the Montagnais-Naskapi in respect to the assumption of a Catholic origin for the later phase of their belief in an anthropomorphic supreme deity. [4]

We cannot pass by without comment the testimony now accumulated both for and against the belief in a supernatural overlord among the Indians of this territory. Among the Montagnais-Naskaspi, who at present are subject to classification as nominal Christians, we find the term *Tce'mɔntu,* "Great Spirit," in common use to denote the Christian God. *Kantautci'tuk^ω,* "Our Creator," and *Kantce·'tɔpeltɑ'k̯,* "Our Great Master or Owner," are also used. [5] With the lapse of time that has intervened since first contact with the priests, it would seem quite impossible now to produce proof in support of the opinion that this concept is an aboriginal one. The impression remains, however, after questioning widely among the older men that *Tce·'mɔntu* is the author of creation; that he is not anthropomorphic. It is, however, on just such a subject that the effect of missionary teaching would be first noticed, for to teach the savages of the Supreme Deity was ever a responsibility weighing heavily upon the missionary conscience. The Montagnais themselves appear to share the feeling of the impossibility of ascertaining the ulterior origin of the conception.

The general opinion prevails among the laity of the bands, that *Tce·'mɔntu* is a spirit having neither body nor form, that he is creator and controller of the universe. McKenzie (1808) defines the Great Spirit belief of the Naskapi in the same terms, adding that they never worship him, "because being all goodness. . . . it would be against his nature to do them any mischief, and will do them. . . . good. . . . without being teased into it." [6] Like non-extreme monotheists elsewhere, the statement they made in answer to my inquiry concerning the form of *Tce·'mɔntu* will cover the feeling of a number with whom I have talked. Says the Mistassini headman: "He is a spirit (*mɔntu'*) like the sun, moon, and stars, who created everything, including them. As to form or body—ah! that is something no one can know because no one has ever seen him. The priests! Ah! they do not know any more about that than we ourselves do!

4. They likewise employ the term "Owner" (St. Francis Abenaki, "*Dabaldák*"; Penobscot, "*Debéldak̯*") and *Kétci N̯ickskam,* "Great Being." The general correspondence between the life of the Labrador bands and the older culture of the Wabanaki tribes, that is, before *circa* 1770, the period of Iroquois contact, are striking.
5. The terms *Kak̯i'uc'hitak̯'ω,* "Our Maker," and *Otipe'litck̯e'o,* "Our Owner," have become disseminated widely among the northern bands through the use of the gospels in the Cree syllabary.
6. James McKenzie, in Masson, *op. cit.,* p. 414.

They talk about it, but it rests a mystery, for they have not seen him."

The actual question as to the origin of the Great Spirit concept in this region remains unanswered for all that I can see in the testimony that can be obtained. Perhaps a deeper insight into the concept might be gotten from a shaman, could he be found and approached with the question, for it is plausible to expect here, as elsewhere among the aborigines, that several types of religious mind exist in the same community. The vision of the average hunter here is limited in his religious horizon to the supernatural forces that directly affect his affairs.

Before dismissing, however, the discussion of *Tce·'mɘntu* as a fiction of missionary teaching, let us make one point favoring the affirmative in respect to native origin. [7] In the native system of thought the various families and genera of animals constitute races and tribes among which the human is included. They are dominated by their spiritual overlords, who rule their destinies and govern reincarnation through succeeding generations of their kind. Conceive a similar hierarchy ruling the cycle of existence of man, and the positive indications would seem to be affirmed. Man, then, has his Owner, and this is the High God. As man comes first among earthly beings, his Owner is implied as dominating the theocratic forces.

Referring, in 1624, to Indians "down the river towards Tadous' sac," Father Le Caron says that they and almost all the Indians of New France have no divinity; are almost incapable of ordinary common and natural reasonings on this point, while Lalemant (1626) notes a belief in "One who made all, but they do not render him homage," among the same bands. [8] Another missionary, Père Arnaud (1861), told Hind that the Naskapi, like the Montagnais, believed in two divinities or manitous, one good, the other evil. [9]

While it is rare that statements can be obtained from informants regarding the "good spirit" that would point to a phase of belief antedating the teachings of Christians, we have one poetic thought which is reminiscent of other Algonkian conceptions concerning the

---

7. That a certain dissemination of teaching by missionaries has taken place to emphasize the concept of the Supreme Deity, it would be hazardous to deny. In illustration of the point, we find as far into the interior as Lake Mistassini the use of the printed gospels in the Cree syllabary common among the converts. Here the Supreme Deity is called *Ke·'tce Mɘ'nitu*, which is a Cree, not a Mistassini form. This intrusion of idea and term is recognized by the Indians themselves.

8. *Memoirs of Father Joseph Le Caron* (1624), as quoted by J. D. G. Shea, *First Establishment of the Faith in New France* (New York, 1881), I, 215. Also Charles Lalemant, *Jesuit Relations, 1616-29*, IV, 203.

9. Hind, *op. cit.*, II, 101-2.

Great Spirit and trees when the wind is blowing.[10] Mistassini informants say that when the wind is blowing hard, bending the trees down all in one direction, it is the Great Spirit combing them as a father combs the hair of his child.

And amid the array of positive testimony in favor of a native belief in a Supreme Being, we have the statements of Father Le Jeune in 1633 and 1637 that the concept was embraced in the term *manitu*, which with modification good or bad denoted God and the devil.[11]

The term *mɔntu'*, is, however, important and of native origin. This has been briefly discussed, for it is cognate with the universal Algonkian designation occurring in so many forms throughout the range of this widely scattered family.[12]

Of similar origin, and even more obviously of European extraction, is the antithesis of the deity just noted, *Mɔtci"mɔntu'*, "Bad Power," which designates the devil.[13] This being is now an actual reality in the opinion of the northern Indians. It has become, possibly, an augmentation to their demonology, an addition invading their beliefs with considerable ease, since it furnishes a feasible embodiment for the source of all their miseries. Following the teaching of the missionaries the "Bad Power," or "Evil Spirit," as the writers prefer it, is a major ogre; but, quite unexpectedly from the missionary point of view, has become associated with a native cannibal demon, *Atce'n.* It is interesting to observe how the Christian theurgy has become expressed in the native tongue, and we can allow the imagination to construct an idea as to what is meant to the savage mind by the names Good Power, Spirit (*mɔnomɔntu'*), applied to the Holy Ghost,[14] as the third divine personage, or "the Great-Power-who-is-three-in-one" to the Holy Trinity. Again, the crucifix is "ghost-wood (*tci"piɔtɔ'k*), and the scapular is *aiamieu' tapcka'gɔn*, "neck ornament," or *tapcka'gɔn*, "neck suspended."

10. The Delawares believe the trees to be "praying" under such conditions. F. G. Speck, *A Study of the Delaware Big House Ceremony in Native Text* (Harrisburg: Historical Commission, 1931). The Cayuga Iroquois regard plants as representing growth on the body of the earth. Even the Hebraic prophet Isaiah in a rhapsodic vision beheld joy so intense that "the trees of the field shall clap their hands" (Isa., 55:12).

11. *Jesuit Relations*, 1633, p. 17; 1637, p. 49.

12. A discussion of the term with implications most eloquently offered to show the native concept of the Supreme Deity as present in the belief of the Algonkian, is classically treated by P. W. Schmidt, *Die Ursprung der Göttesidee* (Münster, 1929), II, 456-63. Father Schmidt infers that *manitu* is an individualization of an original Algonkian conception of magic power (op. cit., pp. 396-407). Analysis of North American monotheism is also essayed by J. R. Swanton, "Three Factors in Primitive Religion," *American Anthropologist*, Vol. XXVI (1924), No. 3, pp. 362-63. In a recent report Dr. John M. Cooper (*The Northern Algonquian Supreme Being*, Cath. Univ. of Amer. Anth. Ser., No. 2, (1934) pp. 35-36), gives information furnished by Dr. W. D. Strong on this point.

13. Also McKenzie, in Masson, op. cit., p. 414.

14. Also *pɔli'ki atca'k,'ɯ* "pure, clean soul" (Mistassini, East Main and Moose Cree), taken from missionary sources and incorporated as a teaching wherever the syllabic gospel system has been introduced.

The designation for religion, aia'miewin, with the meaning of practice of prayer, is an application of an old native concept to Christianity, while its opposite in the Catholic sense is mənto'ci·win with the converted meaning of "deviltry" and includes the native practice of conjuring, of which we shall have more to say in its proper place. The same base, mantu', is, however, recurrent in many terms not distinctly connected with diabolism, as we have seen in the different terms for manifestations of the orthodox deity and also in such terms as "zealous," mənto'kacun, "he has spirit for something, he has bravery," "to strive for something"; mantokacu'n, "take courage" (Lake St. John); and mantu'c, "little power, spirit," "insect, worm, small snake." As Dr. Hallowell has discovered among the Cree and Saulteaux, the term is not commonly used in the plural to denote the spirit-forces as it is among the central Algonkian.

Again, we encounter the term mante'o, "stranger," for which no ready explanation is to be had from informants. Also in mantu-wia'n, "mantu-skin" or "cloth," referring to the finer grades of manu-factured broadcloth, one observes the spiritual idea standing forth.

In conclusion of this brief discussion of the changes brought about by the missionaries, we see the old terms and concepts rehabilitated by ecclesiastic authority in a manner hardly more clarified for the simple mind of the Indian than to the conventional mind of the European peasant. By embracing Catholicism, the Naskapi and Mon-tagnais spiritualist becomes "one who prays" (ka aia'miat), or "one who makes the sign of the ghost-wood for his prayer," since the cru-cifix is known as tci·'pi·atək', "ghost-wood, or dead person's wood," occasionally acəte'atək', "crossed wood" (Lake St. John). And we can smile at the naïve designation of a Protestant as apoaia'miat, "one who does not pray," a synonym in Father Lemoine's Mon-tagnais dictionary for "miscreant." The same term also denotes the heathen. [15]

Probably enough has been said to indicate the extent of influence which modern religious efforts have had upon the spiritual mentality of these Indians. What remains will enable us to comprehend the mode of thought of an aboriginal people who have changed little from the backwardness of one of the prehistoric cultures of the far north.

15.   And hereby the Jesuits have leveled off an old score. For the Protestants of the seventeenth century con-sidered them to be the most "devilish" of all Catholic monks; for example, see the poem of Phineas Fletcher, "The Apollyonists" (1627).

CONCEPT OF THE SOUL

Chapter Three

General Beliefs

IN THE religious system of the Montagnais-Naskapi the soul of the individual is the focal center of attention. Whatever we mean by the term "soul," its lexical equivalent in the language of these nomads is *atca'ḳʷ* (diminutive). The same word designates one's shadow.[1] Another native term embracing the same word element which, so far as I have observed, has escaped the notice of others, is met in the term for "mirror," *wa'pən'atcakwoma'n,* "see-soul-metal." It is interesting to observe that over much of the territory in America where Algonkian languages are spoken, the same stem and even most of the linked concepts are found. In a study of Montagnais-Naskapi soul beliefs it is at first rather confusing to encounter several synonyms for soul in discussions as well as in the texts. One of these, *mista'peo,* "Great Man," will engage considerable attention in the progress of our investigation. Another term, *nictu't',* is in frequent use, more especially among the native bands toward the southwestern portion of the peninsula. The latter really means "spirit" in the sense of "intellect, comprehension"; hence, "mind," as for instance *nictu'tsəm,* "my mind, spirit."

Besides the common term, a proper name exists which is more descriptive of the soul's function: *Mista'peo* (Mistassini), meaning "Great Man." This is the term by which the soul in its active state is referred to, and, as we shall see, the active state of the soul is one which means guidance through life and which provides the means of overcoming the spirits of animals in the life-long search for food.

---

1. The inclusion of the idea of shadow with that for soul gives for this classical homonymy a still wider geographical extension than was thought of by Tylor and by Frazer. Direct evidence on this point has been obtained from all the Montagnais and Naskapi bands so far visited, and from the Algonquin and Eastern Saulteaux as well. Nor is the phenomenon restricted to the Algonkian family, since to cite one example the Siouan Catawba include under the element (*hi·*) *dá'* (one's) "soul," "life," "shadow," "portrait," "footprint."

After many discussions with individuals in various bands who would talk on the subject, I have the following summary to offer on this most important and difficult subject. Naturally, exact definitions and translated correspondences in single terms are impossible. In presenting discussion, I have quoted as nearly as possible the ideas of the Indians, adding explanations as I understood them after instruction, which followed questions on points not well understood at first.

The term *nəwaye'm*, "my friend," is a customary circumlocution for the soul. It is used in referring to one's own soul and also, I believe, to a slain animal's spirit. When the hunter has performed an act of satisfaction to himself, in the form of ceremonial smoking, acting in response to a dream motive by drumming, singing, or feasting, he may declare *nəwi· məlowe'ltaman nəwaye'm*, "I wish to content, or satisfy, myself"; literally, "I wish to make my friend [my soul] feel good."

The most explicit information comes from Joseph Kurtness, now chief of the Lake St. John band, whose father, Ka'kwa, was a religious authority of the old school at Mistassini. I have, however, tested and elaborated the soul theory wherever I could find sympathetic attention among the various groups, and can scarcely doubt its uniformity throughout the area. This comes out in myths, in hunting experiences, and in the individual rites for getting game which are referred to throughout the discussion of the religious life of the people as a basis of thought and performance.

As a mathematician has vaguely associated the "soul" with a radiating vibration that goes on and on and when set free by death seeks another envelope, its conception is not so far from that of the savage. He is also less definite than the classical philosophers who sought for more definite grounds upon which to reason: Homer, who saw the soul as a kind of image of the body that escaped through the mouth; Anaxagoras, who associated it with the intelligence; Socrates, with the idea of good. Even scientific opinion has not failed to suggest the heart as the seat of the soul, as does this strange creature whose beliefs we are considering.

Since the natives discuss soul matters under the proper name of *Mista'peo*, "Great Man," I shall follow their practice. Now the Great Man seems to be located in the heart (*wute'i·*); it is the equivalent of the *life* embodied in human beings and possesses the characteristic of surviving the body, which entitles these Indians to be ranked among those people in a primitive state of culture accredited with the almost universal belief in immortality. I can see no reason for not regarding the Great Man very nearly as we do the ego, in the same sense the essential of man. And again I feel that we are correct in describing a concept analogous with that entertained by the peoples of classical antiquity by portraying the soul, the Great Man, as the seat of the appetites, emotions, and passions, again in correspondence with the traditional terms, heart and mind.

Let me give a summary of the Great Man belief as expressed in the native order of thought by my principal informant at Lake St. John in an attempt to enumerate the qualities of this inner force. Vague parallelisms were the only possible mediums in the transfer of his own feelings into a foreign language.

The Great Man reveals itself in dreams. Every individual has one, and in consequence has dreams. Those who respond to their dreams by giving them serious attention, by thinking about them, by trying to interpret their meaning in secret and testing out their truth, can cultivate deeper communication with the Great Man. He then favors such a person with more dreams, and these better in quality. The next obligation is for the individual to follow instructions given him in dreams, and to memorialize them in representations of art. (Fig.

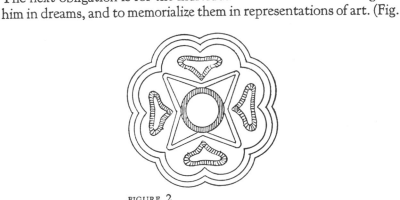

FIGURE 2

Design representing a hunter's Great Man (*mista'peo*) on a beaded shot pouch (Ungava band).

2.) This, as we shall see later, is an important religious peculiarity of these tribes. The process of self-study, of dream cultivation and submission to dream control becomes a dominant idea in the inner life.

We encounter the warning against neglect of dreams, against indifference to their vague suggestion lest the Great Man of the individual cease to appear to him. And cessation of revelations as to when and where to go for game, how to proceed, and how to satisfy it when it is slain, would result in the loss of a powerful and far-seeing guide, the individual's "Providence,"—and a doom of failure and starvation. Thus, autistic thought and behavior become dominant factors in life.

An ethical factor is also present in Naskapi soul philosophy, for we learn that as the Great Man becomes more willing and more active in the interests of his material abode, the body of the individual, he requires that the individual tell no lies, practice no deception upon others. In particular he is pleased with generosity, kindness, and help to others. Besides these ethical precepts, there are others directed toward the satisfaction of animal remains—ethics toward animals—which will form the discussion of several chapters to follow. Here we have the basis of the noteworthy "good behavior" of the uncivilized nomads, which has caused travelers to remark upon native honesty and generosity before they have been spoiled by emulating the traders, whose examples tend to make them irreligious.

Cannibalism

Let us consider a most interesting illustration of such a principle; namely, the accusation of cannibalism which has more than once been made against these tribes. They have a distinct belief in the existence of a man-eating mania which may be possessed by individuals from time to time. And indeed it may have been true in the past among them as it is among the Eskimo. Yet anthropophagy, for which the northern tribes have been occasionally reproached, rests largely upon the *on dits* of the travelers. Admitting its existence for a moment, we may consider it as but the logical consequence of being under pressure of extreme hunger, a circumstance by no means peculiar to these regions. At present, however, it should be noted that there is not a single authentic instance of anthropophagy within the area among the Indians themselves, although one actual case within the last twenty years is on documentary record where whites were guilty of it and an Indian the victim. Returning to native belief, we learn of the *wi·'tigo* (see pp. 73-75), who uses his Great Man in overcoming human beings as he would game animals, but this only in the winter. In the winter periods of starvation he employs his power to wage conquest over the Great Man of a weaker person, then slays and eats him for food. I might add that starvation, to which whole families occasionally succumb in their remote haunts, is attributed often to human cause of the sort just mentioned. In native esteem this is the worst aspect of the dominion of the soul-spirit—the Great Man of some unknown wrongdoer.

When a man had eaten human flesh he became *wi·'tigo*, and by having eaten so powerful a form of "game," his spirit, or *Miĉta'peo*, would grow so strong that they would be afraid to attack him, so a conjuror could destroy him only by sorcery. He would then try to get the *wi·'tigo* spirit into his power by luring it to a fight. The conjuror having succeeded in this, the man would be doomed (see p. 73).

The rumors of actual cannibalism have been confused with fact. The Indians feel that *wi·'tigo* is a reality—therefore they believe cannibalism exists; but they themselves are not the agencies, as hearers would think when such cases are heard of. William Cabot, who has had an intimate acquaintance with conditions among the Indians of this region for many years, gave me his opinion on the alleged cases of eating human flesh during times of famine in saying that "there were stories of the thing on a larger scale, but they came down to the one instance." [2] The case he cites as the only authentic instance between 1899 and 1913 was reported from East Main River.

The first instance of cannibalism on record for the "Montagnais" of Champlain's time, is described as having been witnessed by Champlain and his associates at Tadoussac on the twenty-fifth of May, 1615. [3] An atrocious spectacle awaited them. Six young slaves belonging to the Montagnais had just taken two prisoners from another tribe, and under the eyes of the Frenchmen tortured them and devoured parts of the victims, to the moral dismay of the four Franciscan priests who were of the party. [4]

Hind, who had access to many verbal sources of information on the Naskapi, which, unfortunately, he does not always refer to,

2. Correspondence, April 4, 1921.
3. This notice has been the cause of the degradation in literature of the northern Canadian tribes. I have never felt sure that the savages referred to were Montagnais.
4. An interesting essay on the ecclesiastical history of early Canada is that of Georges Goyau, *Les Origines Religieuses du Canada* (Paris, 1924), p. 29.

reported cases of cannibalism through starvation in 1857, in which the natives were accused of using the dead bodies of their companions as food, and even bleeding their own children to death to sustain life with the bodies. [5] And Low affirms that previous to 1889 three families hunting in the neighborhood of Wabamisk Lake all perished of starvation or cannibalism, except a woman and a small boy. He adds, however, that the case was not proved. [6]

That anthropophagy is not an institutional trait among the northern Indians, is, however, clearly shown by cases reported throughout the area of starvation, in which Europeans as well as the savages have been driven to it as an economic resort. [7] Harmon (1800) mentions cases among the French-Canadians of the Northwest and among the Saulteaux and Cree, [8] while for the latter we also have the direct testimony of Skinner. [9]

Turning to the gentler aspects of the soul-spirit system we encounter some theories and practices which are strikingly rational, at least from the point of view of some schools of modern spiritual thought. The birth of ideas of any nature whatsoever, either in dreams or in waking moments, is attributed to the generous revelations of a well-cultivated soul-spirit. It is the Great Man of the teacher that makes him strong and wise, of the leader that gives him fertile schemes and influence over others, of the successful hunter who garners game for him, of the warrior who garners enemies for him. By the same explanation, too, these primitive men of the North explain the power of leaders, inventors, and wealthy men among the whites. They think that in the departments of civilized culture the same possession of a powerful soul-spirit is responsible for the growth of the marvelous intellects who produce the conceptions of steamboats, phonographs, firearms, airplanes, architecture, science, music and other arts which they have come to learn about in the outside world. They comfort themselves, however, with the soothing thought that the master spirits which produce the latter would not fit into the aboriginal scheme; that the Great Man of the Indian

5. Hind., op. cit., I, 14, 244.
6. Low, op. cit., p. 85.
7. It might be argued that the eating of human flesh is so natural to savages (as it is also to Europeans) when faced with starvation, as not to furnish a problem in primitive behavior. That such is hardly the case, however, is shown by the fact that the South African Bushmen, living in abject circumstances more distressing than the Labradorean populations suffer, do not practice anthropophagy even in cases of great hunger. Cf. D. F. Bleek. *The Naron, A Bushman Tribe of the Central Kalahari* (Cambridge: Cambridge University Press, 1928), p. 7.
8. Harmon, pp. 143-44. He refers to Canadians near Great Slave Lake subsisting upon the flesh of dead companions, to another who killed and ate his wife and child. As for the Indians, he says the practice is not infrequent —one woman he heard of having eaten of "no less than fourteen of her friends and relatives during one winter."
9. A. B. Skinner, "The Eastern Cree," *Anth. Papers, Amer. Mus. Nat. Hist.*, IX (1911), 25.

is adjusted to the sphere of the taiga and tundra; that the two spheres, that of the civilized world and that of the wilderness, that of the white man and that of the Indian, are separate and distinct.

In short, I offer for the admiration of those who enjoy an insight into the keen comprehension of some of these old men, a remark illustrating the relation of the Great Man to the body. "The *Mista'peo* and the body of a man are like the chief of the cabin (locomotive engineer) and the fire-toboggan (locomotive engine). He knows his engine and just what he can do with it, and the engine works just as he directs it. Without him it is a dead mass; when it is worn out or when it collapses he goes into another one." With this lucid conclusion my venerable friend and informant, Joseph Kurtness, after some hours of tedious and devious questioning on my part, one evening in the winter of 1922, climaxed his lecture to me on the subject of the Great Man and the body in the hope that I would be able to comprehend. A branch of the Canadian National Railway had been constructed through the little reservation within the previous five years and the sight of the daily "fire-toboggan" (*ckwu-teotaba'n*) monster rolling along with such power to accomplish its purpose on the "iron path" under the control of one small man had furnished the illustration. We may wonder whether the uneducated French-Canadian passengers in its coaches, engrossed with their petty business and social affairs, credit with equal intelligence the stolid Indians from the distant interior, gathered at the little wayside stations to watch its passage.

The Great Man resides in each individual and it comes to the spiritual conception among primitive peoples again. It seems to be a frequent opinion, according to my notes, that the Great Man of the human embryo is the reincarnation of an ancestor who wills to renew its life-cycle in another generation. Its early development in the maternal abdomen is nourished and built up from the body of the mother, fed and stimulated by the semen of the father, since sexual intercourse is not tabooed during pregnancy. At birth the little body contains its Great Man and is nourished externally.

That the soul-spirit may be transferred in some way, rather difficult to understand since the individual's life depends upon its possession, seems to be the case. Napani' of Lake St. John, for instance, being now so old, claims that his *niĉtu′t‵* (as he calls his Great Man) has deserted him—that it has gone over to someone else.

With growth and attainment of maturity the new body, with its Great Man as chief within its heart, is launched forth to essay a career in a new cycle in the environment of the natural world. As to the form of the Great Man we cannot learn much that is definite, it seems, but I am inclined to adopt the conclusion that the soul-spirit often appears as a spark of illumination. For, in tales of conjuring, mention is made of the emergence of a spark of light or a little flame from the mouth of the individual. During the interval between its departure and return, the individual lies inert as though dead. I might add that this may be an old psychic belief among the Algonkian through its frequent recurrence in tales. It seems, moreover, to be definitely assertable for Wabanaki belief. The final event of demise comes, for the Montagnais-Naskapi, when the soul-spirit or Great Man leaves his body for good. And, he thinks, this takes place either as a result of his neglecting the soul's admonitions or through its desertion of his frame for some unknown reason.

Among the Montagnais-Naskapi we do not meet with the seclusion of youths or the fast-vigil for the acquisition of a spiritual guide, or initiatory rites of organized cults such as are reported among the central Algonkian; nor do they exist among the Wabanaki. This negative correspondence I also regard as an indication of the primitive quality of the two extreme northeastern Algonkian culture types.

What has been observed concerning the Montagnais-Naskapi soul-spirit theory is only an exposition of the nature of the soul. In later chapters we shall see how the individual exploits the power of his Great Man for the accomplishment of his desires. This is done by several forms of mental concentration as well as by certain magico-religious practices such as conjuring, wishing, thought concentration, soul projection through space, manticism, and the performance of wonders. These subjects will be treated in what seems to me their natural grouping as unprofessional, or individual conjuring—the minor individual rites—and professional conjuring, the latter to be treated in a separate publication.

We are thus shown how the hunter's success in avoiding sickness, in feeding his family, in prolonging his life, in building a good reputation among his friends, depends upon his bodily conduct in harmony

Upper photographs, Montagnais women (Moisie and Lake St. John bands). Lower left, *Atila'ockwem*, "Atelao's wife," Naskapi woman (Moisie band) showing manner of dressing hair over wooden blocks (*oce'tcəpətwa'n*), which is derived from reference to the bear's neck-and-shoulder meat as it is sliced for the men at the "bear feast." Lower right, man of the Moisie River.

PLATE IV
Boys of the Michikamau and Lake St. John bands.

with the positive requirements or the negations of his Great Man.

In emphasizing the individual nature of these rites, it seems hardly necessary to note the absence of any organized shaman societies this far east. I think it becomes clear that the conjurors' organization of the Mide'win comes out in a later Algonkian culture development than that which we find in the Labrador peninsula.

The rational moralist may see how there may easily arise circumstances under which the mandates of the Great Man might induce the individual to perform acts quite the contrary of righteous. We do indeed encounter this very situation. For no matter how arbitrary, or even eccentric, the imaginary commands of the inner element might be, they would have to be performed by the man who is "good" in the native sense. The law of conscience, as some would call it, could lead to injuries to others considered as reprisals for some imaginary offenses. [10] It could and did lead to contests for supremacy among men who had cultivated strong soul-spirits and were thirsting for rivals upon whom to test their powers. We even discover that gratification of the passions, often leading to dissipation, is intended to satisfy the soul-spirit; then dissipation to an immoral degree becomes condoned as an act of merit. A good Naskapi, for instance, a righteous, self-considering man, could not be a total abstainer from intoxicants, nor from the excessive inhalation of tobacco, nor from gluttony when he feels an inclination toward these excesses. For his Great Man prompts these desires. Even though they upset the physical well-being for a time, their mental stimulation, the ecstatic state, is a sign of his senses that his Great Man is being stimulated according to wish and will afford him full necessary protection.

But perhaps the most forcible example of the immorality of the sheer conscience rule of the Montagnais-Naskapi is the case of imagination prompting him to think that one of his fellow-men has become malevolent and has inflicted upon humanity disease, starvation, accident, or the like, through the agency of his Great Man. In such a case, we can see how retribution of a serious form might be perpetrated upon the innocent.

10. Indeed, the Naskapi could just as well say in the words of Samuel L. Clemens: "There is only one impulse which moves a person to do things. That sole impulse is the impulse to content his own spirit. . . . and winning its approval." Helvetius, a French philosopher of the eighteenth century, taught also that man acts in the direction of satisfying and contenting his own strongest feelings, emotions, and desires, such being the basis of all our ethical teaching.

While we encounter some difficulty in trying to learn the fate of the disembodied soul-spirit, a belief is evident that the souls of individuals become transformed into stars and rest in the firmament until they become reincarnated.

The soul theory here is illustrated by a comparison of the terms which denote "soul" and "star": *atcakwu'c* (diminutive form), "little soul" or "star"; *atcakwuci'ts* (Lake St. John and Mistassini), the plural for both being the animate plural form of *atca'k^w*, "soul," without the diminutive ending. This is evidently an old native concept, since its occurrence is indicated for the early Wabanaki (Penobscot), viz., *keta'nk^wzu*, "ghost," or "spirit of a dead person"; *keta'nk^wzu audi'*, "ghost trail or path," the Milky Way; and *awa'tawe'su*, "star," literally "far-away being." We learn that *tci˙pa'i meckǝnu'*, "ghost trail," is also the designation for Milky Way throughout the Labrador area. In tales and shaman anecdotes of the Northeast the spirit is occasionally mentioned as leaving the body temporarily in the form of a spark or ball of fire. While it might be thus indicated that a falling star would be interpreted as a manifestation of a falling soul, inquiry among the Indians fails to show this.

We learn, furthermore, in comparing star and soul identity, of a saying among the Indians that newly born babies come from the clouds, *nack^w*, *na'ckwu*, "cloud," to be compared with *wa'cko*, "heaven," or what is pointed out as the starry universe. Another term, *micta i'cpamits*, "in the great heights above," is applied to the upper realm. (The latter suggests analogy with Penobscot, *spǝ'mkik*, "in heaven," or "in the above.")

The Montagnais have the habit of telling children who ask where their baby sisters and brothers come from that they came from the clouds. The Canadian-French under similar circumstances speak of babes being brought by the crow or raven, the Sicilians an angel, while generally among English-speaking peoples the event is attributed to the stork. It is interesting to compare these sayings with that of the Penobscot who assign the visitation of birth to the generosity of the frog! Dr. Hallowell adds that the same belief is current among the St. Francis Abenaki.

That the abode of souls of the deceased is in the sky, that they manifest themselves there in the form of stars, that they travel over the Milky Way, that they congregate in a dance and illuminate the night sky as the northern lights, are indications of the fundamental eschatology of the peoples of the Northeast.

As might logically be expected, with such a belief in mind, *Tsəka'bec*, the hero-transformer of Labrador mythology, at the termination of his career among the people on earth becomes transferred to the sun or to the moon, according to the version, and assumes his place as the supreme soul-luminary of the sky.

Since much the same phenomena are recorded among the Wabanaki, I feel that matters of correspondence between these two long-separated and isolated types of Algonkian culture may be regarded as fairly archaic.[11]

With the Milky Way conceived as the "Ghost Road," and with it the idea of deceased souls residing in the sky, we encounter the combination of ideas given in conformity with the conception of the spirit realm recorded in far distant Finno-Ugric mythology.[12]

Burial

The fear of the ghosts of deceased relatives, so marked in some "primitive" cultures, and often attributed without cause to some American culture areas, seems to amount to little in the region under consideration. And yet neither placation rites nor evidences of sentiments of hospitality toward the soul are met in the present or in the earlier life of these tribes.

The scene at the deathbed is very solemn. In the case of the young, as I have seen it, the parents remain near the afflicted, endeavoring to tranquilize the last moments of life with endearing terms and caresses, themselves suffering in deepest but repressed dejection of spirit. I have never seen them abandon themselves to emotion nor utter their lamentations above the tone of smothered sobbing. Within a day or so of the event, according to the place and time of year, the body is put in the ground near a lake, facing the water. The trees are cleared in front so that the deceased can see persons passing by. Then a fence is built about it. In the case of an important hunter a pole, upon which are fastened bear and beaver skulls, is

11. E. O. James in "The Concept of the Soul in North America," *Folk-Lore*, XXXVIII (1927), 338-57, reviews some of these forms of belief.
12. W. Holmberg, *Mythology of All Races* (1927), Vol. IV, chap. v, "Finno-Ugric, Siberia."

erected near the grave. Bodies of those who die far from home are often transported, frozen, by dog-sled to their home territories.

The question of tree burial seems to remain yet an open one for this region, one to be settled in the future only by repeated archaeological proof. Bodies are interred to face the forest. At Lake St. John, for instance, they face southwest, away from the lake and toward the nearest woods. I was told that to bury a man standing up would be done through vengeance, as in the case of a slain enemy. It would prevent his soul from resting.

In Hind's time (1853), the body was buried three feet deep, either placed on its side in the sleeping posture, or, sometimes, sitting. It was wrapped in a blanket with weapons and tools. Occasionally, dogs were killed and left with the corpse. The body was laid with the head to the west, feet to the east. Hind records that a "medicine man" harangued the soul of the dead, giving it advice! Over the filled-up grave a birch-bark hut was built and an opening or window left in it through which the widow inserted food.[13] In 1631, when first visited by the Jesuits, the Montagnais did not remove the corpse through the door of the dwelling, but through an opening in the side. Among other details in the *Relations* of 1631 we learn that when demise took place in the winter, the corpse was placed upon a scaffold ten or twelve feet high and left until the ground thawed, when it was buried in a "cemetery."

13. Hind, op. cit., I, 170.

CONCEPTS OF MYTHOLOGY
AND THE UNIVERSE

Chapter Four

A REVIEW of the content of mythology among the tribes of the peninsula discloses neither ritual narratives nor the background of religious philosophy. The tales incline to resemble those of the Eskimo in their narratives portraying human characteristics, in which shamanism, nature transformations and magic principles are illustrated. No mythical revelations of ceremony, no historic creed explanations, help us to understand religious origins. Traditional narratives are little more than tales. They seem to imply some understanding of the underlying principles of shamanism and conjuring, and they do the same as regards the habits of animals in general, which possess, by all appearances, the characteristics of human beings at times. But beyond these assumptions the tales only register miraculous wonder-workers, in either human or animal guise, whose conduct has the magical effect of producing transformations in the physical world in much the same manner as the conjurors of today can work them out. Hence, continuity is apparently a principle of some importance. There is no world genesis. In the category of mythical heroes, or more properly perhaps, traditional heroes, we come to one in particular who eclipses his contemporaries and in him we encounter the focus of human importance; the trickster-transformer, under the sobriquet, is *Tsəka'bec*. Only for the reason of his performance among other human hero-transformers does he merit this distinction. This estimate of *Tsəka'bec* is strengthened by the appearance of altruism, his noteworthy devotion to human welfare, a common characteristic of Indian mythology in America, but here in Labrador less emphatic than elsewhere among other Algonkian-speaking tribes.

Tsəka'bec is essentially a human personage, but one endowed with the shamanistic power of a cosmic champion and possessing, above all in the native esteem, the attribute of altruism. So he becomes in a sense the national character hero and might, were his career developed by literary and religious pressure, reach the magnitude of a national prophet or semidivine figure.

Tsəka'bec stands forth as the personification of those aspirations held highest in the mind of the Naskapi, as the master of that conjuring craft exerted over man and animal which the hunter strives so hard to develop within himself.

The character of *Tsəka'bec* is worthy of a review in this connection. The repetition of a complete cycle of his career seems hardly called for, since one series of the tales has been offered in print. [1]

Tsəka'bec lived with his grandmother and his sister. He killed the various evil monsters and cannibals wherever he learned of them. When about to start on a journey to attack one, he deceived his sister as to his intention by saying that he was going to kill squirrels. His sister was tender-hearted. Before starting he would sing and strum his bowstring. Among his achievements was his slaying of the giant cannibal, *Mista'peo*, "Great Man," and his wife, and his marriage with their two daughters in company with *Wiskedjanape'o*, "Whisky-Jack Man." He killed the cannibal girls who lured victims to their swinging rope. He transformed many animals: the mink, the bat, the white whale. He caught the sun and the moon in a snare. He employed "contrary speech," saying "no" if he meant "yes," for instance.

When he had finished his labors of transformation on the earth, he took his mother, sister, and wife to a mountain and caused them to ascend to the sky behind an arrow which he blew upon, and all withdrew to the sky where they now are. He promised the Indians to return to earth again and destroy evil. He may bring about a war. He has selected men abroad in the world who are preparing to perform his commands.

Tsəka'bec is an ancient term, possibly one that cannot be accurately etymologized. One rendering would seem to be "young man who trails a line behind him," from *tsəka'beo*, "he who trails a line" (Mistassini); another, "small man."

The closest mythological analogy with this cycle is to be found

1. F. G. Speck, "Montagnais and Naskapi Tales from the Labrador Peninsula," *Journal of American Folk-Lore*, Vol. XXXVIII (1925), No. 147, pp. 1-32.

in the hero-cycle of the Wanabaki. Undoubtedly, a genetic relation exists between the two series of tales. Most convincing is the element of deceit in the hero's attitude toward his family which, in the Wabanaki, is the basis of his proper name, *Gluska'be*, "Deceiving-Man." In the Penobscot *Gluska'be* cycle, the episode of trailing a cord behind him also occurs as an incident of the hero's career. Future study and more extensive collection of versions from different groups of Labrador may bring to light links with the trans-Laurentian series, now effaced by time and distance.

The great mythical personage of the Cree, northern Ojibwa Algonquin, and some central Algonkian peoples, under the proper name of *Wisa'kadjak* and its variants, appears here among the Labrador tribes as an insignificant character. *Wiskedja'n* occurs only in one or two tales. This is an important fact for the mythologist because it serves to determine the eastern terminus of the hero-cycle with *Wisa'kadjak* as the transformer's name. At the same time we may note that the earth-diver theme does not cross to the eastward of the same culture boundary. This important line of demarcation from what we know at present seems to be at the St. Maurice River. [2]

A survey of the available Montagnais-Naskapi tales betrays little indication that they serve any religious end beyond providing explanations of existing phenomena in the natural world. The explanatory motive averages fairly high in the stories. Existing conditions, the forms and behavior of animals and the geography of the country, are largely the result of *transformation*. Consequently, transformation becomes an abstract principle in the system of thought of the nomads. We see how mammals, fish, birds, and natural landmarks are produced in their present guise by metamorphosis under the power of the conjuror, a shaman of a mythical period. Another important fact is that the trend of Montagnais-Naskapi evolutionary theory is from man to animals. We have a declaration on this point from the old Mistassini ex-shaman, Ka'kwa: "The animals were once like the Indians and could talk as we do. But some of them were overcome by others while in some animal disguise and forced to remain as such. Others assumed animal shapes so much that involuntarily they became transformed permanently."

To arrive at a definite idea of how the manifestations of nature are pictured in the native mind is one of the most difficult of matters.

2. The Mistassini may be an exception to this limitation.

The situation is not indeed so different from what we experience in our own case when trying to visualize trees, waterfalls, lightning and the like as semivolitional beings, as poets do, for instance. The Labrador Indian naturally perceives the objects of nature as they appear outwardly to the eye, but then only as tangible embodiments of volitional beings. Such an attitude is as real to him as it is unreal to a sophisticated mind. Beneath the exterior is the inner element which, in the native mind, is the very "soul" of the thing. This may at times take human form and be encountered abroad in the world with little about it to indicate its normal character. These animations of nature may, like the souls dominating the animals, be induced by the control of a shaman to do various services for man, likewise, against him. They too have their sensitive natures much as man has, and so the control of the shaman over them depends upon his power to call and please them. The power they possess and also the power they submit to in such cases is likewise *mɘntu'*. The number and form of manifestations in the sky and upon the earth would seem to be without limit. Those which are mentioned either directly or in the tales include the properties of nature in all its aspects; winds, seasons, the cardinal points, stars, mountain depths, sea depths, trees, rocks, plants, thunder, lightning, the aurora, mirage, cold, heat, rain and clouds being mentioned in one way or another. The shaman conjures with and employs them in his work as much as he does the animals. And it would seem that some of them rise from the level of vagueness to the specific form of beings who produce the visible phenomena of which they are the spiritual representations. What it is beyond their great influence upon the Indian mind that causes some of these forces to be personified more than others is difficult to say. The selection seems to be arbitrary and also to vary much among the different bands and indeed with individuals. In the western portion of the peninsula, the Lake St. John and Mistassini informants hold definite attitudes toward certain ones. For instance, here we find *Tci'wetinowi''nu,* "Man of the North," as the impersonation of winter and the northwind. Waugh states in his notes that he did not record this being at Davis Inlet, although Cabot refers to it there. The reason may have been that he did not have the correct form of the name. He asked about "*Kiwaytinoshuh.*" [3] He is held in fear. His name even is mentioned with timidity. And this

3. A Cree form meaning "North Being."

fear commands observance of a most interesting rule in respect to the position in which the toboggan is stood against a tree (as is the custom in the woods when it is not in use); namely, that the curve of the toboggan head would be turned toward the south out of consideration for "that Man of the North." If this direction is not feasible, the toboggan may be stood with the curve facing the east. Otherwise, it is feared that the owner may soon freeze or be taken sick, or the game will go away from him. The curved front of the toboggan, among the Naskapi of the east, is frequently ornamented with red paint, or the head-fastening cross-piece of wood may be carved. Figure 3 shows the design painted in vermilion on a small

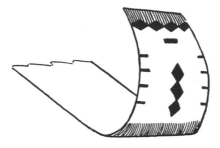

FIGURE 3

Painted toboggan head. The design exerts a magic influence upon the Man of the North (Ungava band).

toboggan from Ungava. Figure 4 shows the carved head-piece from a toboggan brought from Lake Michikamau. The Eskimo of the east coast of Labrador share this carved figure with the Naskapi, as is shown in a specimen of a miniature wooden sled in the collections of the museum of McGill University, Montreal. Here the front crossbar of the sled has an identical carved contour. Among the more

FIGURE 4

Carved head of toboggan decorated to favor the Man-of-the-North spirit (Michikamau).

civilized bands these decorative protections are not so common and few know what they mean. Incidentally, we note that similar protection is insured against the Man of the North in placing the tent. When the wigwam is built, the door is made to face the south or east, toward the warmth of the sun. There is, mentioned by the Lake St. John people, in this connection an aesthetic motive—to face the sunrise. The reason is that one must not be too familiar, too friendly, with "that Man of the North." He will bring misfortune.

The generalized concept of the form of the earth, which is termed tsi'tətci''nau, "our world, universe" (Mistassini), appears to be that it is shaped like a hill and floats upon the water. Questioning fails to evoke the belief that it rests upon the carapace of the tortoise or that it is the carapace itself, as is believed by the Algonkian southward. It was stated by a Mistassini informant (Charley Metowe'cic) while discussing the matter, that the earth's form comes to be known only from the testimony of a person about to die. In the vision that comes at this time the mind can view the universe and sees all around the earth as it rises above the water. And he feels it rocking!

The concept of the earth seems linked in some imaginative fashion with that of the mountain. The latter is venerated apparently through its association with the idea of its being the abode of a spirit-force. The fear of evil consequence resulting from the ascent of high mountains is general to Algonkian tribes of the Northeast. And we may trace the connection of this observance with the belief in the great mountain in the far northern part of the Labrador peninsula wherein dwells the Master of the Caribou and where death lurks for the human intruder. The details of this topic, which is an extended one, are reserved for treatment in another place (see p. 84). In tracing the area of distribution of this religious association, namely, the mountain as the dwelling of the giver of game, one is not surprised to discover its existence among the Algonkian peoples as far south as the Delawares and the tribes of the Susquehanna, [4] and in the mythology of the Siouan and Algonkian tribes of the Great Plains where it is wrapped up in the origin myth of the Sun Dance and the origin of the bison. But when we encounter a similar attitude of fear and veneration for certain mountains in Finno-Ugric Asiatic localities, the explanation of certain common properties in the belief

4. For the Delaware version of the belief that the giver of big game lives beneath a hill, see M. R. Harrington, "The Religion and Ceremonies of the Lenape," Indian Notes, Museum American Indian (1921); Louise W. Murray, Historical and Archaeological Investigations of Aboriginal Life Along the Susquehanna, MS, pp. 62-63.

within the circumpolar area thrust themselves forth with some insistence.

Inasmuch as ordinary human souls may take the form of stars, we naturally infer that the sun and moon might be soul manifestations of extraordinary magnitude. So it happens that the greatest of human personages, the mythical hero-transformer *Tsəka'bec*, appears in the form of the sun and moon. The two luminaries are counterparts, the sun being termed *pi·'cəm*, and the moon, *tebiskau' pi·'cəm*, "night sun," or luminary. There is however, no evidence of formal sun worship. The transformation is accounted for in the following specimen myths from several parts of the peninsula.

Tsəka'bec Snares the Sun and Becomes Transformed into It (Escoumains Band)

In ancient times there was an old man who had a wife and a son whose name was *Tsəka'bec*, "Finished Man." They were the only people living and *Tsəka'bec* was the first finished child. The old man was the master of all the birds and small mammals of the earth. They lived in the woods near him. When he wanted any of them, he had only to call them to him.

The sun was so hot in those days that these small animals and the birds could not live, and the old man was in great distress because his birds and animals were being killed by the sun. Accordingly the old man planned to capture the sun and so put an end to the trouble among his beasts. He built a dead-fall of logs where the sun arose from the edge of the world, intending to capture it by this means. But the boy, *Tsəka'bec*, when he saw what his father was doing, said, "That will not do! If you are going to capture the sun it will have to be with something better than a wooden trap. I, however, will make a snare for you that will catch the sun."

That night he made a loop-snare of *babiche* (rawhide thong) and set it at the place where the sun rises. The next morning when the sun rose it was caught in the snare and held. Then the world remained in darkness. When the beasts woke up in the morning all was still dark, and they thought that the end of the world had come and that they would all perish. Different ones among them tried to approach the sun and cut the snare, but in vain. The rabbit tried, but it was too hot for him; he got his fur burned. The birds could not approach the place, because they could not see well in the dark. Then the field mouse tried, who runs very near the ground; and the mole, who goes under the ground; but they could not approach near enough to cut the snare.

When the old man's wife woke up she saw that it was still dark, although it was late in the day. She said to her husband, "What have you done? Have you captured the sun?" "Yes," said the old man, "I only tried to capture the sun, but *Tsəka'bec* succeeded in snaring it for me, because it was burning up the whole world." "Well," said the old woman, "you have done a bad thing, for it is now dark and we cannot see to gain our living. It is no good thing that you have accomplished." Then even *Tsəka'bec* tried to approach the sun to cut the snare. He held a piece of hide in front of his face, but could not go near enough to cut the snare. All this time every-thing was quiet, as the sun did not cry out. There was only the moon left to light up the world and it was very hard for the old people to get about to gain their living in the darkness. Only the owl and some few of the other animals had eyes large enough to make their way in the dark woods.

Soon the old woman took her hook and line and went out to fish in the lake. *Tsəka'bec* was standing near her as she cast her line; sud-denly the hook caught in his eye and tore one of his eyes out. There he was with only one eye left. "You have been punished," said his mother, "for snaring the sun." He went home and said to his father, "I have had my eye torn out and now I cannot see at all. Call your birds and take an eye out of the owl's head and put in in place of my eye. The owl has a good big eye to see in the dark. He can go every-where in the dark. Take an eye out of him and put it in me." So the old man called the owl to him and plucked out one of his eyes and put it in *Tsəka'bec's* head. Then *Tsəka'bec* found that he could see everything with the owl's eye much better than with his own. He went hunting and could see fairly well. So he went back to his father and told him to call the owl and give him another owl's eye like the first one. Then the old man called the owl, took out his other eye and fastened it in *Tsəka'bec's* head as he had the first. Then *Tsə-ka'bec* had two good eyes for the dark and could see to travel every-where he wanted to. He had two big round eyes like those of the owl.

Soon *Tsəka'bec* grew up and wanted to get married so he traveled about to find a woman. At last he found a creature whom he took for his wife. The first night instead of lying down with her, he said, "Follow me." All night he led her here and there in the woods hunting. Since she could not see so well as he, she could hardly follow him. She bumped into trees and fell down so that he thought he would do well to have her eyes changed for a pair like his own. He took her to his father and said, "Get her an eye like mine from the owl." So the old man called his birds and took an eye from an owl and put it in the woman's eye socket. Now she could see fairly well as they traveled about in the dark.

Soon the wife of Tsəka'bec bore a son. They named him Tsəka'bejis, "Little Tsəka'bec," after his father. When he was born he had two big round eyes like those of the owl and his parents. He could see in the dark as well as any owl. When he grew a little older, he said to his father, "You have snared the sun, you! That is why it is so dark and why we have such big eyes." "Yes," said Tsəka'bec. "Well then," said Little Tsəka'bec, "I am going to snare the moon (night sun)." So he made a snare and set it where the moon emerges. This was in the path where Tsəka'bec walked as he tended his traps. As he walked into the snare Tsəka'bec was snared instead of the moon. He was caught by the legs and there he hung, head on the ground, feet in the air, and crying loudly for help. Then Little Tsəka'bec came up and said, "You are caught instead of the moon. Now you are punished for catching the sun. You can stay there and give light yourself." So he left his father, who became the sun, hanging there by his feet attached by the line. And Little Tsəka'bec continued to live with his mother.

Tsəka'bec Snares the Moon (Mistassini Band)

At that time there was no night. Both the sun and moon had their paths in the sky and one was above the horizon all the time. Tsəka'bec decided to change it. His sister had given him a few hairs from her head and said, "Whenever you want to get anything, get it with this." So one day Tsəka'bec began singing and asked for another hair. The sister said, "You are up to something." "No," he answered. Then she gave him another hair, and it was a snare. He set the snare at one end of the moon's trail and caught it. It was dark for a while. Then *Tsəka'bec* went to his sister, and he was crying because of what he had done.

He had, once upon a time, taken all the small animals and put them in a bag: mice, moles, squirrels, shrews, insects, and small creatures. He asked his sister to bring him his bag of animals. She said, "What do you want to do?" "Oh! nothing, but bring me them." He took them and went to loosen the moon from the snare. One after another they tried and died, until at last the shrew succeeded, and the moon came up as it is now, and so it followed that the sun and moon became as they are now, and day and night are regulated for the good of man. [5]

Tsəka'bec Snares the Moon and Gets Into It, Becoming the Man in the Moon (Escoumains Band)

"*Tsəka'bec* lived with his sister. He had a good hunting road. One day he got ready to leave the camp in search of game. 'Where are you going?' his sister asked him. 'I am only going to snare some hares," he answered. So he departed. He went to the place where the moon comes up (at the edge of the world) and there placed his snare. When the moon came up, it was caught in the snare. When *Tsəka'bec* came and saw what had happened, he was pleased. He liked the moon so well that he got inside it. Then he turned it loose and now he looks out from it as the 'man in the moon.' " [6]

In none of the bands have prayers or ceremonies been found to indicate that any more benefit may be derived from these sources than those so graciously and constantly bestowed by spirit-forces without insistence or recompense from the tongue of man. Acts of minor sacrifice, respect and submission seem to be sufficient to avert malevolence.

Among the supernatural forces at times mentioned as personified beings, are a group of poetical concepts: *wa'banu,* "day sky"; *wabanicu',* "east wind"; *tci·we'tənicu',* "north wind"; *tci·we'tənɔc,* "little north [west] wind"; also *nəkabehe'ncu; cawənɔcu',* "south wind"; *nemictcu'wɔts,* "thunder"; *wute'ia'tɔkʷ,* "heart of tree" [sap]; *tamwini·be'gʷ,* "deepest part of the sea"; *tci·'cɔgwɔts,* "skies, clouds, days." The wind names may be rendered as "man of the east,"

5. *Journal of American Folk-Lore,* Vol. XXXVIII (1925), No. 147, p. 26.
6. F. G. Speck, Montagnais and Naskapi Tales from the Labrador Peninsula," *Journal of American Folk-Lore,* Vol. XXXVIII (1925), No. 147, p. 5.

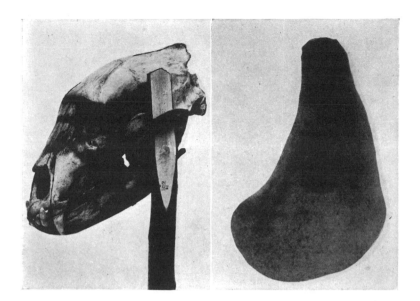

Left: Skull of black bear erected on alder stick out of respect for slain animal. The jaws are lashed with thongs, the forehead painted with two black bars, and a piece of tobacco wrapped in birch bark inserted in the cavity (Lake St. John). Right: Grease ladle of bear shoulder blade used in response to dream (Lake St. John).

PLATE VI

Birch-bark food tray (*wi·ya'gən*) used by a hunter when eating game, especially beaver, killed after receiving a dream admonition. Side and bottom views showing decoration. Length, 23.5 inches. The particular significance of this emblem lies in its being known as *tceka'cəko pi·'cəma'*, "sun illumination," by which is meant the spots of light cast upon the earth by the sun shining through a canopy of thick clouds. The Mistassini conceive this beautiful and impressive phenomenon of nature to be a revelation from *Ketci·'manitu'*, "Great Spirit," to the hunter, betraying to him the whereabouts of game. To see this manifestation of nature, either in reality or in a dream, is a blessing for which the devout and observant native is always yearning.

"man of the north," and so on. The preceding are all given in the Mistassini dialect.

The winds, next in rank of power below the Creator, are pre-eminent as spirits of the four quarters—forces controlling the universe; the life and growth of man and of animal and plant life. An explanatory myth (Mistassini) satisfies our quest for the origin belief of this condition of nature.

Origin of the Four Earth Winds

There was a hunter long ago when the world was being formed who dreamed that he would meet with good luck if he killed a lynx and ate the whole of it. The next time he went out he caught a lynx and ate it all. His dream had told him that his good luck would be to kill something big. So when he went out to find what was promised him he suddenly came upon something truly big but not what he expected. It was indeed a *wi'ndigo!* But by the help of spirits which came to his aid he finally killed the *wi'ndigo*. And there it lay dead on the ground while all the people came to look at the creature. They formed in a half-circle around the body of the *wi'ndigo* standing facing the east, some on the north side, some on the west and some on the south but none on the east side. They were waiting for the Man of the East, the Man of the North, the Man of the West and the Man of the South to come and take their shares as was done when they lived on earth among the creatures.

While they were standing thus waiting, the Man of the East [East Wind] the most feared of all, came walking from the east. He came within the circle of the people and started to take his share. He cut off the head of the *wi'ndigo*, then his right arm and leg and finally his heart. That was more than his share for it should have been divided among the four spirits equally. That is why he is called the Stingy One. He takes everything without regard for others, so when the east wind blows ever after he takes all the game and fish away from the people. When the Man of the East had taken nearly all the best part of the *wi'ndigo*, the Man of the North came for his share. He too is hard and cruel and he took more than his [quarter] share, the other leg and arm. Then the Man of the West came for his share and he took the rest of the meat from the body of the *wi'ndigo*. Last of all came Man of the South. He is the most gentle and mild and so all he got was the back bone for his share. [Since then the four spirits of the winds and the four quarters have acted in the same way as they did then and are known by these characters.]

The Lake St. John and Mistassini hunters declare it to be the truth that when the east wind blows there is no use to go hunting or fishing because they will get nothing in their nets and no animals can be found in their traps nor to be shot.

Other celestial phenomena seem to be unpersonified physical

properties, phenomena created as the result of force rather than spiritual entities themselves.

The rainbow bears a designation which can hardly be considered descriptive or theological, but seems rather to be traceable to artistic symbolism. In the various Montagnais-Naskapi dialects the rainbow is "legging," or *pi·ca'gənwi·abi*, "legging string"; *ləgəpeja'gən*, "legging" (Escoumains); *wikwela'kapecagən* (Coast Montagnais); *wiu'kbecagəniabi'*, "striped legging string" (Mistassini); *wiukweabi'* (Mistassini), "vein string"; *wi·lukweabi'* (Cree); *nəkəpeha'gən wiabi'*, "legging string" (Nastasquan); *nəkəpeca'gənwiabi'* (Michikamau); *pi·tuləkəpeca'gən* (Seven Islands). In the Lake St. John dialect, however, we find another, namely, *pi·'cəmwiabi'*, "sun string," which suggests a clue to the origin of the name, in that the rainbow may have been conceived of as the "legging string of the sun." The designation *pi·'cəm* may have been elided from some of the terms in the course of time. The Indians themselves do not seem to bother with further explanation of the term.

The rainbow, in the words of Alex Denis (Escoumains-Tadoussac band, 1921), brings the water. "But if it did not hold back somewhat there would be a deluge, for it also holds back the water. When the rainbow fails to hold back the water, then it rains hard, and a quantity of frogs and toads falls down." It is interesting to note the belief in the "rain of frogs and toads" among these Indians corresponding to that of Europeans. It may possibly be of Old Testament origin. In June, 1920, a very peculiar rainbow appeared while I was with the Lake St. John Indians. It was during a hot, calm and dry spell of weather. At eight in the morning part of the arc showed at a great height, although there was no sign of rain anywhere. This was observed by the hunter with whom I was staying and pronounced a sign of bad weather soon to come. It soon did come.

Another weather phenomenon and sign of an approaching storm is the sun dog, *nembuckutwe'o* (*pi·'cəm*), "deceiving, false sun" (Escoumains).

Along the coast of the St. Lawrence the weather conditions in summer often produce very beautiful minor mirages causing the distant shores and islands to appear elevated to magnified heights. This is called *ili'twacteo* (Escoumains). Its only significance is the sign of good weather.

The aurora borealis, however, is remarked by all the bands and much commented upon. It is called *wawa'ctockwao*, "[night] lightning illumination," and *wawactockwu'n*, "shining clouds" (Lake St. John), and is explained as caused by the "spirits of the dead dancing" (*tci·pa'its nimo'wuts*), in the northern sky where they abide. Waugh's notes on the Davis Inlet Naskapi inform us that it is here called *beskwadinau'* (possibly meaning "bursting [in the] north"). This belief suggests Eskimo influence. It is current among the Indians throughout the peninsula. Said old Napani' of the Lake St. John band one night, during an auroral display that brought many of the men forth from their tents to behold it, "He! There is my old grandmother dancing!" They regard it as a sign of high wind for the next day. The belief accords with the idea of the souls of the dead residing in the sky as stars (see p. 50).

The Milky Way has another spiritual connotation running without variation throughout the peoples of the peninsula and likewise through the entire Hudson Bay as well as the Wabanaki region. In Montagnais-Naskapi it is called *tci·'pai meckɔnu'*, "ghost road," or, as some might prefer to see it rendered, "dead persons' path." For anyone to observe the forking branch of the Milky Way is a sign that someone among his relations is soon to die.

Constellations are not especially noted, contrary to what might be expected among people who are abroad much at night. I noted only the names of the Pleiades, *wutci·'manɔc*, a term evidently too archaic for the present informants, and *nictotcima'uts*, "three chiefs," applied to Orion's Belt.

The "falling star," *petsi'natcɔkwu'c*, seems to figure only as a weather sign, meaning that the wind will blow in the direction designated.

As regards the comet, Hind learned from Père Arnaud that among the Naskapi northwest of Lake Manikuagan the comet of 1853 produced the utmost consternation among the Indians, who reported the sight as a new one to their experience. [7]

The North Star is generally throughout the area known as *mɔcɔ'o wɔtce'gɔtɔk*, "great star," sometimes specifically *tci·we'tɔn atcɔkwu'c*, "North Star" (diminutive) (Mistassini and Lake St. John).

From Ka'kwa's son, my religious mentor among the Mistassini, at Lake St. John, I was told in the winter of 1920 the following

7. Hind, *op. cit.*, II, 101.

origin tale of the North Star, the only one of its kind that I ob-tained. "People of another world were living in a village. They knew that a new world was going to be formed. One day some of them started to quarrel. Among them was North Star. They fell upon him and were going to kill him, but he fled and soared into the sky, all after him. When they saw that they couldn't get him they declared, 'Well! Let him be, he is the North Star, and will be of good use to serve the people of the world that is to come as a guide by night on their travels.' So the North Star became the guide of the people." The conjuror, we might add, does not allow himself nor his audience to eat during his performances until after the North Star has become invisible toward daybreak.

The morning star itself is *wa'bənatcəkwu'c*, a literal equivalent known in general among all the bands.

The Naskapi who gather at Seven Islands know the evening star as *miĉtəwətce'gətək*, "great star." At the time it was pointed out to me and noted it was, I believe, Jupiter (July, 1925). The Mistassini and Lake St. John Indians give the name *tci'cəga wət-cəkwu'c*, "day star," for, they say, it can be seen like a spot of silver in the daytime. Our most explicit information concerns the con-stellation Ursa Major. This group is known among all the bands as *wətce'kətək*, "fisher star," and is the basis of an explanatory tale. The fisher-marten becomes transformed into the stars of the famous constellation. The legend is so characteristic of the region that it seems advisable to give the Mistassini version in full, as narrated in that dialect in 1915 by Ka'kwa, the religious authority of these remote hunters, whose name has been mentioned before. This is the most extended version I have recorded of the story. It is a free translation.

The Origin of Summer and the Fisher Transformed into a Constellation

A long time ago there was a child who had lots of lice. And they left him. Then other people came and took him to bring him up. One of them killed his lice, all but two which he left on him, one male and one female. He said, "*As long as man lives it will be a pastime for him* [*to pick lice from his head*]." Then he went away carrying his kettle on his back. He went to see the man who was the owner of the child. When he came to them, he stayed with them. He lived with them, but he did nothing while he was there, and then he went away. In the morning when he left them, the child cried. Then they started off. The child was always crying, even when they gave him things to play with. They even made a bow for him. But he kept on crying just the same. "What can we do?" they said, "For he does not stop crying." Then the child said, "Not until I have summer birds that I can shoot with my arrow will I stop crying. Only then will I stop." Then after the boy had said this, the people said, "We are ready [to go and get what he wants]." Then they started out to get the Summer. "How shall we ever manage to get for him what he wants so that he will stop? What shall we do? It is so far away. Let us leave the otter behind. Don't let him go with us. He has the habit of laughing too much. He will spoil it for us." "What do you say about me?" said the otter. "You stay, don't you go, because you will get more when they divide the grease." "No," said the otter, "I will go, for I too pity him, that boy, for crying. You keep your grease," he said. When they got started, they came first to the house of the beaver. He was going to share the grease. As they were dividing up the grease, when they got halfway with it, the otter started laughing. And then they jumped on him. Then they tickled him, when he was crawling out. At last he could not hear on account of so much laughing. Then he gave back what he had (his share of the grease). Then they went back to where they had started from. When they arrived there at their camps, the boy was still crying, and they said, "We will try again to go. But we will go without the otter." "I am going to go too," said the otter. "If only you go you will not be able to enter the beaver's house when we reach it." "That's all right," they said. Then they started again and when they came to the beaver they told the otter not to bother about going in. They said, "We will bring out your share." "Oh, that's all right," he said. Then they went in, the rest of them. After they had all sat down with the beaver, they were going to share up the bear grease. Then again he gave the strangers something to eat. And they said to the beaver, "There is one of our companions who did not come in." He gave them each something to eat. After they had eaten they gave the beaver some tobacco. When they went out they carried to the otter his share of the grease. "My share must have been bigger," he told them. "You must have eaten some of it." When he had told them this, they started out again and arrived where the Summer was. There was a very big long wigwam. "Wonder where the Summer is lying in there?" they said. "Someone go in first." "Who will it be who goes?" They said to one of them, "You go." This time it was the bird. "No," said the bird. "When I fly I make too much noise with my wings. Someone else go." But they said to him, "Let us see. You fly close to our heads." And he flew close to their heads, but they could hardly hear his wings. "That's the one," they said. "Let him go." Then he flew over and alighted on the tent. He looked through a hole in the door. And he saw where the Summer was kept. And those in the tent (feeling that someone was looking at them) said, "Someone is looking at us. We had better look for him. It seems like a stranger, by the way he acts." Thus they spoke. "From which direction does he seem to be looking?" Then they told one old man, "From the daylight direction. That is the direction from whence he is looking at us," said he. At last they saw him. Two small eyes. "Here is the one who is looking at us," they said. "Who is it?" Some said, "It appears to be a stranger. What can we ever do with him? However, don't let him come in." Then they tried to see him, and they ran out, but they saw nothing. "Nonsense, it is nothing but imagination," they said. "It can't be anything." Then they beheld a muskrat swimming far out in the water. They said, "A stranger appears to be coming. Invite him to come in." And they called to him, "You swimming, who are you?" And he answered, "I am muskrat, always going around alone," he said. "Haven't you any neighbors?" "No," he said, "I am always alone." "Then swim ashore." And the muskrat swam ashore. "Come ashore," they told him. "I never come ashore on the land, only on the rocks" [said the muskrat]. "If you come ashore, we will give you some grease to eat," they said. "Oh, throw some over here to me," said he. Then they threw him some grease, and he ate it. "I can't find any taste to it," he said. "I made a mistake, I mixed water in my mouth. Throw me some grease again," he said, "This time a bigger piece." And they threw him some grease again. "If you come ashore you will get a bigger share," they said. When he had eaten it, they asked him, "Is that good? If it is good, come ashore," they said. "It is good," said he. "Only it is too rich." Then he started to swim away. "Don't tell anybody that you have seen us," he was told. "No," he said. Then he spoke to himself, " I am going to tell it pretty soon," he said. Then he dove. Then no more thence was the muskrat seen by them. Then he searched for his companions. Together they arrived with that bird who had peeped in on the sly, upon the Summer. Just the length of the big tent, the ridge pole just at midday points, leaning exactly toward where the Summer lies. Then the muskrat said [to his friends], "Every morning they paddle after moose over the narrows." (He referred to the habits of the people who were guarding the Summer.) Then the muskrat was told, "Tonight you go and gnaw their paddles and likewise in their canoes you bite through the bottom," so he was told. "And soon as it is morning you will swim pushing the root of a tree over there in the narrows in the place where the moose generally swim across."

Now, the sucker and the sturgeon were accustomed to guard the Summer, so they were told. Accordingly, the muskrat swam pushing the tree so that it looked just like the antlers of a moose swimming by. Now, as it was coming daylight, they saw it appearing just like a moose swimming by. Then one of them said, "Moose is swimming over there." Then they all ran out. Then they jumped into their canoes. But the sucker and the sturgeon, the keepers of the Summer, stayed back. They they pursued the moose a little way out there in the water. Thereupon, the People of the North rushed in [from their hiding places]. And some of them dipped up some sturgeon glue (from a vessel standing near) and pasted up the mouths of sucker and sturgeon. Then they were not able to cry out for help when the People of the North ran in. Then they (the People of the North) took hold of the Summer. Then they ran outside and ran off with it in a birch-bark container. Then the sucker and the sturgeon could not call for help because their mouths were glued up. Then one of them picked up an arrow, punched it in his mouth and called out, "Our Summer, they have taken from us." That's what they said, that sucker and sturgeon. "They have taken from us our Summer," so they said. "Sho! paddle back quickly." Then they tried to paddle back hard and their paddles broke, while others sank to the bottom. But after a while some of them ran in to the camp. "What's that you said?" they asked of the sucker and the sturgeon. "They have taken our Summer away from us," they answered. "Then we will go after them," they said. And they started in pursuit, and soon they caught up to them. "Now they are overtaking us," cried [the pursued]. "Who will engage them and delay them?" "You will!" the otter was told. "Run under or inside a stump!" he was told. Then he ran into one. Then the pursuers came up. "*Ma* (hello)!" they said, "Where is one of them? Oh! Here he is in this hole! Get hold of him!" Then they seized him. "What will be his manner of death?" Then one of them said, "Throw him into the fire." Then the otter said, "You will all make yourselves sick and die when the flames spread out if you do that." Then it was said concerning the otter, "Strike him to death!" "That will cause your deaths when I bleed from the wound!" "Then let's drown him in the water!" Then otter said in great terror, "*Nawe, nawe, nawe* (horrors)!" Then they seized him and threw him in the water. And after awhile over there, way out in the water he emerged. Then he said, "My habitat (natural element)! To die here is impossible for me."

Then again they started off after those who were fleeing with the Summer. And these again they almost caught. When they came close, the pursued ones said, "Who will engage them again to delay them?" Then the fisher was told, "You, fisher!" "What shall I do?" he said. "Run up a tree," they told him. Then he ran up a tree. And the pursuers came up. One arrived first. "Where is he?" "He must be up in the tree. Look for him!" Then they saw fisher up in the tree. And they shot at him. But they only ripped off a little of his tail, for he ran around behind the tree so fast that they could not do anything to him. They said, "Where is the most expert bowman?" "He was not yet arrived." But at last he came along. "Now!" he was told, "We cannot do anything to fisher. It is your turn." Then he shot at him. Twice he shot at him, but he did not hit him once. Then he said, "This time I'll shoot you with an arrow right." Then he shot him. Then fisher blew off toward the sky with the arrow sticking in him. They did not know how that was. Then they looked in the sky and saw fisher. "We could kill him," they said, "*But it will be a sign for man when he comes here in the future, the Fisher Star.*" So they said. And again they wanted to pursue him. But everywhere, all about, they heard the summer birds and saw them at the same time. At the same time they saw the child shooting the birds with an arrow. And when they saw it they went back in different directions.

As to the "Fisher Star," or Great Bear, the second star in his tail is the spot in the tail of the animal where he was shot with the arrow.

A most important fact is brought out by this tale; namely, that the identification of the Ursa constellation with the bear which holds for the Wabanaki and Iroquoian peoples does not pass northward of the St. Lawrence in its distribution.

The solar eclipse is *akwucəmo'pi·'cəm* (Eastern Naskapi), "concealing sun." All through the territory the Indians observed the eclipse of 1925, but the old hunters of the Michikamau band, whom I questioned, did not know any reason for it, which struck me as somewhat strange. At Lake St. John, where it is called *sekᵂskwe'-*

can pi·'cɔm (also Mistassini), the Indians were much frightened by the eclipse, thinking that it was caused by a forest fire, although they did not smell the smoke. Some of them prepared to flee across the lake in their canoes.

Similarly, there was among the same people no spiritual explanation for the earthquake which was very severe throughout the peninsula in the same year. It is called nenɔmickwo'as·i·', "shaking earth." The only cause suggested, by a very old woman of this band, was that a sinkage of the ground had taken place. "It was no spirit or monster that did it," and she laughed as she motioned with her hands to show her idea of land dropping.

The thunder is anɔmistsu' (often used in the plural form, anɔmistsu'ts'). While in general it seems that no mythical associations for the phenomenon are forthcoming, there is nevertheless a tale related of one of the bands of the Barren Grounds of the interior of the peninsula. "The Indians for a long time did not know what caused the thunder. So they conjured a while to find out about it. At last a conjuror got to work and brought it near the earth (when it was thundering). One of the men shot directly into the noise. A great bird resembling a goose fell wounded from the sky. He had hit it. And it fell into a big lake. It was so hot that it made the lake boil so much that the fish living therein were cooked."

As a weather sign nowadays, thundering in the spring means a stretch of fine weather coming. And when a thundercloud appears on the horizon with a threatening appearance, it may be split asunder and rendered harmless by placing an ax in the ground so that its edge is directed toward the storm, according to the statement of a Mistassini chief.

A list of lunar divisions, each beginning with the new moon, obtained from the Lake St. John group is given below. They correspond with the designations given in the Montagnais almanac printed for the mission services. The correspondence is so close that it would seem that the Indians are versed in the formal classification of time standardized by the early priests for their use throughout the North.

tce' pi·'cɔm,	"old moon," January
e'pcɔmɔnckweo,	"shortest (moon)," February
wi·'nɑck' pi·'cɔm,	"woodchuck moon," March

ci'cip̓ pi·'cəm,	"duck moon," April	
onicko' pi·'cəm,	"goose moon," May [8]	
wa'pəgwun pi·'cəm,	"flower moon," June	
ceta'n pi·'cəm,	"Ste. Anne moon," July [9]	
opo'pi·'cəm,	"flying-bird moon," August	
ocaka'ᵚ pi·'cəm,	"(go to) bay moon," September	
waĉtesi·'u pi·'cəm,	"leaves change moon," October	
tsi·'pi pi·'cəm,	"dead moon,"	} November
kəna'tsi·u pi·'cəm,	"falling leaves moon,"	
pi·'cəmuc,	"little moon," December	

Forest Beings

The number of apparitions inhabiting the forests and barrens is rather small considering the opportunity for the play of fear-inspired imagination offered by these immense solitudes. This condition somewhat resembles that of the Eskimo. There are cannibals, giants, dwarfs, and distorted genii.

A prominent spirit of evil nature is the personification of a cannibal giant known among all the bands as *Atce'n*, "Old Man" (Moisie, St. Marguerite, Michikamau), *Atci'n* (Ungava), *ətce'n̓* (Escoumains). Father Laure (1720) referred to the same creature in the Mistassini region. This fearsome creature is described as being formed like a man but as tall as the trees. He is described in a tale, from a woman of the Escoumains-Tadoussac band, as being so large as to carry a child enveloped in one of his mittens. The monster's wife is also mentioned, and a crude carving of a face on the hilt of a bear-bone skinning tool from Seven Islands once was designated to represent the wife of *Atce'n*. The monster is accredited with a certain degree of stupidity and, as he appears in the tales, can be outwitted without much strategy. He is not always in a malignant humor, for the tales mention his coming to a wigwam and being fed by the ancient Indians, who upon that occasion were not much afraid of him. And in another Escoumains legend he restores a lost starving child to relatives and keeps it warm inside his mitt.

There is, on the whole, much to confuse the identity of *Atce'n* with that of *Wi·'tigo*, the second man-eating personage. *Atce'n*,

8. Also known among the devout as *Ma'ni·pi'cəm*, "Mary moon."
9. Named after the patron saint of the Montagnais.

— 67 —

however, is a giant and remains one, while Wiꞏ'tigo may not be distinguished at times from an ordinary human being. At Lake St. John, Atce'n is regarded as being about identical with the latter; a human being who has eaten human flesh and become a semispirit. Both are alike in that they can only be killed by means of conjuring, not by ordinary mechanical means.

The nearest analogy in name and character with Atce'n among neighboring peoples is the Chenoo (Tce'nu) of Micmac legend, according to Rand. Hind mentions Atce'n (which he spells Atshe'm) as the "terror and bugbear" of the Naskapi, a monster who assumes the form of a dreadful conjuror of olden times wandering through the forest in search of human prey, adding that when a report spreads in a camp of his tracks having been seen, the poor creatures fly from the neighborhood. [10]

For those who may think of the Canadian-French contact with the Montagnais, I might add in concluding my notes on Atce'n that he corresponds to Loup-garou among the Canadian habitants of the bush.

Everywhere the Indians speak of the apci'lniꞏc (Lake St. John), "little people" (apciꞏ'niꞏc, Mistassini and eastern Naskapi). The dwarfs here have attributes strikingly similar to those believed in over the whole continent. They are generally amicable to man, frequently give to human beings warnings of danger, and are fond of playing innocent pranks. They abduct children and carry them to distant places, leaving them there to be found and raised by those who either have no offspring or have lost theirs by death. Among the Mistassini there is now a poor foundling whose name is Meme'o. He was found in the forest, left by the dwarfs. No one knows where he was born and "he himself does not know who he is." The dwarfs become invisible to human beings when the gaze is removed from them or when they have dodged behind a tree or rock.

Tambe'gwilnu, "under-water man" (Eastern Naskapi, tambe'-gwiꞏnu), is a being of whom the Montagnais speak as something corresponding to a merman. [11] He is regarded as the owner of springs, for whom travelers when passing by leave a present of tobacco in return for the privilege of drinking the cold water. Cabot

10. Hind, op. cit., II, 102.

11. This belief is a close correspondent to the Wabanaki reference to Alambe'gwinosis (Penobscot), "under-water little man."

noted the belief among the Barren Ground Indians, but Waugh did not record it there.

The *memegwe'djo* (Mistassini) are creatures human in form, with narrow faces and eyes almost concealed in a mass of hair. They live in rocky ledges, and pass in and out of their abodes simply by pushing against the stone. The narrow-faced elf is smaller than a man, and is friendly to him. We hear of them eastward and toward the interior among the Naskapi, and again under the same name and description among the Algonquin and Ojibwa. At Seven Islands I learned that these fairies have stone canoes. *Kwakwadjə'o*, "wolverine" (eastern Naskapi), although animal in form, seems to be a personage of malignant disposition.

In the character of Wi·'tigo we have the Montagnais-Naskapi analogue to the widespread northern Algonkian *wi'ndigo*—a being human in form with supernatural qualities, whose main object of existence seems to be the killing and eating of his fellow human beings without being detected. This individual may, at times, mingle with the Indians as a stranger, in which disguise he achieves his purpose. He is much discussed among them and is the subject of some narratives, a few of which are given from translations. "It is a belief from the ancient times that they [the cannibals] appear just like the Indians. In the summer he lives like other people and eats the same food. But he changes his food completely in winter. For he changes and eats people then." (Thoma Ka'kwa, Lake St. John, 1919.) The Indians associate the urge with insanity more prevalent among the full bloods.

It becomes necessary for the cannibal to be killed. But this can only be done by the magical performance of the shaman. Ordinary men are powerless in such a case. Again I will let a native informant, this time a competent hunter of the Mistassini, give the appropriate discussion in his own words. "When a person has eaten human flesh he becomes a *wi'ntsigo* (Mistassini). And through having eaten such powerful "game" as man, his soul-spirit (*mista'peo*) becomes so strong that others less powerful are afraid to attack him. So the conjuror has to finish him by sorcery. He then tries to get the cannibal's spirit into his conjuring cabin by challenging it to a fight. He can induce the bear, for one, to get underneath the cannibal's spirit and send it off the earth into the air. Having succeeded in this

the cannibal is without his spirit, and though still alive he is doomed."
(Joseph Kurtness, 1924.)

There is some reason to conclude that the immortal cannibal, Wi·'tigo, is a shaman gone wrong by indulgence in eating human flesh—that of his victim. The characters in the tales are often cannibals. Mista'peo even, the father of the two girls whom Tsəka'bec takes for his wives, was one and shared this disposition with his wife. The girls, however (to their great moral credit), neither inherited the horrid craving from their parents, nor acquired it through parental example—an aboriginal lesson in the line of eugenics!

There have been some other wi·'tigo characters in Montagnais-Naskapi mythical history. One is described in a narrative by Pitabano'kwe'o, a woman of Lake St. John (1922), under the sobriquet of Mamiltehe'o, "He Who Has a Hairy Heart." The shaman's method of obtaining control over the spirit of the cannibal, just mentioned, is illustrated in the story.

The Cannibal, Mamiltehe'o
("He Who Has a Hairy Heart")

Mamiltehe'o was a very dangerous cannibal who lived during the winter by eating human beings. But in the summer he lived like a good man eating game like other people. In the summer, however, no one knew him or they would have killed him. He was a most powerful sorcerer.

But there was another sorcerer named Kanewe'o, "He who kills at a great distance [with an arrow]," who even surpassed Mamiltehe'o in power. This is the story of their struggle. One time Kanowe'o decided to try to kill Mamiltehe'o. He went to meet him by the shore of a lake. Beavers lived in the lake. Kanewe'o pretended to be very poor, cold, and hungry; when Mamiltehe'o saw him he did not know him and came down to ask him what he was doing. Said Kanewe'o, "I am dying of cold and hunger. If you will come and help me, I will not starve." Then said Mamiltehe'o, "Oh, I will come again tomorrow and help you kill the beavers! I have sons. I have seven of them. They are going to aid you to work and kill your beavers." But Mamiltehe'o said to himself, "What a pity he is so thin! I am going to fatten him up." Then to his wife, when he got back to camp, "When Kanewe'o is fat we will kill him." So Mamiltehe'o spoke to Kanewe'o and said, "Go get your family and come here to camp, and I will call up my family so we can all live together." So that evening he went back to his wigwam and sat opposite the fire. He began to cry. One of his sons said, "What is the matter? Our father cries so. Perhaps he has seen Kanewe'o who everybody knows is so powerful." Mamiltehe'o answered, "It is not he that I saw. The man I saw was almost dead of hunger. He was very sad. I fear we cannot eat him, for he is too thin, unless we work for him and his wife to get food for them so that they will get fatter. To-morrow we will go and camp with them. We will help make them into good flesh." The next day they met and camped together. *Mamiltehe'o* had seven sons, *Kanewe'o* had two little boys. Now *Kanewe'o* said to the sons of *Mamiltehe'o*, "Go down far into the woods and cut some wood so that we can close up the hole to catch the beavers. Your father and I will go out and cut a hole in the ice (so we can bar the entrance to the beaver house when you bring the wood)." The boys went. Then *Kanewe'o* said to his companion, "You cut the ice, I will watch you. For me, I am too weak to work." Then *Mamiltehe'o* took the ice-chisel and commenced to cut the ice. When the hole was big enough *Kanewe'o* took his chisel and struck *Mamiltehe'o* in the back. Then he pushed him into the hole under the ice. *Mamil-tehe'o* disappeared dead under the ice. Now *Kanewe'o* had hidden an otter-skin quiver of arrows near at hand. When the seven boys came back loaded with wood as he had commanded, he killed them all with his arrows! Whereupon the wife of *Mamiltehe'o* came running up with nine old women that they were keeping to fatten up for eating. *Mamiltehe'o's* wife was ahead of the others. She asked *Kane-we'o*, "Where is my man?" *Kanewe'o* answered, "I was using your man to close up the entrance to the beaver house. He is frozen now." The wife of *Mamiltehe'o* laughed, "Ha! You liar! My man is too powerful for you to have done what you say." At this word she took the ax to kill *Kanewe'o*, but he struck up the ax and cut her back in two. Then *Kanewe'o* asked the other old women, "Do you eat people" They all cried, "No!" But two of them exclaimed to the others, "You do eat them yourselves. Just look at us two who do not eat Christians [*sic!*]. Look at our stomachs." *Kanawe'o* looked and saw many cuts of the knife which *Mamiltehe'o* had made to see if they were fat enough to eat. These two cut ones, who were slaves, *Kanewe'o* kept and spared. But the others, he killed them all. That was the finish of the family of *Mamiltehe'o*. Afterward when *Kaneweo* pulled *Mamiltehe'o* out of the lake he beheld that he actually had hair to the length of a hand hanging from his heart like a beard, as his name indicated.

ANIMALS IN SPECIAL RELATION
TO MAN

Chapter Five

TO THE Montagnais-Naskapi—hunters on the barest subsistence level—the animals of the forest, the tundra, and the waters of the interior and the coast, exist in a specific relation. They have become the objects of engrossing magico-religious activity, for to them hunting is a holy occupation. The animals (awa'cɔts) pursue an existence corresponding to that of man as regards emotions and purpose in life. The difference between man and animals, they believe, lies chiefly in outward form. In the beginning of the world, before humans were formed, all animals existed grouped under "tribes" of their kinds who could talk like men, and were even covered with the same protection. When addressing animals in a spiritual way in his songs, or using the drum, the conjuror uses the expression ni·tcimi'·tc'tc ni·tcɔtce'·tce'k̟, which means, freely, "you and I wear the same covering and have the same mind and spiritual strength." This statement was explained as meaning not that men had fur, not that animals wore garments, but that their equality was spiritual and embraced or eclipsed the physical.

There has been no change in these native doctrines since they were first recorded in the seventeenth century in the words of the French priests. "They believe that many kinds of animals have reasonable souls. They have superstitions against profaning certain bones of elk, beaver and other beasts or letting dogs gnaw them. They preserve them carefully or throw them into rivers. They pretend that the souls of these animals come to see how bodies are treated and go and tell the living beasts and those that are dead, so that if ill treated the beasts of the same kind will no longer allow themselves to be taken in this world or the next." [1]

1. J. D. G. Shea, *First Establishment of the Faith in New France* (New York, 1881), I, 220, quoting Father Le Clerq, 1691.

The belief of this same character among the central Algonkian is expressed succinctly by William Jones: "It was thought that every living creature possessed a soul and that to get control of the soul made it possible to get control of the possessor of the soul. It was on such a theory that the Ojibwas hunted for game."[2]

The killing of animals, then, entails much responsibility in the spiritual sense. Since the animals' spirits at death are foregathered in their proper realms to be reincarnated later, the slaying of them places the hunter in the position, theoretically, of being their enemy. But he is not that in the ordinary sense of the term, because it is the ordained manner of procedure and one to which they are adjusted and inured. Requirements of conduct toward animals exist, however, which have to be known and carried out by the hunter. His success depends upon this knowledge, and, they argue, since no one can know everything and act to perfection, the subject of magico-religious science becomes, even from the native point of view, an inexhaustible one. Therefore, failure in the chase, the disappearance of the game from the hunter's districts, with ensuing famine, starvation, weakness, sickness, and death, are all attributed to the hunter's ignorance of some hidden principles of behavior toward the animals, or to his wilful disregard of them. The former is ignorance. The latter is sin. The two together constitute the educational sphere of the Montagnais-Naskapi, and the schooling is hard enough in reality although it may seem to the civilized imagination a mere travesty of mental training.

Women are neither physically nor spiritually disqualified from the pursuit of game, as frequent testimony proves. Widows, even those extremely old, are to be found in every band whose records of prowess in hunting and trapping are the talk of the country. Such a one, for instance, was old Marie Louise, a nonegenarian at Kiskisink, who lived alone for over forty years, making an average year's hunt as good as the men's, finally losing her life by breaking through the ice in springtime while on her way from her hunting grounds, typically a man's fate!

In concise terms, when gifted with the sight of game waiting to be killed somewhere within the hunting territories as the result of conquest by the hunter's soul-spirit, and adjusted between him and his quarry through the medium of dreams, the devout native appears

2. William Jones, *Archaeological Report of Ontario* (Toronto, 1905), p. 146.

on the scene to fulfill the destiny of the animals. He does not—or perhaps more properly should not—dash impetuously into the midst of them, but bides his time patiently to take cool and quiet advantage by killing them when they have taken to the water, or by posting himself at a point where they will pass within range of his weapon. [3]

So, blessed with a feeling that they owe a debt to the animal world for its sacrifice of life in their behalf, they have developed a system quite profound and rational in the spiritual sense. This we are now to examine.

Much could be quoted, as I have heard it discussed, to show how the very spirit of religious thought and practice is aimed to exert influence upon the spirits of animals, developed to an extent that converts animals into creatures comparable to supernatural beings. It is through them that life, health, and happiness come to the lot of the native while living, and hence they become the primary objectives of religious zeal. After death the soul of the individual is not annoyed with cravings of the flesh. Its fate is a matter of no concern, since continuity of life's pursuit without pain is assured. There is no soul jeopardy, no retribution betrayed in aboriginal Naskapi theology; therefore, no religious observances tending toward soul salvation. One of the professed rewards of the ordeal of death (*ni·bo'wo·*, a term akin to that denoting "sleep") is that the individual will "see" the High God, *Tce·məntu'* (see p. 37). But our quest at this point is for light bearing upon animal associations.

The animal first in order of importance in the vital sphere of these tribes is the caribou: in the northern treeless portion of the peninsula the Barren Ground variety (*Rangifer arcticus caboti*); in the forested southern districts, the woodland form (*Rangifer caribou caribou*). The caribou is more essential to life of the Naskapi than the other beasts, while next in importance to all the subtribes of the region, and of prime importance to some in the forested regions, is the beaver. South and west of the Saguenay River and in the Lake St. John area the moose is found, and economic culture centers largely around that animal. Of late years it has been observed that this animal is pressing gradually farther to the east than it has hitherto been seen, although in the earlier accounts the moose is reported abundant in the Saguenay country. And the Virginia deer has

3. The roving Naskapi of the more remote regions who hunt in a more aboriginal fashion still largely employ the caribou pound or fence, the description of which belongs in another sphere of treatment of native life.

PLATE VI

Bear skulls and beaver skulls suspended from branches of trees to satisfy the spirits of the animals. Left, two bear skulls near Lake St. John. Right, two bundles of beaver skulls at old Indian cemetery at Escoumains (1919).

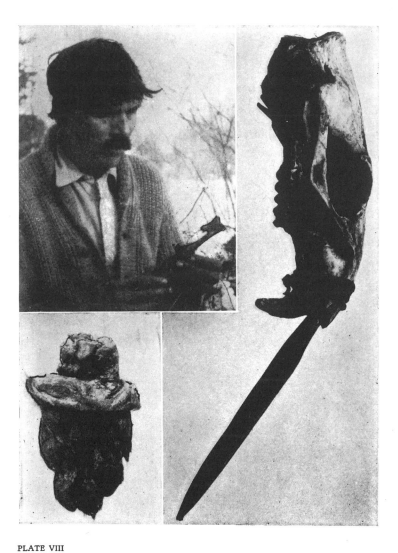

PLATE VIII

Upper left, a hunter of the Lake St. John band, examining a beaver pelvic bone which he had just burned for divination. Lower left, otter-paws divination. Right, woodchuck skull used in tossing-up divination game (Lake St. John).

penetrated into the base of the peninsula on the southwest, moving up from the Ontario forests—possibly as a result of the same factors of distribution and shift, whatever these actually may be. But neither of these animals figures prominently in the religious thought of the Indians, the latter I might say almost not at all.

In the estimation of the natives themselves, next in rank as a food source, but first in rank in respect to ceremonialism—is the bear. The subject of bear ceremonialism is an important and complicated one. Its discussion, involving correlated phenomena distributed through northern Europe, Siberia, northeastern Asia in general, entirely across northern America, presents one of the many topics of intercontinental culture distribution. In view, however, of the extended treatment of this theme by Dr. Hallowell, my contribution to the religious position of the bear in Montagnais-Naskapi ethnology will be only to place on record notes recorded from the various bands and subtribes; notes which Dr. Hallowell has consulted to some extent in the preparation of his monograph. [4]

Fish are entitled to a high place of importance in religious observance, at least in the case of the Naskapi to the eastward.

And, finally, come various other food- and fur-bearing animals whose spirits are invoked by rites and influenced by rules of behavior. But they all fall under secondary consideration by comparison with the beasts just mentioned in respect to ceremonialism. It might appear that the economic value of the seal to the Montagnais contiguous to the coast, and even to the interior bands when they emerge for the summer rendezvous at the coasts, would call for some noteworthy ritualistic observances. But such is not the case, for the seal appears neglected in the performance of magic rites, so far as existing sources of information permit a conclusion. I do not understand why.

Food preferences and uses may account for the respect shown in different degrees toward various animals. In some cases aversion may amount to a local food taboo. For instance, the varieties of fish inhabiting the salt water are not eaten by the Indians of the interior about Lake St. John—such as salmon and cod, and the eel. This applies also, and even with more force, to the seal and the porpoise. They dislike the greasy flavor and say that the meat of these creatures is too strong. A most peculiar restriction is met in their aver-

4. A. I. Hallowell, "Bear Ceremonialism in the Northern Hemisphere," *American Anthropologist*, Vol. XXVIII (1926), No. 1.

sion, likewise, to the meat of the Virginia deer, an animal which is recently penetrating the lower part of the peninsula in an apparent northward migration. Even the Têtes de Boule, who have long had the deer in their midst, do not ordinarily eat deer. They feed the deer meat to their dogs. At Lake St. John they do not even shoot at the deer unless they are short of food. Lately, since the caribou have begun to decrease, they have stopped killing caribou so as to allow them to "replenish the country" with their kind.

Certain animals absent from the faunal horizon of the bands are also out of mind in legend and ritual. Absence may thus account for there being no serpent or tortoise references; the eagle is not prominent, nor the raven, owl, nor hawk. That the seal or the sea mammals do not figure with prominence is noteworthy among the coastal Montagnais, who pursue them in season. Can it be that the cultural origins of the circumpolar Indians were couched in a continental hinterland—the subarctic barrens—not along the coasts until a later epoch of migration? My impression thus far is so.

The taboo at Lake St. John against non-indigenous food does not stop with the deer; the clam, eel, seal, porpoise, and whale are also in the forbidden class. And when it comes to mutton and chicken, beef and pork, the feeling is even more intense. Nevertheless, the changing conditions of the time force them to eat pork and beef. They realize, however, the impurity of these viands, and attribute their bodily ills, even the decline of their race, to the eating of domestic animals. The use of salt also is avoided in preparing pure wild meat. [5]

It should be noted, however, that the eating of shellfish, seals, porpoise, and whale is not avoided by the Montagnais living on the coast. These taboos are evidence to link the Lake St. John Indians with those of the northern interior. Hence, the distinction between eating the flesh of the native herbivorous game animals and domestic beasts is of fundamental significance. Native game is to them *notcimi''umi'tcɔ'm*, "forest food," tantamount in meaning to "pure food."

The holiness of hunting and the holy character of the animals that are hunted has been alluded to. We note a most important and logical belief, at least from the angle of native thought: that the food of the native game animals, the caribou, moose, bear, and beaver, being vegetal substance, and the vegetable kingdom being the original

5. The Indians returning to trading posts after a long sojourn in the solitude of the "bush" often dissipate in salt-eating and become ill.

source of medicine agency, the virtues of plant pharmacy are conveyed from the original growths to man through this diet. No wonder, then, the proper food of the tribe being either directly wild fruits or indirectly vegetable through the diet of game animals, that with their food in whatever form consumed, the Montagnais-Naskapi are "taking-medicine." Thus, the native game diet is prophylactic to mankind. A deep significance lies beneath this doctrine.

Sacrifice is mᵊtᵊste' haman, "he sacrifices to an animal." An offering of the cooked flesh of every animal eaten was a general custom and is still frequently observed. If three kinds of meat were eaten, a small slice of each was thrown into the fire. At Lake St. John one of the hunters, I learned, never fails to cut a piece of meat from each animal consumed and give the pieces to his dogs before eating of it himself. This is a sacrificial rite to satisfy the spirits of the dogs who track his game for him.

The conception of chance in the universe affecting the welfare of the individual is approachable only through the analysis of native terms for that vague expression "luck," which so many of them use without defining. Good luck (in the Lake St. John dialect) is kamᵊlᵊn-to'hᵊt‘, which also means "making a good hunt"; while the opposite is kam ᵊtcinto'hᵊt‘, "bad luck or bad hunt" (kas‘inu'tcetci‘'mᵊlo'pᵊ-li‘'n, "all forms of good fortune"). The fatalities of life are represented in starvation, freezing, accident, and disease for which the animals, animal overlords, plant spirits, the demons of nature, and monsters are responsible. The individual has only to rely upon their benevolence for his welfare. His own soul is his medium of power in the struggle against their force. The importance of divination in the religion of the region appears chiefly in learning what the future has in store, with little chance, however, of altering greatly its outcome. If the preceding comments satisfy any of the qualifications of the definition of fatalism, then the Montagnais-Naskapi are pronounced fatalists.

The Caribou

Among the specific animals whose pursuit furnishes the natives of the region with their vital activity and at the same time brings into play certain religious forces, we find the caribou occupying a most conspicuous place.

These noble animals are believed by the Naskapi to compose a race living under the control of an overlord, having their established social life, executing their migrations, and carrying out other modes of conduct not unlike those of the human inhabitants of the great peninsula. Great intelligence is attributed to the caribou.

The belief is general to these tribes, if not over most of the New World, that the mechanical devices for killing animals play only a part in the chase, that the auxiliary practices of magic and religion are perhaps more cogent than the instruments of slaughter. So while the aboriginal bow and arrow, spear and snare, and the modern gun and rifle are naturally indispensable in hunting, the spiritual preparation, the willingness of the beasts to submit to the weapons, and the permission of their deific "owner" are of utmost importance.

Let us review the character of evidence that is forthcoming from various portions of the peninsula concerning the overlord and owner of the caribou. The belief is most developed among the subtribes toward the northern and eastern interior. It seems to take a different form among the Montagnais proper in the southwest. Among the former groups the Barren Ground caribou is absolutely controlled by the master of the caribou, and none is permitted to fall victim to the hunters without his release. This has to be sought by spiritual devices which we shall consider later. Among the latter groups the belief in the master of the caribou is not so compelling in its force. Here, where other game besides the caribou is more abundant and sustaining, it is thought that the caribou (the woodland variety) are under the leadership of a master, but he is accounted for as a transformed Indian; in fact, at Lake St. John he is considered an actual historical personage. Hence, I suspect the latter phase of the legend to be an extension of the original belief subjected to certain modifications which have tended toward its dissolution and re-interpretation. Among the Lake St. John Montagnais, the cari-bou-man tale seems to be on its frontier horizon, if we consider its dissemination as from the northern area, where it is most elaborate. In support of this suggestion it would seem that the legend is wanting farther west, say among the Têtes de Boule and their Algonquin allies beyond the St. Maurice, where the moose hunt replaces the totally different caribou drive. My statement may be corrected with further investigation and, therefore, I feel that it is wiser to offer it as a prospect than to press it as a conclusion, so far as the tribes outside the Montagnais-Naskapi group are concerned. It may be noted that the tale and its associated religious significance are entirely wanting among the Wabanaki tribes, and I know of no definite Ojibwa cognate. It is a matter that will have to be inquired into by direct questioning among the adjacent tribes, since it has not independently come to light in studies so far conducted among them.

Among the Naskapi of the northern interior we meet the story in its greatest force and definitely localized. The Ungava versions of the story are likewise shared by the Eskimo, as we have it from several sources, and extend without much modification to the Michikamau, Petisigabau, Nichikun, Ste. Marguerite, and Moisie bands from actual narration in my notes. While members of the intervening and neighboring groups have discussed and added to it in conversation, I have not taken down duplicate narrations from their lips. Most recently (1934) Dr. Strong gives some notes on the chief of the caribou and his abode, recorded from the Davis Inlet band (*see* n. 12, chap. ii). Here an inverted triangle with short line in the middle of the base surmounted by a circle represents the caribou god.

The material from the northern interior bands can best be surveyed from the transcriptions of the informants themselves:

To you will be related a story; the caribou-man story. Once an old man and his son were very expert in hunting. And it happened that the son dreamed that he cohabited with the caribou. It seemed that he killed a great many caribou. Once, then, it happened that during the winter he said to his father. "I will depart. And I will kill caribou enough for the whole winter. So do not wait for me as respects anything. I will come back. For, indeed, I am going to go with the caribou." Then he sang: "The caribou walked along well like me. Then I walked as he was walking. Then I took his path. And then I walked like the caribou, my trail looking like a caribou trail where I saw my tracks. And so indeed I will take care of the caribou. I indeed will divide the caribou. I will give them to the people. I will know how many to give the people. It will be known to me." [So he sang, and continued:] "He who obeys the requirements is given caribou, and he who disobeys is not given caribou. If he wastes much caribou he cannot be given them, because he wastes too much of his food—the good things. And now, as much as I have spoken, you will know forever how it is. For so now it is as I have said. I, indeed, am Caribou Man ('Ati'k'wape'u). So I am called."

This narrative explains the origin of the being famous among all the Montaganis-Naskapi of the peninsula in the words of an informant (Nabe'oco, by name) belonging to the St. Marguerite band. It is a literal translation of a text recorded from him in August, 1923.

This short tale concisely covers the two points of importance: the human-historical origin of the hero (incidentally, his mission undertaken through the all-important factor of dream control); and his assumption of the prerogatives of dispenser of the caribou with the obligations of frugality that he imposed on subsequent hunting. Some description of the dwelling of Caribou Man and the localization of his abode are given in the next narrative, that of Alexandre Bellefleure of the Ungava band (1925).

Ungava Version of the Tale of Caribou House

In the interior between Ungava Bay and Hudson's Bay is a distant country where no Indians will go under any consideration for the following reason. There is a range of big mountains pure white in color formed neither of snow, ice, nor white rock, but of caribou hair. They are shaped like a house and so they are known as Caribou House (ati'ᵏ wədzwa'p). One man of the Petisigabau band says there are two houses. In this enormous cavity live thousands upon thousands of caribou under the overlordship of a human being who is white and dressed in black. Some say there are several of them and they have beards. He is master of the caribou and will not permit anyone to come within some one hundred and fifty miles of his abode, the punishment being death. Within his realm the various animals are two or three times their ordinary size. The few Indians who have approached the region say that the caribou enter and leave their kingdom each year, passing through a valley between two high mountains about fifteen miles apart. And it is also asserted that the deer hair on the ground here is several feet in depth, that for miles around the cast-off antlers on the ground form a layer waist deep, that the caribou paths leading back and forth there are so deep as to reach to a man's waist, and that a young caribou going along in one would be visible only by its head.

Wapistan Pien says the mountain is partly of stone and caribou hair but he thinks there is no chief. He added, "The mountains are near the sea between Ungava Bay and the Atlantic Ocean. No Eskimo or Indians go there, for they would certainly die. One can see the mountains a great distance away. The caribou tracks are as deep as one's shoulder. The hair is of the same thickness. The mountains are shaped like a wigwam, that is, dome-shaped." The story is generally common to all the Indians who gather at Seven Islands. A conjuror can visit the caribou house and find out what cause keeps the caribou from coming out to the hunters, then can make them follow him.

That the caribou live here during the summer and come out to the country in the fall, passing between the mountain portals to the caribou house, is the general belief of all the Indians. The "white man" (another name of their supernatural owner) allows only such members of his flock to be killed as he wishes, granting to the hunters whom he favors a certain number of victims and no more. And if for any reason he is displeased with a hunter he refuses him an allowance, and the hunter, in consequence, may hunt in vain.

One informant of the Michikamau band of the far interior, Alexandre Mackenzie (1925), in giving corroborative testimony of the general belief in the "chief of the caribou," or "boss" as he also styled him by analogy with the foreman of the log-drivers, referred to a proper name besides the common sobriquet Ati'kwənabe'o, "Caribou Man," in his dialect. He said, "Kanəbənəgasi· we'o ⟦a proper name⟧ is the 'man of the caribou.' He was formerly a man ⟦Indian⟧ like other men. He is now there together with the caribou. Chief of the caribou. His house is called Caribou House (ati'kʷudz wa'p). And so he is chief there in the white mountain. It is he who gives the caribou to the hunters."

As an example—to the Indians even a proof—of the supposed ferocious character of the animals in this region and their enormous size, the following narratives are recorded.

"A hunter who had wandered into the forbidden region without being sufficiently aware of it, found himself coming down a mountain in a place where before him a ledge of some yards' extent lay below. Upon this a huge wolf lay asleep. The beast was fully three times the size of the largest ordinary wolf. He shot at the wolf twice in succession from close range and both times hit it in a vital place. Although so wounded, the animal sprang up and pursued him for a day. He had all he could do to keep it from killing him until he came to a branch of the bay and crossed the water. At the water's edge the beast stopped its pursuit. He took it to be a guardian of the forbidden region."

Upon another occasion three hunters were watching for caribou at one of the usual crossing places (acwo'pan, "watching-place") bordering on the forbidden frontier. They saw five caribou coming down a caribou trail worn so deep that only their heads and backs were visible. Then as they were waiting to shoot them at a distance of two hundred yards the caribou suddenly turned into five men coming toward them. The astonished hunters turned about at once and fled. And again one time a band of hunters reached a gorge between the two mountain portals previously mentioned. There they observed thousands of caribou coming towards them and seemed to descend a declivity just below their line of vision and disappear as though going into the ground. They watched the swarming herd for a while, and desiring to learn what had become of them went to the place, but when the place was reached they could see no explanation for the disappearance.

Two sled parties of Eskimo once tried to get to these mountains to hunt and all lost their lives but one man. Even the dogs died. Alexandre Bellefleure tried in vain to hire an Indian for seventy-five dollars worth of goods (rifle, cartridges, suit of clothes, and two pounds of tea). The Naskapi declared that no matter what he received, if they got there they would die and it would do him no good.

I think we may see in the foregoing legend the source explanation of the familiar "king of the caribou" belief which is current throughout the whole peninsula. The mountain abode of the game king and his subjects, its inviolable boundaries, its miraculous qualities, all indicate that it is the abode of the caribou tribe, both of the living animals and the caribou ghosts. The living caribou emerge in a migration from their summer domain apportioned to the hunters whose religious observances have been properly carried out under the instructions of their individual dream mentors. And next the souls of the slain caribou return to the "haven" with their king, where they remain until they are again ordered to issue forth to be killed.

A word more should be added: the conjuror of the family or local group may appeal to the "white man" for an allowance for the hunters. In his conjuring lodge he submits to his spirit control and communes with him and then he receives instructions. If he observes them success comes, but not otherwise. Should he disobey, he may lose his power for a year.

It seems to me very probable that this belief centering around the movements of the Barren Ground caribou is a version of the original myth; the source from which the various tales of Ati'kwabe'o farther south among the Montagnais-Naskapi of the peninsula (from whom I have fuller records) have become detached and, finally, through modification by time and space, appear in connection with the woodland variety of caribou, forming an important element in Labrador religious mythology as far as the Lake St. John band. Naturally, the tale retains a greater religious importance the farther north it is mentioned. For instance, it plays a greater part in the religious beliefs of the Naskapi of the Seven Islands region than it does about Lake St. John, where moose share the status of a major game animal with the woodland caribou.

The Labrador Eskimo in general have similar tales and beliefs in caribou reincarnation and allotment to hunters under their master, according to Hawkes, Turner, and Wallace. This I believe to be an Eskimo borrowing from Indian mythology. Yet it should not be forgotten than an idea of lordship is present among both Indians and Eskimo, as seen in the Eskimo Sedna tale. Dr. Wissler's earlier conjectures, in his understanding of the northern influence in the culture of the plains Indians (especially in his paper on the Missouri-Saskatchewan area) have shown a number of instances of northern borrowings; and I wonder if circumstances might not sometime point to the above game-lord concept as the possible source of the story among the plains tribes describing the mountain in which a supernatural being possesses and supervises the bison, and which has become the origin legend and testament of the sun-dance ceremony (Arapaho, Cheyenne).

Our sources of information are, however, somewhat ambiguous in regard to the distribution of this episode among the Eskimo. Boas relates several tales of origin of the caribou from Baffin Land, in which the protector and overlord of the animals is not present, but then refers to a tradition reported by Lyon in which the element is present, and concludes by saying that he himself could find no trace of it. The tradition referred to is so pertinent to our investigation that I quote from Boas. "I could not find any trace of the tradition reported by Lyon—that *Anautalik, Nuliajoq's* father, is the protector of land animals, nor of that of a being to whom he refers by the name of *Pukinna* [from *pukiq*, the white parts of a deerskin], who lives in a fine country far to the west and who is the immediate protectress of deer, which animals roam in immense herds around her dwelling." [6]

Comparing eastern Eskimo and Indian beliefs on this point, we

6. F. Boas, "The Central Eskimo," *Sixth Annual Report, Bureau American Ethnology, 1884-85,* pp. 587-88, quoting Capt. G. F. Lyon, *Private Journal* (London, 1824).

— 85 —

may glance at the version given by Hawkes from the coast of Labrador.

There was once a great *angekok* who felt it his duty to find out for the people the place where the caribou went to when they passed in great number into the interior. So he asked his *torngak* to show him where they went. His *torngak* told him the way to go. He told him to walk on and on, and not to stop until he told him. So the *angekok* started off. He walked day after day. For two moons he walked. His boots did not wear out because his *torngak* was with him.

At last, one day, his *torngak* said, "Stop! Make no noise, and wait till the sun sets. Then you will see the resting place of the caribou. You must not wish to kill what you see, or I will turn you into a mouse."

So the *angekok* did as he had been told. When the sun went down he saw a very large house made of turf and rock. Standing across the door was a very big deer. It was king of the caribou. He was so big that the other caribou could walk in under him without touching him.

The caribou came up in big bands, and all passed under the king into the house. When the last one had passed in, he lay down and kept guard over the others.

The *angekok* went home and told the people what he had seen. But he did not dare tell them where to find the wonderful place, for fear that they might desire to kill so many caribou and his *torngak* would turn him into a mouse. So the Eskimo know that there is a place where the reindeer live and stay with their king, but although they are always looking for it, they can never find it. But they hope to do so some time. [7]

The occurrence of these mountains with religious associations in the belief of the Eskimo rests upon several evidences in the literature dealing with the Labrador Eskimo. Dillon Wallace passed the *endroits* of these mysterious mountains in 1905, accompanied by Eskimo who spoke to him of Torngak, the spirit of death, who, from his cavern dwelling in the heights of the mighty Torngaeks [the mountains north of the George River toward Cape Chidley], watches them always and rules their fortunes with an iron hand, dealing out misfortune, or withholding it, at his will. It is only through the medium of the *angekok*, or conjuror, that the people can learn what to do to keep Torngak and the lesser spirits of evil, with their varying moods, in good humor. He estimated the height of the mountains to be full seven thousand feet. [8]

We look in vain for the caribou-man tale among the earlier documents concerning the Athapascan of the Northwest. The only

7. E. W. Hawkes, "The Labrador Eskimo," *Canada Department of Mines, Geological Survey,* "Anthropological Series," Memoir 91, No. 14, p. 154.
8. Dillon Wallace, *The Long Labrador Trail* (New York, 1908), pp. 227, 248.

exception is the mention of the tale among the Chipewyan by Birket-Smith.[9]

Strong alludes to a version of the same tale and belief among the Indians of George River (Barren Ground and Davis Inlet bands). "According to Indian belief there is a high mountain in the Barren Grounds of northeastern Labrador that is called Caribou House, ah-tee-which-oo-ap,[10] where the chief of all the deer lives. It is here they believe the caribou spend the summer. As a result of the slaughter in former days there are great heaps of deer bones around Indian House Lake, which have been commented on by all travelers in the region. The caribou smelled these bones, the Indians say, and were offended, so that they returned to Caribou House and told the caribou god, who directed the chief of the caribou to take them into his mountain. Since then the caribou god has refused to let the herd come south, and as a result the Indians have been starved out of their interior homes. Today they are extremely careful in observing all the varied rites pertaining to the caribou and thus hope to appease the anger of the god.[11] His version of this now classic tale is recognizable despite its local application to modern conditions.

I have mentioned the occurrence of the caribou-man tale among the bands on the southwest. At Lake St. John there is the general belief in the Caribou Man, known here by the same name Atəkwa-be'o, who at one time was an Indian like the rest. His dream-vision and adoption of the life of king of the caribou run much the same as it was given by Nabe'oco at Seven Islands. This Indian, in their belief, consorts with the main caribou herd and has offspring by the does. He sleeps between the bodies of the animals to keep warm, he eats moss as they do, and when the animals are pursued he rides upon the back of a big bull. He also allows only an alloted portion to the hunters under conditions which he indicates to them in dreams. In short, his general status in the religion of these bands seems to be similar to that already given. One fact of importance, however, is that the tradition is placed in chronology at a period of some fifty years ago, when the event took place in which the Indian hunter became the caribou leader. And again we find a deviation from the versions among the northern Naskapi in the belief

9. Kaj Birket-Smith, "Contributions to Chipewyan Ethnology," *Report of the Fifth Thule Expedition* (Copenhagen, 1930), Vol. VI, No. 3.
10. *ati'k'wi'dzwa'p*, "caribou house."
11. W. D. Strong, "Notes on the Mammals of the Labrador Interior," *Journal of Mammalogy*, Vol. XI (1930), No. 1, p. 2.

here that certain hunters have actually seen the caribou man in the living form, coursing over the tundra-barrens with his cervine subjects, and have talked with him from a distance. One of these favored men is old Napani' of the Lake St. John group, almost a century of age, who claims to have enjoyed such an experience when a young man. The traditions taken down from some five or six authorities at Lake St. John (1918-23) are as follows:

Atə'ḳ'wabe'o, Caribou Man

Atə'ḳ'wabe'o, Caribou Man, was the youngest of four brothers. They were hunting caribou and were following a herd near which they camped one might in an open shelter. That night he dreamed that a female caribou came forth from the herd and spoke to him, and called him out to come and live with the caribou as her husband. The next morning Caribou Man left camp alone and went forth to the place indicated in his dream. There he saw a caribou doe which appeared to be waiting for him. Laying down his bow and arrows he approached her and when he reached her she led him to where three other caribou stood, evidently watching as scouts. They led him away and he joined the herd.

Caribou Man thenceforth lived with the caribou. He still lives, eating the same food, the moss, as the deer. He wanders with them from place to place, sometimes riding on the back of a big buck. His clothing is of caribou skin. When he needs clothing they permit him to kill several for the purpose. His offspring are caribou like the rest. At night he lies down and some of them lie close to him to keep him warm. There he survives contentedly, they say, year after year passing his life with the caribou as one of them, and as their chief and protector. [12] Caribou Man has been occasionally seen by the Indians. When they are hunting caribou and encounter his herd, they refrain from killing the deer. And several times conversation has been had with him.

It is reported among the Indians that this strange being was last met some seven years ago by some of the Montagnais hunters cruising under an old man named St. Onge from Bersimis. The place of encounter was near Lake Michikamau. Caribou Man has told the Indians that he was twenty-one years old when he abandoned his kind and that the time was some forty years ago. It is believed at Lake St. John that he belonged originally to the Seven Islands division of the Naskapi. He has told the Montagnais that their troubles in life arise from killing the caribou too freely. When they meet his herd he allows them to kill only as many as they need to feed them and to renew their tents and apparel. From him is also derived the name of a small stream flowing into the Ashuapmouchouan below Oasiems-

12. The French-Canadians who have heard of him through the Indians call him *le roi des caribous*.

kau, a larger stream emptying on the northwest into Lake St. John, and also a small lake, namely Tikouapi River and Lake. The actual tale of Caribou Man is not associated with this stream by all the members of the Lake St. John band, for I have heard that the name was derived from an individual, bearing the name, whose hunting territory embraced those waters. Since, however, the latter hunt south and west of Lake St. John and are affected by contact as well as by blood and marriage with the Têtes de Boule, the same might be expected. The tale seems not to have reached the Têtes de Boule so far as the direct inquiries of Dr. Davidson and myself show; inquiries were made with the object of discovering any knowledge of the tale among the members of this division, from Obidjouan eastward to the hunters of the now dispersed band at Kokokash (Cococache), some of whom are now domiciled at Lake St. John. The above is the testimony of the Montagnais of Lake St. John in general. I might add that if some of the Montagnais of the western and southern districts of the peninsula trace the identity of Caribou Man to one of the Seven Islands bands, the latter on their part are unconscious of the application, and, as we have observed, turn the scene of his origin far again to the north. The tradition, indeed, seems inseparable from a northern locale.

In respect to ceremonial treatment of the remains of caribou slain by hunters there is rather less than might be expected, in view of the general importance of the animal. Caribou disposal rites are almost nothing in comparison with those which mark the treatment of remains of the bear. One obligation, however, of general occurrence all over the region is that all of the carcass be utilized, from head to tail. We learn, for instance, that among the virtues of Montagnais-Naskapi life is the spirit of generosity in sharing with others one-half the carcass of all large game falling to the hunter's weapons. This ruling applies with much force to disposition of caribou meat. Its neglect is a sin. Besides the total consumption of the flesh and the use of the skin, the rules of utilization also apply to the bones and antlers. At Lake St. John the obligation to use for tools the bones of each caribou killed has almost the force of a command. Thus is accounted for the abundance of bone implements everywhere, in present as well as in past life. A glance at the material culture of the Labrador bands discloses the employment of caribou bone and antler as the materials of manufacture of every conceivable tool: beamers, scrapers, fleshers, skinners, drills, handles for iron awls and crooked knives made of files, snowshoe needles, mesh straighteners, drum beaters, harpoon heads, arrowheads, fish hook snags, the "cup-and-ball" game, and the like. The religious associations of these articles will form the substance of a separate chapter (see p. 217). In the utilization of the skin of the caribou, besides the indispensability of the material in thong (babiche), clothing, moccasin and tent-cover making, we find even the tail used as a tip for the "cup-and-ball game," the ears for human ear-warmers, and stiff leg skins carefully prepared for construction into the legskin bags used as tool bags and food containers universally among the Naskapi of the northern interior, where birch-bark receptacles are not at all common. The Ungava, Michikamau, and Barren Ground bands of Naskapi seem to have the custom of gathering together into heaps the antlers of slain animals after a caribou drive, as a propitiatory rite. This is not done toward the southwestern area. These antler heaps have been noted by many Labrador explorers. Hind notes that, on the upper Moisie River, the antlers of the first doe killed after the Indians leave the coast, are preserved to be placed on the ice of a lake, so as to sink when the spring ice breaks up, that they may not be gnawed by animals.[13] And universally the rule holds that dogs must not be allowed to munch caribou bones. The Mistassini and Lake St. John people claim that dogs allowed to eat caribou bones will become thin and sickly or choke to death on the splinters. It is a general practice, when caribou are killed, to gather the bones and crack them with the ax or with a stone maul to obtain the marrow. The intestinal contents are taken and eaten, the blood is drunk crude and warm by the tired hunters, or collected and kept in the form of a thickened pudding; the esophagus is removed and treated to be made into a container for grease (similar to fig. 23), and then becomes a personal grease bottle with ceremonial associations, about which we shall learn later when dealing with shaman's rites; and the unborn young in the abdomen of the females are taken out, their carcasses eaten with gusto, and the tiny tender skins converted into delicate baby coats, with the head of the little calf-to-be forming the hood or capuchin. The little coat then becomes a protector of the child. And finally we find the caribou scrotum skins prepared into tobacco pouches—both substances rich in latent magic power (mɔntu').

13. Hind, I, 186.

These remarks will serve to illustrate the absolute fidelity with which the orthodox Naskapi adhere to the taboo against wastefulness of the caribou enjoined upon them by Caribou Man, in whatever form they believe him to exist.

Our picture of the ceremonial procedures connected with the occasion of a successful hunt could hardly be complete without mention of the formal manner in which the returning Naskapi announce to the inmates of the wigwam the glad news of having found a herd of the ever-needed caribou. "The hunters, having hunted the caribou trail, now arrive at the camp. One throws a small stick against the tent cover and cries, 'You go home! You can eat!' [Tci webət'acəme! acəmenanəme'! a formal cry.] Then the people rejoice and proceed to beat the drum and dance, eat and sing. 'For there are thirty deer! Already the deer are killed! We shall all eat!' they cry. And to the old men, there at one side of the tent, they call, 'Ye patriarchs, you shall eat!' " (Translation of native dictation in the Michikamau dialect, 1925.)

For most of the important game and fur-bearing animals the Montagnais-Naskapi have a ceremonial pack string, or drag string in case it is winter and the carcass can be dragged to camp over the snow, which is associated with dreaming and the final satisfaction of the slain animal's spirit. This important and at the same time useful fetish is called ni·ma'ban, and the development of symbolism and magic connected with it is so great that it forms an independent topic to be discussed by itself. Yet while speaking of formalities associated with the killing and disposal of caribou, the drag string used in hauling the caribou carcass should be mentioned. This is a three-ply length of caribou rawhide, one end of which is fastened to the caribou antlers by which the body is dragged head first on the snow or ice by two men. The drag line for caribou which I obtained is ungarnished with beads or ribbons as are those for many other beasts. The material is not dyed red as are many of these pack-strings for smaller game, and there are no ornamentations of beads, yarn or ribbon. The white color of the caribou drag string accords with the color symbolism for this creature, which is white. The white connotes not only the body color of the caribou but the snowy realm in which it is sought.

It is believed that caribou spirits constantly visit the hunter in his dreams when food is exhausted, and then he imagines that song accompanies the visitation. So being under the obligation of using the song with his drum or the skin hand rattle, the caribou lure-song becomes part of the successful hunter's individual hunting ritual. The words of several of these are offered for exemplification of this native idea.

A chant that was used by an old Naskapi of the Michikamau band named Jérôme Antoine, now long since dead, was repeated by his grandson at Seven Islands in 1925. "Because he who comes [referring to the caribou seen approaching in the dream] looks so fine!" This refrain was repeated many times accompanied by a rapid drum beat. The old man dreamed the song and kept it throughout his life, and finally others learned it.

Another plaintive refrain was chanted for dictation by a young hunter of the Ungava band (Antoine André). This song likewise originated in a dream and belongs to the same category, ati"ḳ'nakə-mə'n, "caribou song." The originator dreamed that he was travel-ing with an Eskimo, which is a good omen. Then he killed some caribou and had a good supply of food. The song then became a means of regaining the same good luck. The words are vague and disjointed. "First time I could eat in the land of the Eskimo, when I danced." Again the melody was repeated over and over again to the rapid striking of the drum, about five strokes to a second.

Another dream recorded also from the Michikamau people is "When a man dreams that his wife meets one of his friends he is pleased, for there at a lake he will find caribou. (This means that he dreams of his wife associating in familiarity with one of his own friends—a vestige of the sexual hospitality custom.) If I in my dream see one of my gentleman friends or a chief (otci˙ma'u), I take a drink of whisky, and then there at the river I shall see the caribou." The narrator added that in default of whisky a drink of tea might be substituted to secure the benefit of the omen. We could scarcely, however, attribute the substitution to the influence of prohibition teaching. In reality the hunter is giving his soul-spirit a libation to pay for the revelation and to induce its fulfillment. In this instance it is a stimulation in both senses of the term.

Observances Concerning the Bear

Coming to consideration of the numerous formal practices con-nected with the dreaming of, the hunting, the killing, the consuming

Upper photograph, cup-and-pin game; lower photograph, eighteen-inch, double-headed drum with two hoops and snare of bird quills (Lake St. John band).

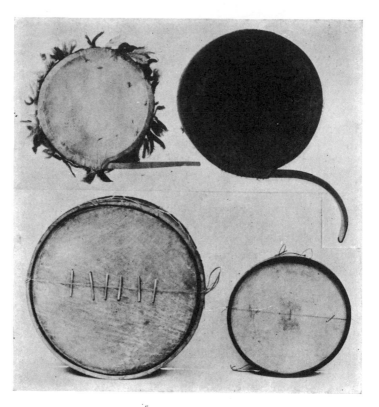

Upper figures, Naskapi hand rattles (four inches and five and a half inches). Lower figures, left, drum of Montagnais (eighteen inches); right, single-headed drum of Montagnais-Naskapi of Seven Islands (thirteen inches).

and the disposal of the body of the bear, we meet with true magico-religious formalities. They form, perhaps, the closest semblance to a religious institution encountered in this area, where religious assembly ceremonies are lacking. Why the bear should be singled out for ceremonial approach and reverence in a region where other animals are accorded reverence in lesser degree is a matter possibly to be explained by analysis of bear ceremonialism over the whole circumpolar region, rather than through an intensive study of the matter in any single group of tribes such as these. The range of related practices and theories connected with the bear from northern Europe across both continents to Newfoundland and Labrador has been given serious attention by Hallowell, whose conclusion suggests it be an old diffusion among boreal hunting cultures, with a starting point possibly in Asia in the Amur-Tartary region developed to its highest.[14] The original concepts of bear ritualism seem similar in content to those attached to other animals. But a more serious religious attitude toward the bear seems to have focused attention and feeling upon this animal. In the Montagnais-Naskapi culture area it seems apparent that the rites of the bear show analogies to those addressed to other mammals and even to the remains of large fish. The Indians themselves, when questioned as to why the bear is so highly regarded, propound as a reason his supremacy over other beasts by virtue of his human physical characteristics and his almost human intelligence—their own ethnological theory in the matter. When I asked a religious man of the Mistassini if, like the caribou and the fish, the bears formed a tribe with an overlord or chief who controlled their fates, the answer was, "No, every bear is a chief himself." But why do they not accord the caribou, for instance, an equal consideration? The fact, as has been observed, that the hunter does not kill more than a half dozen bears or so each season may have to be considered as a quantitative factor in the case.

Again we will open the presentation of the subject with a native dictation. In the words of old Ka'kwa, late a converted shaman of the Mistassini band, and recorded in that dialect in the winter of 1915, the testimony is as follows:

When they kill "Short Tail" [a polite epithet for the bear], before they bring him in the young unmarried women cover their faces. This is done so that they may not see the "great food" [another epithet] coming in, lest they become sick

14. Hallowell, *op. cit.*, see n. 4, p. 153.

on account of having insulted him. Only the married women may skin him, and only the men can cut him up. Then only the oldest men can eat his head. The tail must not be severed lest he be insulted. The right arm [of the bear] is cooked beside the fire. It must not be cut from the paw. Only the oldest man in the camp may eat it. This is the regulation they follow. Only the men eat the heart, and only the men can pick the leg bones. If the women should pick these bones, they would have sore bones and could not get up to walk. And when they kill a bear they fry the guts, and throw the fat in the fire. Then they throw a wooden spoon-ful of the grease with some meat into the fire for the Mista'peo, "Great Man" [their soul-spirits], so as to satisfy him. And they drink it using a wooden spoon to satisfy their Mista'peo. The "great food" must not be eaten out of doors for it would be improper. It must not even be chewed outside the tent by the children, as this would be improper in respect to the "great food." The skull is very im-portant, and it is picked very clean. And if "Short Tail" is killed in the fall, the skull is carried all winter, and then at the place where they gather in the spring-time, a "flagpole" (a peeled fir tree, mist'ɔkʷ) is made and trimmed and peeled very carefully and erected. And there the bear skull is hung up, and tobacco is put in his nose—and his chin and lower lip are fully cleaned and beads are worked on it by someone, so that the "one who owns the chin" will be satisfied. And the "worm under the tongue" [the tongue sinew of the bear] is finely dried and attached to the end of the dried chin, so that it will look very pretty. And the chin is carefully preserved and kept in a birch-bark receptacle so that he will be well satisfied when he thinks about and remembers his chin and tongue. Even the claws are not to be burned lest he could not dig out his den in the fall when it comes time for him to go to sleep in his bed.

This interesting narration, furnished by an old religious character who could speak neither English nor French, covers the general subject of bear observances for the whole area. There are some facts to consider in this account itself, besides a number of variations en-countered among other bands of the Montagnais-Naskapi. We learn from the Mistassini that unmarried girls may not look upon the carcass of the bear, because they are not respectable, in the sense of being "worthy" enough. For this reason, the carcass is better kept covered with a blanket or sheet. Some of the particulars mentioned in the Mistassini record are not recognized with equal force in other bands, while there are notes recorded among the Naskapi more to the eastward which are not forthcoming from the Mistassini. The subject is, however, an extensive one and will undoubtedly continue to develop new aspects when definite inquiry is aimed at the details in different subareas.

In the Mistassini declaration we meet with the characteristic cir-cumlocutory names by which the bear is referred to in order to avoid using the generic term, *mɔck*,⁴⁰ general in the Montagnais-Naskapi as well as in the Cree dialects. Here we have *təkwa'yəwagən*, "short tail," *katəkwa'socəwi·'* (St. Marguerite), *tštce'mi·tcəmiyu*, "his great food," *kawe''kwa'kwənit*, "the one who owns the chin," and, besides, among the Mistassini, as well as widely through the peninsula, there is also *kaopa'tc mi·tcəmiyu* (Mistassini), *kwəctewa'o mi·'tcem* (Escoumains), *kak'ᵘctewə'tc mi·tcəm* (Moisie), "black food." Skinner has recorded practically the same list of epithets among the Cree south and west of Hudson Bay. These sobriquets all appear to possess the nature of compliments. Only one possible exception to this rule occurs in my notes on the subject, and that is in a song coming from a member of the Michikamau band, in which the bear is called *kanaya'pewut*, "chicane, clown." Since the latter occurs in a song it is somewhat outside the category of an avoidance term, and the idea of the bear as a chicane need not be opprobrious in this instance.

I shall pass over at this time the reference in the foregoing text to satisfying the *Mista'peo*, "Great Man," since this relates to the soul of the individual and was treated in the previous chapter.

The progress of the bear hunt is everywhere throughout the peninsula marked by certain formalities, which link up with similar customs reported across the continent and even to parts of northern Asia. It cannot, however, be said that among the Labrador populations bear ceremonialism is as highly developed as it appears to be in Asia. South of the St. Lawrence, among the Wabanaki tribes there is even less development than in Labrador. Here at any rate the bear is enshrouded with much reverence both before he is killed and afterward. Let us review the circumstances in the order of their progression.

The inner self or spiritual element of the bear is one of great power and influence among the spirits of animals. It has control over them much as the physical bear is their superior in respect to strength and sagacity. His soul-spirit knows especially when the hunters are on his trail, and so he does what he thinks best to do in order to save himself or else he allows himself to be overtaken and killed.

A hunter at Seven Islands opened some discussion concerning what these Indians believe to be a fact, namely, that the female is never killed and found with young in her belly. I have found this since to be a general belief among the Naskapi, and even when incidentally mentioning the matter to some Nansamund bear hunters in the Dismal Swamp, Virginia, learned that they too could never recall having killed a gravid she-bear. The Montagnais-Naskapi assert that, knowing in advance the nature of her fate, she passes off her embryo, or else refuses to be killed, escaping all human endeavor to take her, and then brings forth her cubs. A narrative illustrating this self-preserving ability, coming from a hunter of the Mistassini, mentions that some men chasing a fresh bear spoor found that it led to a round pool containing quicksand on one of the portages leading to Lake Mistassini, and there disappeared. The animal had dived in to escape the men, because she was not reconciled to being taken.

Sweat lodge preparation for the bear hunt.—In connection with the formal preparation for bear killing, our attention is drawn to that important ceremony, the sweat bath. The association of the sweat bath with bear hunting is, so far as I have been able to learn, a feature occurring nowhere else over the wide territory in America and Asia where this practice is common. Apparently it has become a unique development in the Labrador culture area, and so it is necessary to mention it while speaking of the religious rites belonging to the bear. First, let us glance at the myth of explanation coming from an inland hunter, Simon Rafaël, of the Lake St. John band, and recorded in 1921 at that post.

Me'jo Talks to Himself

Me'jo always talks to himself. He once went along a small lake and saw beaver tracks. "Oh, what a lot of beaver! I'll have to eat some." Finally, he found one asleep on the shore and went up to it. "Ah! a dead one. I'll roast him." So he tied his hunting sack to its neck to mark it and went to make a roasting stick.

While he was gone the beaver awoke and jumped up and then dived for the water with the sack. *Me'jo* saw him and said, "Ah! There's another beaver. I will get him and then I'll have two." But when he saw the beaver with the sack on its neck, he called for him to come back and give him back his sack. But the beaver only laughed and dived, with a whack of his tail. And so *Me'jo* wandered along the shore talking to himself again; soon he saw other tracks. "Ah! Here is a nice one; he is dead." Then he saw an otter asleep, and went up to it and grabbed it by the chest, feeling to see how fat it was. This tickled the otter and he laughed. "What are you going to do with me? "he asked. "Eat you," *Me'jo* answered. Then the otter jumped up and dived into the lake. Then *Me'jo* went upon the big mountain and suddenly found a bear. The bear jumped up, and *Me'jo* said, "What are you going to do?" "Eat you," said the bear. "Oh! Wait awhile. Don't do that yet. I came here to play, so let's do it first." The bear agreed to this. So *Me'jo* built a cabin for a sweat lodge and heated stones to put into it. Then he entered the sweat lodge and showed the bear where to go. Said he to the bear, "Here is where I sit, and you sit there."

So they went in and *Me'jo* began singing. The stones threw off great heat. Soon the bear was overcome with the heat and fell over dead. Then *Me'jo* cooked him and got his meal. (*This is the origin of the sweat lodge which is used among the Montagnais to call the bears so that they can be killed.*)

Next he went on to camp among the beautiful birches which are covered with smooth bark with no "eyes," or knots. So he looked at the birches and said, "Indians will have too easy a time with such fine bark to make camps, canoes and vessels." So he grabbed the birch, shook it, and caused the knots. Then he took a switch of spruce and lashed it hard and made all the streaks and "eyes." So that is why birch is not better than it is now, though it serves Indians every useful purpose even as it is.

The Naskapi nowadays resort with great fidelity to the magic influence of the sweat lodge, and in regions scant of game, where the bear furnishes a large quota of their food supply, the sweat lodge is a most important religious performance. It is so with the Naskapi of the Natasquan band toward the eastern reaches of the peninsula; their name, *Notackwa'nwi·nu't*, "bear-hunting people," being an appropriate one. Mr. William Cabot, for instance, in the summer of 1920 traveled inland with the chief of the St. Augustine band of the region and witnessed the old man engage over thirty times in the sweat-bath rite during the forty-odd days he was in his company. Although Mr. Cabot did not learn definitely what reason lay beneath such persistence, it is sufficiently clear to us.

When the "black food" has been overcome in spirit by the hunter's *micta'peo*, or soul-spirit, it remains for the killing to be accomplished by locating the animal and slaying it with mechanical devices—deadfall, gun, ax, arrow, or spear. Ordinarily, the hunter receives his hints as to the whereabouts of his victim in a dream, but he may chance upon a sleeping bruin in his winter lair without any previous introduction. Spring hunting is indeed one of the most common pursuits, and so our principal information on the matter of formal address comes from this occasion. At Seven Islands, old Nabe'oco of the Ste. Marguerite band and Peta'banu of the Ungava band gave some reviews of the procedure of address when the "great beast" is encountered in his "winter bed." Apropos of ursine hibernation, it should be noted that every person questioned among these bands will confirm the belief that the bear sucks his forepaws while sleeping. They maintain that the proof of this fact is that when the animal is killed in winter (in a winter den) this paw is always at the mouth and that the skin of the sole is raw. Hallowell has collected many references to this widespread belief and discussed it. Moreover, among the Montagnais it is claimed that the animal places a dottel of moss and earth in its rectum to prevent soiling the lair.

When the den of the hibernating beast has been discovered and the exact spot ascertained by the air hole, stained yellow with the animal's breath, is seen, the hunters stand about with their weapons. It is considered proper to attempt to finish the animal with a blow from an ax. Some hunters in doing this have knelt before the exit and used the ax with the cocked rifle lying at hand in case of failure or emergency. One of the characteristic customs of the Montagnais-Naskapi is the following form of address to the bear in this situation. The hunter issues the call olawi·'namucu'm‘! "Come out grandfather!" (coast dialects Montagnais) as much as three times if there is no activity within. If, however the bear is a female she will not respond to "grandfather," so the call is changed to olawi·'namoku'm‘! "Come out, grandmother!" For some reason the animal is aroused, growls, comes forth to be attacked. A variation to this address was recited by a hunter from Ungava: namocu'm neka cackwa'wac tsucpwa'gan! "My grandfather, I will light your pipe!" This refers to a custom mentioned below. From the Escoumains band we have a variation of the address: Olawi·'namucu'm cac cactcite'u tcetci·' olawi·'n, "Come out grandfather, already it ⟦the sun⟧ is warm enough for you to come forth." And then follows an exhortation still more coaxing: Wabatli·'tctagwa'n namucu'm, "Show me your head, grandfather." This, they say, may have to be repeated several times before the beast emerges. We have a belief connected with the den which may be noted here; namely, that the den where a bear is found and from which one has been taken, may be made to have again an occupant the ensuing winter if the successful hunter will be so generous as to place a plug of tobacco therein. This seems to be done throughout the peninsula.

As soon as the beast is dispatched, the hunters collect themselves about the carcass and light their pipes for a libation of smoke. And they do not slight the victim, for everywhere among these bands, the old order of conduct toward the bear required them to put some tobacco in his mouth (Lake St. John and Mistassini) or make a pipe of birch bark (fig. 5), and putting a charge of tobacco in it, insert it in the victim's mouth for a friendly smoke with his conquerors (Seven Islands, St. Marguerite to Ungava). The Mistassini Indians, after killing a bear, smoke a pipeful of tobacco over the carcass. In their case the individuals have their own stone pipes of a special form (pl. XVII). They do not have the custom of the bark-pipe offering that prevails farther east.

This is all done at the time and place of killing. We find another illustration of reverence for the victim's feelings in a custom among the eastern Naskapi of saying something like this when a hunter refers to having killed a bear: *nəpəta'n mi'tcəm kak⁰cto'wats,* "I have killed black food." One man at Seven Islands added that he did this so that the spirit of the bear, hearing the words, would not know who was referred to or who had killed him.

FIGURE 5   MUSEUM OF THE AMERICAN INDIAN
Birch-bark rolled pipe (Lake St. John band), length six inches.

To give the newly slain bear a small amount of tobacco in his mouth is a practice observed in one form or another everywhere among these tribes. The more conservative Indians will not skin or cut up the bear until this is done. A story along this line is told by the hunters at Lake St. John of a father and two sons a number of years ago who had killed a big bear in March, when the weather had turned warm for a short spell, about a day's journey by snowshoe south of the former trading post of the Hudson's Bay Company at Metabechouan. They, being on their way out of the bush for the first time that spring, had exhausted their winter supply of tobacco some time before and, consequently, had none to offer to the "great food." The father, however, decided to camp at the place and send one of his sons in haste to the post for the needed drug. It took the boy two days and a half to get to the post and back, and by that time the carcass was too much blown by the flies to use, and the meat was lost. A sacrifice to orthodoxy! We might note here also that when the skin is to be removed from the bear, the incision is made at the throat and the skin cut toward the tail. The reason given for this variation from the ordinary way of starting to skin animals, is that the bear likes to be treated differently from the other beasts. The same practice is known to the Penobscot of Maine.

We have already seen how the preparation of the bear for eating requires the observation of certain taboos. Salt is usually avoided in the preparation of the meat. In respect to not cutting the forearm from the paw, to cutting off and preserving the chin and the tongue sinew, and the elevation of the skull, sometimes ornamented with spots and bars of red ochre or black, on a trimmed tree, the distribution of these observances is general. In regard to the bearskull pole, or "lopstick" as it is called by the English-speaking traders and travelers in the Cree country—the French call it le mât, mast or flagpole—we must note that more often among the Montagnais the skulls of bears are simply tied to the branches of a living tree without further elaboration. At Kiskisink, a village of the Lake St. John band, south of that water, I have seen two bear skulls and a dozen or so beaver skulls all tied promiscuously to the branches of a balm of Gilead tree growing at one side of a log-and-birch-bark wigwam inhabited by a very old woman, a widow, who for many years has hunted and trapped as a solitary being, carrying her canoe and provisions wherever her pursuits led her in the surrounding wilderness. Another typical scene emblematic of the coast Montagnais' treatment of the remains of the bear is at Escoumains, where, on a poplar sapling bordering the little Indian graveyard, hangs a collection of similar skulls—some generations of the remains of both hunters and their victims foregathered within the common precincts until their next reincarnation (pl. vii).

Waugh in his notes on the Naskapi of Davis Inlet records the following observation: "Two bear skulls, one facing north, the other south, were lashed near the top of a pole with stones piled around the bottom to keep it upright. The skulls were painted with vermilion, a circle around the snout, circles around the eyes, ears, around the top of the head, around the lower edges of the jaws and a strip from between the eyes down the top of the nose."[15] It is a belief among all these Indians that one of the sources of spiritual satisfaction to the slain bear is to have his skull set high upon some prominent

15. Unpublished notes of F. W. Waugh, p. 113.

point of land near a waterway frequented by the Indians, so that long after his demise he can enjoy the sight of the world afoot in winter, afloat in summer, as he did while he was living. The custom may be a form of tree burial, a recognition of an immortality like that of man. Hind recorded a belief of the Naskapi that to remove these skulls would bring vengeance for the indignity. [16]

Bear Feast.—The bear when killed is usually made the substance of a feast to which all the people within reach are expected to come. It is accompanied, when ceremoniously observed, by a dance. The feast of game, no matter what kind, is called *cab∂towa'n* ("passage lodge," referring to the two opposite doors) and the ceremony of feast and dance *maguca'n* (Naskapi), *muk"ca'n* (Montagnais). So far as I can determine, there are few differences between the feast of the bear meat and that when mixed sorts of meat are consumed. The general characteristics of the *cab∂towa'n* are that the meat must be eaten under the cover of a tent, that all must be eaten, that no dogs are admitted lest the spirits of the animals consumed be offended. Among the Mistassini Indians we learn furthermore that the tent must be very clean when the bear is brought in. The men who have dreamt hunting songs and who own them as a spiritual working property entertain the audience with them and with drumming, and the assembled company dances. I learned of no traditional ordinances that the bear must be brought in through a specially made entrance. The usual door is used.

Those present dance in order to exhibit the respect they have for the spirits of the animals whose lives are so freely sacrificed to give them nourishment and life. The *cab∂towa'n* as an independent cere‑ mony will be discussed as a later topic, but to complete the survey of rites of the bear, I shall give an outline of the fiesta as described by a hunter of the Michikamau band which took place at Lake Michikamau. In this instance the carcass had been cut up by the married women and the masses of meat placed on bark trays where they would be within reach of all present. The feast was celebrated by a group comprising two families living in a single tent, with two fires, one at each end. Incidentally, this tent was composed of seven sewed caribou skins on each side. The ground plan is given in outline (fig. 6).

16. Hind, I, 184. Also Masson, II, 415‑16.

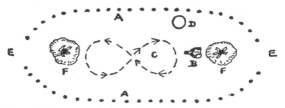

FIGURE 6

Diagram of feasting lodge (*cabətowa'n*) from native drawing by man of Michikamau band. (A) Spectators' seats; (B) bear skull, when feast celebrates eating of
bear meat; (C) direction taken by dancers; (D) tambourine drum hung from roof
poles; (E) entrances at ends of lodge; (F) fires on flat stones.

The bear's head was laid at one end of the tent facing inward,
while during and after the feast the company at times danced as the
line in the diagram indicates. The head was passed around the
assembly in a birch-bark dish, and they ate from it without using
knives. This procedure was continued all night until the entire
animal was devoured. The bones were then all thrown into the
fire. We learn also that the bear was not referred to by his proper
designation during the feast, but by the usual circumlocutions:
"great food," *tcitcəwe mi'tcəm;* "black beast," *kəckte'wədjiu;* "short
tail"; and especially *nəmucu'm,* "grandfather." When the bear
was ready to be brought into the tent, someone called out, *peta'-
gən kətəkgwa' pisico,* "Bring him in who has a short tail." A most
interesting sidelight is thrown on this procedure by the nature of the
following allegorical reference to the bear's neck-and-shoulder meat
when it was cooked and ready to be eaten by the men feasters: *oce'-
tcəpətwa'nəck,* "hair bobs of the bear." This denoted the twelve
slices of the neck flesh, six on each side, one of each being a portion
for two men, the figurative expression alluding to the "bobs," in
which fashion the Montagnais-Naskapi women dress their hair (pl.
iii). During the recitations of the feast, some ingenuity was exer-
cised in the attempt to avoid direct reference to the bear.

This group also punctiliously observed the usual taboos mentioned before—of not allowing dogs to eat any of the meat, of eating
the head without knives, of the women not eating the head. After
this feast the skull was cleaned and decorated with vermilion across
the forehead, over the eye and ear sockets, and placed away on the
rack for the drying of meat above the fires, where the spirit of the
animal could thenceforth see his "friends" (pl. v, left).

I have inquired in vain among the Montagnais-Naskapi for certain bear customs reported among other tribes within the circle of the Canadian North comprising the sub-Arctic cultures, such as the taboo of bringing the carcass in through the door of the tent, the requirement of sexual abstinence before the bear hunt, and leaving the skin attached to the head. Nor is it formal for the hunter, having slain a bear, to announce the event when returning home by throwing a stick against the tent cover without voicing any other signal, as is noted among rites of the caribou. [17]

From another quarter of the peninsula, from the Montagnais of Godbout, we have a narrative description of the bear feast attended and written by N. A. Comeau. This interesting account I quote in full:

Our common black bear is looked upon by most people in Canada as a very dangerous animal. This dread is even shared by our Indians, and when bears are spoken of it is always with great respect. In fact, the name is seldom mentioned, but the bear is referred to as "the Black Beast" or simply "the Animal." When caught in a steel trap or seen at a distance he is spoken to and asked that vengeance be not taken for his death. Even the bones are held in respect. They are never thrown to the dogs like other refuse, but placed in the fire and burned. The skulls are hung up in a tree. Some parts of the animal, like the paws and head, are never allowed to be eaten by women or children. These last, if by some accident they eat any meat, are supposed to be liable to suffer all their lives from cold feet. At certain times bear feasts used to be held, at which no women are allowed to be present, and special wigwams were built wherein to hold the feast. At these feasts nothing else but bear's meat was allowed to be eaten. This was prepared in various ways: either roasted on the spit, boiled or stewed. Blood pudding, fat pudding and pure fat of the bear are other dishes prepared from parts of the animal. "Fat pudding" is prepared in this way: About three or four feet of the large intestine is cut off with all the fat adhering to it. A ramrod or thin stick of suitable size is then inserted in the gut and one end tied to it. It is then pulled inside out and cleaned. Berries are sometimes stuffed inside with the fat. The ends are then tied, and the gut put to boil for about an hour, and then laid aside to cool, as it is always eaten cold. It is served up in its full length on a birch-bark platter, and each guest cuts off with his knife whatever length he is able to manage; the more he can stow away the greater being the honor he is paying to his host.

Being in luck one day, I chanced to supply the necessary viands for a feast in the shape of two bears, and of course had to be invited. Outside of the Hudson Bay Company's factors, few whites have ever had that honor. Some of the hunters were away, so that the gathering was no large one, some fourteen or fifteen guests being present. A long strip of white cotton served as table cloth. This was laid down on the balsam branches, fresh cut for the occasion. A plate and knife and

17. As far away as Lapland this trait extends as noted by Holmberg, *Finno-Ugric Mythology*, p. 87.

some thin sheets of birch bark were laid before each person, but no fork or spoon. When necessary to take a piece of meat out of the platter, a wooden skewer was used. This, as well as the only ladle allowed, was made out of the mountain ash,— the bear's favorite tree. For some reason that I could not find out no one sat at what we would call the head or foot of the table. The two eldest men sat opposite each other at one end and after that, towards the foot each guest according to his age or rank as a hunter. Everyone being seated, the first course was served. A large bowl of hot bear's grease took the place of soup. In this was the wooden ladle. The bowl was set before the chief; after helping himself and sipping from the ladle what quantity he chose, the bowl and ladle was passed on to the next man in rank and so on to the end of the table. If there was a mighty hunter—I should rather say eater—able to distinguish himself by drinking three or four ladles full of the fat, it was always greeted with a round of applause. The first course through, the bowl was laid on the middle of the table and the ladle taken away. The second course was the bear's neck and head roasted on the spit and the spit left in it, as it served to pass it around to each guest. It was stuck in front of the chief who made a sort of address to it. He boasted of the bear's strength as a tree climber and of its power of endurance as a faster—referring to its hibernations—and paid it all the other compliments he could think of. The end of the spit was then raised and a piece bitten out or torn with the fingers, as no knife must touch this sacred *pièce de résistance*. Like the bowl of fat it went around and each one had to take a small piece or bite as he fancied, but no one was allowed to take more. What was left was then put into the fire and burned for the absent ones—the deceased hunters. After this second course each guest was free to help himself and eat whatever quantity he chose of roast, boiled, stewed or pudding. Very little conversation was carried on during the feast. The diners were not there for "palaver," but for business, and any special gastronomic feat performed was sure to meet with general approval. After everyone had eaten until he could stand no more, the bowl of fat was placed in front of the chief a second time. With his two hands open he dipped his palms in the fat, and then smeared his long hair with it, every guest following suit. Was this the origin of the use of bear's grease for the hair?

Thus ended the feast. Pipes and strong black plug tobacco were then brought forth, and everyone who smoked enjoyed himself. What was left was quickly taken away by the women for their meal, and the small bones were thrown into the fire. As soon as the cloth was removed, there was a general stretching out of the diners on the ground all around. Had I not been familiar with these feasts I should have expected an invitation to a funeral shortly afterwards, but nothing out of the ordinary happened. Through the efforts of the missionaries these superstitious rites and customs have been partially abolished on the coast, but they are carried on just as soon as the Indians go inland for the hunt. Similar feasts are also held in honor of the caribou and the beaver, and also for birds such as geese and loons. I have never heard of a fish feast in this section. In honor of whatever animal or bird the feast is held, no other kind of meat figures, and provision is always made to have more than will be eaten; they will actually starve themselves for a time in order to collect the required quantity. [18]

18. N. A. Comeau, *Life and Sport on the North Shore* (2nd ed.; Quebec, 1923), pp. 85-89.

The accounts obtained of the bear feast as it was conducted among different groups are much the same. At Escoumains the Montagnais passed the bear's head around among men of the company who ate it with their fingers only. The head was passed in a birch-bark dish which is here called *wuckwi·'lagɔn*, "bark dish"—an undecorated one, though similar in form to those collected from the Mistassini (pl. vi). Again the women were forbidden to eat of the head. And here we are told that the skull when cleaned of meat was hung in a tree, but not decorated with paint. Something of these observances is still adhered to at Escoumains as appears in the photograph of the suspended bear skulls in the balsam tree (pl. vii A, B). At this place also the hunter who killed the bear cut off and preserved one of the beast's ears as a mark of respect and for future luck in hunting.

Parts of the skeleton are used in divination. The patella is made to answer questions put to it by the hunter by placing it upon a hot stone or on the top of a hot stove. When questioned about the game, a slight sidewise wobbling is the affirmative; a failure to move, the negative. This is reminiscent of the Eskimo divination practice. The bear scapula is, among the eastern Naskapi, also used in the burnt divination as will appear in later discussion. It may be added, however, that at Lake St. John one hunter recoiled at the suggestion of using a bear bone for scapulimancy.

As regards the use of the *ni·ma'ban*, or ceremonial pack strap, in handling the body of the slain bear, there is less to say than there is in the case of smaller game. The bear is killed in the season when there is no snow or ice upon which the carcass can be dragged. Nevertheless, from an old hunter of the Lake St. John band, Napani', I obtained in 1920 a strip of moosehide made into a small carrying strap which the old man explained was a pack-strap for portions of bear meat. He said that when he used to kill a bear he would drape this strap over his own forehead and dance several times around the body, then leave the strap on its chest to keep vermin away. The strap in question was decorated in yarn with an outline figure of a bear.

From a woman of the same band I purchased a white canvas game bag with a cloth appliqué silhouette of a bear cropping berries from a bush, and two blotches of red in cloth below it representing blood. The whole was the outcome of a dream and was intended to develop a successful hunting career for her young son.

Bear bones are much in use for utensils. The leg bones are frequently made into skinning knives (mitsəkwu′n), and they are, in
about half the cases, etched or engraved with lines and dots, because
these figure in dream experiences resulting in the taking of game.
The decorations are intended to please the owner's soul-spirit, as we
have seen. Snowshoe needles and bone awls also are made of bear
bones. I have obtained several spoons trimmed out of the bear's shoulder blade (pl. v, right), which were used in feasts to drink grease
with, in the endeavor, it was explained, to attest the hunter's
gratitude for the "great food" allowed him by the self-sacrifice of
the animal. The canine teeth of the bear are often taken out when
one is killed and kept to be drilled at the base and put to service as
toggles attached to the end of a thong for fastening articles. A few
of these teeth may be found in the possession of nearly every hunter.

Bear abductor tale.—South of the St. Lawrence the story of the
little boy abducted by a female bear and kept in her maternal custody
for a season with the result that he was being slowly transformed,
is a common element in mythology. I have made inquiries for this
tale among a number of the Montagnais-Naskapi bands without en-
countering it except in the following instances from the lips of an
old Mistassini conjuror and again from an old man at Seven Islands
belonging to the St. Marguerite band.

The following was narrated by Kakwa in 1918 in the Lake St.
John dialect, though the story, he said, was one from the Mistassini.

A long time ago a bear captured a child and kept him to raise. He fed him on
fishes. For three years he raised that boy. After three years then the man set
out to see his son, that man the one whose son was captured. In the bear's den
they were, the bear and the boy. In that very place [the father] went to search
for his son. By that time he had no clothing left. But the man carried on his back
some clothing for to dress up his son. When he got to the place, that man, over
at the bear's den, the bear did not wish to give up the boy. And then the man
shot him with an arrow, that bear, and killed him. And then he dressed him up
and took him home to his camp. (Said his son, in referring to his life with the
bear), "When we knew that anyone saw us, he [the bear] would put me on his
back and he would run away very fast."

From the Naskapi informant at Seven Islands is a less succinct
though evidently a variant version. This is the translation of the
monologue delivered by the bear foster mother of the Indian boy
just before it was time for her to deliver him up to his parents. It is

hardly more than a fragment. "I always hid so that no one passing near would see us and find us. But now you will find your father tomorrow morning. And you will go away with your own father. For I no longer can keep you. And so I will be killed in the morning. As long as three years I have kept you. Now this is all of it."

For some reason the distribution of the legend does not accord it a prominent place among the extreme northern Algonkian.

The preceding discussion refers to the common black bear, *mack$^{\omega}$*, but we find occasional reference among these Indians to another variety which they call *mata'mən mack$^{\omega}$*, "great bear." They believe it to be a different race several times as large as the ordinary bear. This may refer to the so-called Barren Ground bear of Labrador. I have, however, no more information upon this reputed form than the following statements from Chief Kurtness of the Lake St. John band, and corroborated without expansion by several others with whom I discussed it. This bear does not hibernate in a den but "sits upright in the snow with his head uncovered above the drift." He has a very savage humor and his flesh is more tender than that of the common bear. His claws are so long that he can scarcely climb a tree. But the most puzzling thing about this legend is that something like it is related by the Penobscot of Maine as regards what they believe to be a second species of bear, known as a "ranger bear," inhabiting their own forests far south of the St. Lawrence. The story, one might imagine, could possibly be of a legendary nature. [19]

The white bear, *wabə'ck$^{\omega}$*, is widely known by name among the Montagnais and by actual contact among the Naskapi, who at times encounter one that has wandered inland from the coasts. No ceremonial obligations are mentioned in my notes for this beast. Yet among the Penobscot again the same animal, *wampsk$^{\omega}$* in their language, figures as a hero in mythology.

The following tale is illustrative of certain customs just discussed.

An Old Woman Kills a Bear and Observes the Proper Rites

Late in April once the people had nothing to eat. They rested in a wigwam. There was an old woman who was the second wife of the father of the two men

19. In his discussion of the Barren Ground bear (*Ursus richardsonii*, Bangs), probability of this is given by Dr. W. D. Strong, "Notes on Mammals of the Labrador Interior," *Journal of Mammalogy*, Vol. II (1930), No. 1, p. 5. He summarizes the testimony for the supposed identity of the separate race. I would add to Dr. Strong's references that of Cartwright, op. cit., p. 348, in which he writes of a kind of bear very ferocious, having a white ring around its neck.

of my story. The old woman went out. It had thawed in the morning. Suddenly she found a bear's track. The bear had floundered in the snow. She followed the bear with a gun. She saw the bear going along in snow. At a distance near enough she shot and killed bear. Her name was Malic. After she killed the bear, she took the bear's tongue tendon, *utelni·' ckwan m ɑck'ᵚ*. They went to camp to get a toboggan to bring the bear back but the three men, two stepsons and her husband, a very old man, could not walk to help her, they were so weak from hunger. (Too weak from starvation!) They even had no tobacco, but the old woman had secretly saved a pipeful of tobacco although she loved to smoke even more than the men. When she arrived at camp she took the tobacco, cut it up and smoked it in her pipe. The old man, when she lighted her pipe, smelled the tobacco smoke. He said, "Where did you get tobacco? It's long time since we had tobacco." When he spoke the old woman took her pipe and gave it to the old man. "Smoke!" When they finished smoking she showed the tongue tendon. "Do you know this?" The two weak men, who were sleeping and helpless from hunger, arose and saw that she had killed a bear. The two weak men, they said, "Let us see it." They realized that she had killed a bear and they were so glad that they jumped up and embraced her. "Where is it you have killed bear?" "Take toboggan and follow my tracks and you'll find the bear." The two weak men then became strong and hurried on the traces; and they got the bear, ate, and saved their lives. They were fortified and were able to continue the winter. They would have all died, they were ready to die, if the old woman had not killed the bear. The two men were George and Thomas Metabi of Mistassini; more than fifty years ago.

The Beaver Rites

The third mastership is that of the beaver. This beast detaches itself from the ranks of the wild animals almost as much in the esteem of the savages as the caribou and the bear. They bear witness with all the fidelity of worshippers to its miraculous powers of magic and its sage intellect. The patriarchal giant of the beaver race, the supreme lord and owner, we shall first consider. This legend was recorded some years ago. The giant beaver, *Mičta'mɔck'ᵚ*, mentioned in the tale was master of his kind. It was he who governed the destinies of his race, their return to the world after death, and their allotment as game food to the hunters. [20] The tale explains his movements and final departure from the country.

Mista'beo (Big Man) Tries to Kill the Giant Beavers

Mista'beo went to kill the beaver up at the headwaters of Mistassini where they had a great pond and dam. He broke the dam to let the water out so he could

20. Recent inquiry among the Algonquin of River Desert, P. Q., results in showing the occurrence of similar beliefs in this area. Toward the territory of the Saulteaux and Ojibwa (Mattagama River), the beaver story assumes greater importance, it would seem from investigations made of their economic legends in 1928. Thus it may be expected over a very wide area in the North, as Hallowell reports it from the Saulteaux of Manitoba.

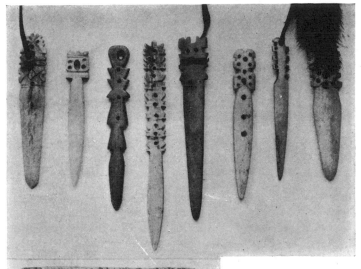

PLATE XI

Upper photograph, carved and engraved bone fastening pins and pipe cleaners.
The first two, the fourth, and the one on the extreme right, are from Lake St. John;
the third is from Seven Islands; the sixth is Moisie, the seventh is Natasquan.
Lower photograph, birch-bark comb case, with etched figure of bears based on
dream experience.

kill them. Then he lay down across the dam to prevent them from going downstream. He intended to stay awake all night to kill them if they tried to cross over his body; or in the morning when the dam got dry, to finish them. During the night the old beavers planned how they could escape. They sent the muskrat to see if *Mista'beo* was asleep. "Go dive near him and see if he is asleep yet," they said. They all used their wishing power to make him fall asleep. The muskrat went near where *Mista'beo* lay and splashed around and learned that he was wide awake. "No," he said when he came back, "he is not asleep." They all used their wishing power again and asked muskrat to go look once more. It was then just after midnight. He went and splashed near *Mista'beo*, who had only closed his eyes. *Pishtegu'm!* the noise he made. But *Mista'beo* was awake. They waited. Later they asked him to again and this time, just before daylight, he went and splashed loud, *pishtegu'm! Mista'beo* did not move. So muskrat came back and said, "Yes, he sleeps." The water was now getting very low so they had to hurry. The female beaver said to the male, "You go first, then the four little ones, then I will come last."

The male beaver went to where *Mista'beo* lay and jumped over him and went down the Mistassini River. Then each of the four little ones crept gently over him without arousing him and got past also. Last came the female beaver. Before she jumped over *Mista'beo*, she took an armful of mud and daubed it all over his face, eyes, nose, and ears. "Now you will sleep." And she jumped over him. They all fled downstream.

Mista'beo jumped up and had to get all the mud off his face. He chased them toward Lake St. John. It was a long chase, over two hundred miles. He chased them across the lake and tried to stop them at the Grand Discharge. But they all got through, swimming between and around his legs, except the female who, to avoid him, dove back into the lake toward Mistassini Point. *Mista'beo* took one step and reached the point. Then she dived again before he could seize her. She came up at Pointe Bleue and he missed her again. Then she dove and passed down the Grand Discharge and escaped. They all reached the sea swimming down the Saguenay. The falls are now called Kastsegau, "where the rocks are cut down."[21]

One of the sitting stations of the giant beaver is pointed out below Chicoutimi on the Saguenay River, under the name *otə'p-mick*ᵂ, "beaver seat." Here is where the giant beaver is said to have rested after his adventure with *Mista'beo* at Lake St. John. To understand this allusion, a habit of the beaver may be recalled to mind; namely, that in the springtime when the animal wanders abroad to seek out new territory to inundate and colonize, he "squats" each night of his journey in a "seat" close to the water's edge, from which he can plunge and escape at the sound of alarm. His shelter is in the open, hence the "beaver seat." The Lake St.

21. F. G. Speck, "Montagnais and Naskapi Tales from the Labrador Peninsula," *Journal of American Folk-Lore*, Vol. XXXVIII (1925), No. 147, pp. 23-24.

John Indians attribute much of the change of contour in the region to the giant beaver. The opening up of the outlet at Grand Dis-charge caused the drainage of the Lake St. John basin to its present level; prior to then the shores reached to the foothills of the escarp-ment surrounding the lake basin, at varying distances of ten miles or more on some sides, from the present shore line. It may also be recalled that Lake St. John has always been known to the Indians about it as a shallow lake with low flat shores, whence its name *Pi·-əkwa'gəmi*, "flat-shore lake." The present large wooded islands rising above its surface, Isle à Traverse and Isle au Couleuvres, were then mere projecting ledges bare of trees, tradition says. The important result of the transit of the legendary giant beaver was that with his exit he drew the other beavers after him, being their master, since which time the animals have not been abundant in the Lake St. John district. Before the expulsion of the giant beaver and the draining off of part of the lake, they believe, beavers abounded in the adjacent waterways.

The attitude of the hunter to the giant beaver is, or was, one of hope for his generosity and obligation on his own part to observe the rules for disposing of the remains of the slain animals. We observe, among other impositions, the necessity of throwing the bones of the beaver back into the lake or river, its native element. This is done so that the spirit of the creature will return to life. It was a mark of special regard for the slain beaver, one much esteemed by its shade, to elevate the skull on a forked stick, as was done with the skull of the bear. The eyes of the animal are also cast into the water after the body has been skinned and butchered. The piece of gristle lying behind the large paunch is cast into the water for the same reason—to cause the animal to return to life. The gristle here referred to is likened to a leech,[22] which develops from the designation *amick*ᵂ*otakəki·'m*, "beaver, his leech."

The beaver, it is believed, embodies extraordinarily high spiritual endowments. It can transform itself into other animal forms, that of geese and other birds being specifically mentioned. The beaver can disappear by penetrating the ground, by rising aloft into the air, or by diving into the depths of lake or stream and remaining any length of time desired. In short, "he can escape or hide himself if he wishes to, so that he can never be taken." Old Étienne, the

22. This the large black leech (*Pontobdela muricata*) of northern waters, called in Montagnais, *a'kəki*.

pretended centenarian at Lake St. John, affirmed that he once saw a goose alight onto the water lying atop the ice surrounding a small island one spring, and when he reached the spot to kill it, it turned out to be a beaver.

Again we are told it is only with the amiable consent of the beaver himself that the animal can be killed, and this consent is in some curious way dependent upon the volition of the giant beaver.

Beaver rites.—The following narrative of a dream experience is a translation from a text in the Mistassini dialect taken down from Ka'kwa in 1915. The rites and observances are best given in his own words and will introduce the topic to which we are about to turn.

Dreaming about the beaver is called "great dreaming." An Indian was sleeping and he dreamt that he saw a man coming toward him. He dreamt, "It was as though he was coming close to me and as though he was giving me a beaver!" He dreamt that he was going to burn the hair off this beaver. But he dreamt that the man commanded, "Cut out *only* the backbone, and then you boil it whole. And after it is cooked you will put it into your dish (*wi˙ ya'gəm*, a special form of birch-bark dish). Don't use a knife when you are eating. For you know how he, Short Tail [meaning the bear], does when eating. And so you do the same when you are eating. So eat then. And do not leave it until the next morning. You know over there is a mountain." He then pointed out a distant mountain. "Over there you will go." I thought he told me all this. "You will look for a birch tree standing and bending directly toward the north. There beneath the root, in there you try to get your food for your children [meaning more beaver]."

In the morning when he arose, the hunter said, "I dreamt last night!" "Wonder what he dreamt!" his wife thought, and asked him. Then I went to look at my beaver traps. And there was caught one big beaver. That indeed was that I saw last night in my dream. Then I took it back to camp and arriving there I singed it, and afterwards I ate the beaver. The next day I started off, and went there to the place that the man of my dreams indicated. I arrived over the mountain and found little else than birch trees standing about and leaning in different directions. Which way should I dig to search for it (the one bent as indicated in my dream). Never mind! At last I walked straight ahead, and while going saw the birch tree leaning over toward the north. "Well sure enough, this is the one," I thought. And there standing close by, I first of all smoked. And then having smoked, I shoveled away the snow. And there, behold, I found my children's food [meaning by this phrase, the beaver promised in the dream]. I obtained a big supply of it from him who was feeding me [the dream spirit, his Great Man] —it was the big food [a bear by its epithet]. It is well known that when once the beaver comes to tell anything, it is not for nothing that he speaks. It is like a great prophet. And so he wants his bark dish [the one in which the beaver is eaten by the hunter] to look pretty with decorations. After this is done just as he likes it, he never fails to grant a supply. Yet he does not like to have different kinds of meat cooked in this dish devoted to his meat, only his own kind eaten in it.

Another Mistassini description is as follows:

When a man dreams that he will kill a beaver and gets it, he brings it home carrying it with his *ni' ma'ban* (carrying string). Then he says to his wife, "Bring here my bark dish." And he singes the hair from the beaver over the fire and roasts the body entire. Then he takes his bark dish from its covering of white cloth and puts the roasted carcass on it.[23] Then he invites the whole camp to come to eat the beaver. When they are ready to eat, the insides of the beaver are thrown into the fire, as these parts cannot be eaten. And also a good piece of meat is cut off and thrown into the fire. Then they all eat. All the meat must be eaten before morning, by which time the feasters depart. The time is spent in conversation and dancing.

Several correspondences are to be noted between methods of disposal of the beaver and bear remains: The elevation of the skull on a "flagpole," the taboo against the use of a knife; preserving the backbone intact—which is also required when cooking a big fish. The association of the bear and the beaver in the dream and the observances just given are other matters to be noted. While the most specific information on beaver observances seems to come from the Mistassini band, the general features appear to be fairly well distributed among other bands. The same style of feasting with the birch-bark dish is described at Escoumains, where we learn of special attention being given to the formality of cooking the carcass. It is hung by a thong and meat hook so that it will revolve before the fire, and roasted until it is crisp and yellow. Then it is eaten in one of the special bark trays. Several specimens of the birch-bark dishes mentioned by Ka'kwa were obtained from the bands visited for the museums and are examples of the finest workmanship to be seen in this material of the North. They are shallow, tray-like basins with the rims higher at the ends than in the middle. The seams of the bark are sewed with red dyed spruce root and some are smeared with red ochre. Besides this are to be seen the five orientated red dots so frequently repeated in the decorations of far northern North America, from the Cree to the Naskapi. These are generally admitted to be signatures of *mite'win*, or shamans. Some of the forms of these feast dishes are shown (pl. VI).

23. The dish is decorated with painted groups of four red spots forming a square, with another one in the center, the symbol of revelation in a dream (see pp. 173, 186).

The beaver is one of the most frequent apparitions in the dreams of the hunters, and his visitation is always portentous of hunting activity. Whatever game is killed after a dream directed by the beaver, is eaten in the specially prepared bark tray. Often the hunter will have this animal's figure etched upon the outside of the bark vessel, directing some woman of his household to make the image. Moreover, should his wife dream of game it has the same significance, and the same things are done. Such a receptacle is, among the Mistassini, at least, kept wrapped in a white cloth. We are informed that a hunter may have such dream admonitions every night for a considerable period.

An interesting specimen of a skinning and scraping tool of beaver bone (*mitsəkwu'n*), of the Lake St. John band, shows the figure of a beaver outlined by incision on the side of the tool (fig. 7). The

FIGURE 7

Beaver figure on handle of caribou leg-bone skinning knife (*mitsəkwu'n*), after the owner had dreamed of a beaver and enjoyed a successful hunt in consequence.

owner explained that he had dreamt of a beaver and consequently, soon after having killed one, he filed the outline of the beaver on the skinning bone to repay the giver of his dream and to bring good luck again.

The most ornamented and carefully made pack strings (*ni·ma'ban*) are constructed for the transportation of the beaver from the locality where it is killed to the camp. These are very often colored red, which seems to be the symbolic color for the animal. The *ni·ma'ban* employed in winter for all small quarry is longer than the one made for summer use, as will appear in subsequent discussion, the winter form of pack string being intended to drag the carcass over the snow attached by a toggle through the septum of the beast's nose. At other than snow time the string is shorter, for then the carcass is slung on the hunter's back with a forefoot–hind-foot attachment. Beaver pack strings are commonly ornamented with strings of beads and ribbons, the red being the symbolic preference for this animal.

When ready to be cooked, the beaver carcass is suspended over the fire by a twisted thong and a hook attached to its throat. Or a sharpened piece of moose antler is put through the nose as a cleat (Lake St. John). Thus, the body slowly revolves over the heat, allowing it to cook evenly. There is, however, more than commodity in the device. There is ceremonial formality in it, as we see evidenced by the suspension thong occasionally being ornamented with color, and the cord and hook being consistently kept in readiness for use among household effects. One specimen collected from a Michikamau hunter is a hook of iron wire with a caribou skin line tanned red.

The skulls of beaver are commonly suspended in trees. At the Montagnais village of Escoumains, in several such bundles there were some thirty skulls, and in others there were two attached as "couples."

The disposition of beaver bones does not include their conversion into tools and utensils to the same degree as those of the caribou and bear, on account of their lightness and smallness. The teeth were originally made to form a knife, as tradition says. But the shoulder blades of the beaver, as well as the pelvic bones, are important among the devices of divination. The beaver's patella is at Lake St. John employed in divination the same as the bear's. Scorching the beaver scapula, signs result from the cracks and burnt spots which may be deciphered as a revelation of where and under what condition game (in this case the beaver) may be found. The pelvic bone is employed to elicit a reply of yes or no from the beaver's spirit in response to questions concerning the prospects of the hunt. These matters will, however, receive discussion and illustration under a subsequent heading, that of scapulimancy (see p. 160). The foreleg bone of the beaver is also employed in divination. The hunter who can break this in his hands by bending it will soon kill a beaver. More will be said of this practice later. A very strong medicine is made by charring beaver's teeth and grinding them to powder. Put in water, this is drunk by the hunters (Mistassini).

The account of the beaver should not be concluded without mention of a tale, localized in the country north of Lake St. John, and narrated by the Indians there in 1919. The tale has the general similitude of the caribou-man story without, however, the control feature having developed as far as to become a cult-story, although its trend may be in that direction.

A hunter once had a dream in which a female beaver appeared to him and desired him to join her kind and become her husband. He followed the instructions of his dream and went to live with the beavers. Before this time the beavers did not know how to build dams across the streams. But the man taught them how to construct dams to raise the waters of their ponds for their protection. They always, however, lived in the beaver "cabin." The place where this took place is known as *wətəbəmi'ckʷ*, "beaver set," a cranny far up on Oasiemshkau River where a deep cave is to be seen in which this man dwelt. At the foot of a waterfall here is a rock appearing in the form of a beaver. This is the transformation of the beaver husband.

The Master of the Fish

Like the caribou and the beaver, the fish also have an overlord, or master whose characteristics of control and sensitiveness toward waste of his creatures are practically equivalent. In the case of fish, it is the moose-fly (*Tabanus affinis*), that torment of the northern bush (fig. 8 A). It is called *misəna'kʷ* by the Naskapi bands in general who emerge at Seven Islands, *mici·cakʷ* "big biter," by the Mistassini, and among those who come to Lake St. John, *mictsina'kʷ*.

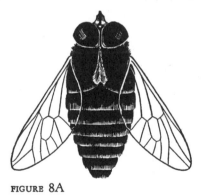

FIGURE 8A

(Three times natural size.)

The moose-fly (*Tabanus affinis* [?]) known to the Naskapi as *misəna'kʷ*. This is the master of the fish to whose favor the Indians owe success either fishing with the hook or the net. The fly hovers about the fish caught to see that nothing is wasted. Wastefulness is an offense to him, hence a cause of failure in taking fish.

— 118 —

These terms hardly submit to specific analysis, especially when we discover that the former is a synonym of terrapin, or turtle, among the bands in the more moderate climate of the southwestern area of the peninsula, where an occasional specimen of terrapin (*Chrysemis picta*, painted turtle) is discoverable in the lakes and swamps. The term obviously refers to the hard back or shell, as we see it again in Wabanaki as *ktcikwəna'k'tc*, the water terrapin of the maritime provinces. All the terms given may, however, be analyzed into the elements, "big hard back."

Something of a question arises out of this synonymy: Could the confusion of identity of the moose-fly and the terrapin be connected with a northward migration of the people away from the haunts of the latter, resulting in the transfer of name and character to the fly? The terrapin as master of the fish seems, however, not to have been reported among other tribes south or west of the Naskapi, as might be expected in case of such an explanation.

In his supernatural estates the moose-fly carries the name *təpə-nəmə'k nəme'c*, "he who governs fish." The particular belief we are introducing seems to belong to the Naskapi bands toward the eastern point of the peninsula and to the northern reaches rather than to the southwestern, for about Lake St. John it was not recognized by informants of the lake band proper when I discussed it before them. The Mistassini, however, share the belief, and in that dialect refer to the master of the fish as *katəpe·'i·mat nəme'ca*, but they designate his identity definitely as terrapin.

At any rate, we find the moose-fly regarded as the dispenser of the fate of the fish tribes, specifically those of the salmon and cod. The moose-fly is observed to appear upon the scene when the fish are taken from the water in the summer, and he is then regarded as coming to witness the treatment of his subjects by the fishermen— his inclination to torment them by his stings (perhaps we should say "her" stings, since it is only the female who is capable of stinging) being an indication of custody over the fish and warning against wastefulness of the flesh. Then, to the observant and economical fish catcher the ration of flesh will be continued, while wasteful fishermen will sooner or later be punished by deprivation. Such warning is seldom merited by the Naskapi in respect to his source of food. [24]

24. McKenzie, in 1808, found the Montagnais attributing the cause of sore throat to fish and wearing a strip of net around the neck to get rid of it (Masson, *op. cit.*, p. 427).

In explaining the belief of the fish master, the following translation is given of a text taken down from the dictation of an old informant, Nabe'oco (Baptiste Picard), of the Ste. Marguerite River band, at Seven Islands (1924). The belief is explained in native terminology, as though the fly were declaiming in the first person—a commandment: "Məsəna'k^ω I am called, the one who is master of the fish. I support them. You Indians will be given fish; you who do as is required are given fish, not him who wastes them. He who takes fish and wastes them will not henceforth secure anything. And likewise he who laughs at the fish on account of his big eyes here, will not catch fish. And he who ridicules the way the fish are formed will not be happy for they will not be given my fishes. Whoever wants to take fish must do right; after this fish will be given him. For I am master of the fish. And as I say, so it will happen here as I say. I the moose-fly, *məsəna'k^ω*, so I am named!"

From another quarter of the Naskapi territory, this time from the Mistassini, comes a dictation in respect to the ceremonial treatment of the fish, revealing something further in the direction of ichthyolatry. It is a free translation of the original text recorded in 1915 from an old man of this band:

Where the northern people dwell, so they do according to their thoughts as they appear in their minds. When a very big lake trout is killed, they boil it whole in a large kettle. After it is cooked, it is spread out on a sheet of birch bark and the kettle is turned upside down over the fish. Then the men eat it. They do not use a knife when they eat the big fish. When it is so they cannot eat it all, then the women may finish eating it, but the children never eat it. Should the children eat it, it would be unlucky, for they might get poisoned by it and made sick, or else the rest of the big fishes might depart and go in deep water where they could not be caught. They never break his backbone. Slowly they pick the flesh from it, and after it is done they peel a pole, *mictək'ʷo'ka'n*, and on this 'flagpole' the backbone of the big fish is hung up. And by so doing, they satisfy the terrapin (*mictsina'k'ʷ*), the master of all the fishes.

Several elements of this narrative are most important. One is that the "eat-all" feature so common in the bear feasts of the northern Indians in general occurs with the fish feast, and also that as the bear's skull is erected on a pole to propitiate the animal's feeling, so the fish backbone is treated. But especially noteworthy here is the interpretation of the name *mictsina'k'ʷ*, who is the usual master of the fish, as "terrapin" instead of "moose-fly."

We may add that from Lake St. John to Lake Mistassini the custom of wrapping up the jawbones of big fish in birch bark and suspending them in trees is common. This brings the hunter good luck and increases the fish supply. At Escoumains when a big fish was taken, the man who killed it cut off its tail and kept it or hung it up. Waugh mentions seeing a trout's skull suspended in a wigwam of the Indians at Davis Inlet.

FIGURE 8B

Gullet fish-hook of sharp bone set in wooden shank, with line of red-and-white rawhide to attract victim (4 5-8 inches.).

Another instance of magic operation, this time through the employment of color, appears in a specimen of native made wood-and-bone fishhook obtained from a hunter who operates near Lake Michikamau and a member of that local group. The rawhide line, by which the hook is attached to the hand or set pole, is made of alternate white and red pieces. The red coloration was explained by its owner as a form of *mite'win*, or conjuring, to lure the victim to the bait (fig. 8 B). This, however, is the only instance that has come to my observation of the decoration of fishing apparatus for magico-religious purposes, none appearing on harpoons, nets, floats and the like that I have seen.

As to divination in connection with fishing, there is something also to say in passing, but the discussion of the practices will be given under treatment of divination. Nevertheless, since the spirits of fish that have been killed are believed to return to the abode of fish souls somewhere beneath the sea, so certain bones of the fish are regarded as being capable of giving responses when asked about the outcome of a fishing operation, or, when thrown into the air, where to obtain fish. This refers to the jawbone and to one of the long bones in the head of the salmon and cod, if not those of other fish.

Although I questioned several of the men besides the one who furnished most of the information about the master of the fish, regarding similar control beings over the seals and other sea game, there seemed to be nothing to add along these lines. It should be also added that inquiry among the Indians about Lake St. John, far to the west, failed to elicit knowledge there of the belief in the master of the fish tribe. Davidson, moreover, reports its absence among the Têtes de Boule—more evidence of an eastern Labrador locale for the legend.

Responsibility to Various Other Animals

While we note the near development of a cult in connection with the behavior of these Indians toward the caribou, there is little parallel in their bearing toward the moose. The Montagnais of the southwestern part of the peninsula rely as much upon the latter as do the Naskapi upon the caribou, and yet we learn only of one act of placation toward the moose—his antlers, with the skull attached, are elevated upon a tree and left there, out of respect for him.

I have already mentioned a similar indifference toward the seal, although this animal is one of great economic value to the coast bands. We hear only of songs addressed to the seal, and references in both dance songs and hunting songs to the joy of hunting these wary creatures in the St. Lawrence. One such melody from the Escoumains band refers to the pleasure of seal hunting when indulged in accompanied by one's wife. The seal is considered humanly wise, as is attested by the Montagnais name for the harbor seal, *ilnadju'k* (*ilnadjogo's*, diminutive), "wise [human-like] seal."

Among the animals which might be considered eligible to selection for reverential treatment when dead, if not as an aid in hunting while living, we may consider the dog (atǝ'm). Despite his universal service in tracking game and in sled hauling among the Montagnais, the dog is totally disregarded as a religious force. Observation and questioning bring forth no evidence of burial rites or spiritual address. In contrast with surrounding culture groups, some of them even of Algonkian classification, they are *never eaten* by any Montagnais or Naskapi even when, during times of serious famine, it would seem that anything providing nourishment would be acceptable as a source of food.

The northern hare (*wabu'c*) may be noted as another neglected creature, although the utmost use is made of both the flesh and hide. We do find a ceremonial game carrying-string (ni·ma'ban) made for the use of youthful hunters who supply the camp with hare meat. For children to achieve success as hare hunters means, generally, that they will have luck later in life when they essay larger game. Ordinarily, the hare is women's or children's prey. The skulls of the hare are often seen hung to tree branches in bundles, while at Lake St. John I found the custom of women keeping a hare's foot as a charm for good luck.[25]

I may refer again for emphasis to the universal northern Indian belief that to keep animal's spirits favorable to man, and also to increase their numbers in the forest by inducing their spirits to submit to reincarnation, the bones must be treated with respect by those who kill the bodies. The bones are, in different respects for different animals, regarded as possessing power, in that sense being more or less sacred. They are often found suspended in trees near where the creatures have been killed or eaten, often being brought for this purpose from the place where they are killed to trees or bushes near the camps. This is especially true, as we have seen, for bear, beaver, and even muskrat and hare skulls. An incidental taboo for bones is that dogs should not chew them, because it is extremely debasing to the owners of the bones to have them fumbled, gnawed and gulped down by the canine traitor who not only helps man to bring them low, but who finally treats their remains with ignominy. McKenzie in 1808, reported a most interesting fact in connection with this taboo against the defilement of animal bones by dogs. He

25. Specimen in Natural Museum of Canada, Cat. No. 37, III C. 92.

says that dogs who had eaten animal bones were killed and their flesh eaten. Each guest present then ate a teaspoonful of the excrements, and the bones of the dog were hung to a tree to appease the angry deity.[26] The fish, however, are more appropriately regarded as dog food since the dog does not help in their death and since he is not one of their own kind. The Indian's regard and respectful treatment of the game animals' remains exonerates him from offense in his attack upon their tribes. But this does not cover the behavior of the dog. It is generally believed, for example, that caribou bones are harmful to dogs (Mistassini), in which superstition there would seem to be an element of spiritual retribution. A Mistassini man, for instance, made the remark that the bones of slain animals are carefully put away with a sentiment similar to that with which the white man puts away his books and other things which he respects, beyond the possibility of harm. Bones, indeed, of every kind seem to be a constant possession amid the bewildering mass of what would seem to be rubbish, cherished in quantity by every family, but which appears ultimately made to fill some useful purpose in their hazardous lives.

The bones of animals killed, either to be eaten or for their fur, are generally not allowed to be broken while the carcass is being cut up. The people become skillful in butchering and invariably strike between the joints with the first stroke of the knife. In nearly every case the joints of the foreleg are not severed, but are left with the breastbone to be roasted entire and eaten by the men alone. While this procedure marks the treatment of most animals, we find it less explicitly carried out than in the case of the bear and the beaver. Some of the taboos prominent in bear observances appear in certain localities associated with animals in general, such as a taboo among the Montagnais at Escoumains against permitting women to enter the tent when freshly killed game is lying inside. Furthermore, it is a custom among those hunters of conservative conduct, that when an animal is to be eaten, an old man of the family cuts a small piece of meat for each member of the family, puts it in a small birch-bark dish, and burns it in the fire. This is to appease the spirit of the slain beast. It applies to all game animals.

26. McKenzie, in Masson, op. cit., p. 416.

Lesser Animals (Otter, Marten, Hare, Seal, and Birds)

As we descend in the scale of ritual importance among the ranks of animals sought by the hunter, it is more difficult to find explicit requirements mentioned for the satisfaction of their spirits. But from personal narratives and discussions of the subject with individual hunters, the following observations are offered:

First, there is the otter, whose killing is accompanied by certain marks of religious reverence. The otter seems to be a factor in dreams. Elaborate pack strings are made by the wives of hunters who are accustomed to take many of these animals. Most of them are dyed red and profusely decorated with bead pendants, wool tassels, or ribbons—the latter often being green, which is a symbolic color representation associated with otter. I have not, however, seen otter skulls exposed in trees. Otter paws were several times shown me by hunters who gave them to me readily, saying that they were taken and kept to please the spirit of the animal.

Marten bones must not be eaten by dogs because they would make the animals thin and sickly (Mistassini).

Birds appear as creatures worthy of consideration in the regulation of human affairs. An instance of this may be mentioned for Wickəd-jaku'c, the Canada jay.[27] His cries have the value of an oracle. An informant of the Lake St. John band says that when he utters the cry, "chip-chip-chip," which sounds to the native ears like whetting a knife blade, it is a good sign; "the Indians are satisfied that they are going to kill big game. Wi'ckədjaku'c is sharpening his knife. The whisky-jack gathers meat not for himself, but he hides pieces for other creatures: birds, martens, squirrels, flying squirrels, weasels, ants, worms, insects and the like. He hides pieces in the bark of trees for them, and they scent them and come to eat. Often when the Indians have killed one they find no meat in the belly. But he (Wi'ckədjaku'c) carried it in his throat until he finds a place to hide it for their supply and protection. Indians never kill him. He comes when he hears the crack of a rifle and arrives at the place of the feast. When a Wi'ckədjak[uc] follows a hunter it is a good sign of getting a big beast." It seems that Wi'ckədjak[uc] is a protector of small animals and helps man kill beasts so that the small animals can eat. Wi'ckədjak[uc] informs a hunter of the luck he will have by his

27. *Perisoreus canadensis.*

— 125 —

cry in imitation of filing the blade of a knife to sharpen its edge. The sound is likened to a shrill chirping with the lips. They do not address Wi'ckədjak⟦uc⟧ for this oracular knowledge but wait for his sign. There is, indeed, a semblance here of a belief in the over-lordship of Wi'ckədjak⟦uc⟧ over small animals and insects.

Other narratives of great interest to the naturalist portray this curious bird as a guide to the hunter resembling the function of the dog in this particular. The call wi·ya's, wi·ya's repeatedly uttered by him is the call of "meat, meat" in Montagnais, which the hunter understands as the joyful tidings of success soon to be had. "One time a hunter out of luck heard far off a Canada jay calling wi·ya's! wi·ya's! He went in that direction, saw two caribou, killed and butchered them, getting an abundance of meat. Then he made his offering to the jay. Crack! went his gun and the jays came in numbers and feasted on morsels of the meat."

If the hunter observes that the jays pay no attention to him while on his route in the woods it is a bad sign for him. The more garrulous the jays, the better the omen for him who hears them. Hind recorded of the Naskapi (1861) that this bird was not allowed to enter the wigwam lest it cause pain in the head, and that the gizzard of the bird was examined to observe by the shape whether a moose or other animal would next be killed by the hunter.

The Indians seldom find the nest of the jay but if by chance one does it is a sign that he may die soon. The jay, they claim, is never killed by the larger birds of prey.

The esteem in which the bird is held is shown by the appellation wi·skədjadja'kʷ, "Wiskedjan's soul," denoting the belief that it is the embodiment of the mythical hero's (Wiskedja'k) soul, whose personality is present in Montagnais folklore though in a much weaker form than among the Algonquin and related bands to the west.

The hold of these picturesque superstitions on the native mind has not lessened; they all adhere to the belief in the wisdom and benevolence of the "soul of Wiskedja'k"!

Despite the bearing of the foregoing remarks, I have recorded a contrary notion of the bird's benign disposition from an aged hunter of the Montagnais at Escoumains (1922). He said that Wiskədja'n· was an evil bird since it occasionally picked out the eyes of children.

The loon, it should not be forgotten, is also a bird of omen to the hunter, for in his movements in the air he must consider the condition of the wind, and so his cries are to be understood as indications of the coming direction and force of the wind—a most important one in the life of these nomads.

DIVINATION

Chapter Six

THE practices of divination embody the very innermost spirit of the religion of the Labrador bands. Theirs is almost wholly a religion of divination. Laufer, impressed with its importance, declares that divination is a fundamental of eastern Asiatic culture. [1] In central Asia, also, divination was practiced from the shoulder blade of a sheep, which was scorched over a fire, and from the cracks thus arising in the bone the future was predicted. Here lies the closest correspondence with divinatory magic as it has developed in northeastern America. Cooper has ventured the hypothesis that northeastern American scapulimancy is genetically related to that of Asia. [2]

Divination in its varied forms is indicated in Montagnais-Naskapi by appropriate terms depending upon the methods involved. For instance, *wapənatca'kwoma'n*, "he sees his soul," being the more generally used term for divining by reflection; *tci·'tc'stewehidje'o*, "he prophesies," meaning either by the use of bones or simply by making a prophetic statement.

General Discussion and Distribution [3]

The device of scorching an animal's shoulder blade for the purpose of obtaining an answer to a question and for divination of the future

---

1. Berthold Laufer, "Methods in the Study of Domestications," *Scientific Monthly*, XXV (1927), 253. This author recognizes four distinct culture provinces in Asia, based on divination with bones of certain animals. I would venture to point out that several of his areas may be paralleled by zones of similarity in North America. Dating from the Shang dynasty (1766-1122 B. C.), ox scapulas have been found on a site dated about 1500 B. C. They show on the underside small holes drilled partly through. Burning charcoal was applied to the cavities, causing slight cracks on the surface from which the oracles would read replies to questions, such as would the sun shine the next day, would it be opportune to undertake a journey, and so on (*Illustrated London News*, June 21, 1930, p. 1142).

2. J. M. Cooper, *Northern Algonkian Scrying and Scapulimancy*, Festschrift (Vienna: P. W. Schmidt, 1927).

3. The substance of the following section was made the basis of a paper read before the Oriental Club of Philadelphia in 1926.

—scapulimancy—has been reported by many authors from populations extending from Central Asia to India, to Europe and to northeastern Asia, among both ancient and modern tribes. A deep significance is attached to this phenomenon since, by the nature of its complexity, it would seem to be accounted for more by diffusion than by the explanation of independent parallel development over the wide range where it appears.

The question of its origin has caused considerable speculation, most of which tends toward the assumption that it arose somewhere in Asia and, from some starting point there, spread to the regions where it has been found in later times. Richard Andree, who has assembled the most complete array of material on the custom, [4] associates it with the sheep-raising industry of Old World antiquity, since he finds it practically everywhere where sheep are reared and practically nowhere else. He has been followed with little hesitation by others who have discussed mantic practices. The question, however, really is—and it seems a natural one to the ethnologist—why place the beginning of a custom in so advanced a culture stage as that of animal husbandry? Being associated with an animal diet, the practice of reading omens from animal bones would challenge attention among primitive observers as belonging in the environment of a much earlier level than that of domestication—in fact in the hunting stage. The use of bones in practices of divination among such peoples in northern Asia, northern North America is, as we shall see, a familiar one. Reading the shoulder blade is one of the manifestations. We find among the hunting nomads much knowledge of animal anatomy—the beginnings of scientific butchery. I propose to show the occurrence of scapulimancy in a much wider distribution, embracing the whole of boreal North America. This is a broader distribution than has hitherto been known, and makes its occurrence much more general as an underlying primitive culture property than previous authors have shown it to be. Like other ethnic traits encountered among peoples inhabiting the margins of the continental areas, we may place it among man's earliest magical practices by similar distribution conditions.

Among Asiatic peoples, we learn from Andree's extensive compilation of references which I quote, scapulimancy plays a prominent

4. Richard Andree, "Scapulimantia," in the *Boas Anniversary Volume* (New York, 1906), pp. 143-65.

PLATE XII

Various beaded and fur neck charms (Barren Ground band): Upper row, tabs of bear lip and otter fur for hunting bears and otters; lower row, for general hunting luck.

PLATE XIII   MUSEUM OF THE AMERICAN INDIAN

Ceremonial game carrying strings (*ni˙ma'ban*) from northern and eastern bands: (A) String for hares and small game, made for a boy (Nichikun band); (B) similar to preceding; (C) string for beaver (Ungava band); (D) string for otter (Ungava band); (E) string for small game (Seven Islands); (F) string for otter (Michika-mau band); (G) string for otter (Michikamau band).

part in the augury practices of the Mongols. Prshewalski [5] describes the shoulder-blade oracle as one in which the Mongols have un-bounded confidence, despite its oft-proven prophetic fallacy. Our direct knowledge of scapulimancy in Mongolia dates back to 1253. In this year the monk, Ruysbroek (or Rubruquis), [6] who was sent by Ludwig the Holy to treat with Mongol rulers, met at Karakorum the Khan Mangu. Here he beheld the operation of the shoulder-blade oracle. The author at that time noted that the direction and length of the burnt cracks furnished the signs in answer to certain questions which were put to the fetish. If the crack ran the length of the bone the sign was favorable for the adoption of the plans under considera-tion; if they ran crosswise or if little pieces were cracked off the bone by the heat, the omen was unfavorable.

With the passage of seven hundred years this custom has changed but little among the Mongols. [7] Andree, indeed, thinks the rite to have originally been diffused from this locale. The wide distribution of the rite among the Mongols is discussed by Prshewalski. [8] He says that the belief in the efficacy of the shoulder-blade oracle among the Mongols is unbounded and that it exercises a deep influence in the religious life of these nomads.

The occurrence of a similar practice among the Kalmuk hordes of Central Asia has been recorded by Pallas. [9] Here the shoulder blade to be burned was allowed to rest upon the coals of a fire. The shoulder blades of the sheep, of the saiga, of roebuck or reindeer, and wild boar were used. The latter was consulted only to learn the outcome of the boar hunt. It was also noted that the shoulder blade of the hare served for prophecy, but only for one day. These two notices are important inasmuch as they correspond in their fundamen-tals with what is recorded in my notes on shoulder-blade divination among the Algonkian Indians of North America: namely, con-sultation of the hare scapula and the use of that of a special animal to ascertain the future in the hunting of its own kind. The Kalmuk used this rite for the divination of good and bad fortune, life or

5. N. von Prshewalski, *Reisen in der Mongolei* (1877), p. 47. Observed also by Dr. A. Hrdlicka in 1913 (corres-pondence. 1928).
6. J. Pinkerton, *Rubruquis, A General Collection of the Voyages and Travels* (London, 1811), IV, 65.
7. A contemporary Mongol seer prophesying from a shoulder blade is shown in *Mythology of All Races*, "Finno-Ugric, Siberian," by Uno Holmberg (1927), pl. LIV, p. 470, but while reference is made to p. 488, none is to be found at that place. Dr. A. Hrdlicka writes me that he has also observed the rite among Mongols. See Dr. M. Sprengling, "Scapulimantia and the Mongols," *American Anthropologist*, XXXV, 134-37.
8. Von Prschewalski, *op. cit.*, pp. 47, 69.
9. P. S. Pallas, *Samlungen historischer Nachrichten über die Mongolischen Völkerschaften* (St. Petersburg, 1776, 1881), Vol. II, pl. 20.

death. Pallas notes that the scapula was divided into a number of imaginary areas, each having a certain significance should the burns appear within them. The meanings were thus predetermined. Scapulimancy in Kalmuk is called *dalla tüllike*. The neighboring Kirghiz are accredited with shoulder-blade divination very similar, in most respects, to that recorded for Kalmuk. From the writings of a Siberian explorer, Potanin,[10] we learn of the details here. The scapula of a sheep is employed after the meat has been removed. Similar to the process among the Kalmuk, this group regards the bone as being divided into separate parts bearing meanings. The Mongolian Buriat on Lake Baikal, who have now become Buddhists, formerly practised scapulimancy before they had changed from their shamanistic religion. Bastian[11] records the practice of a shaman discovering the whereabouts of a chest lost on a journey, by means of a burnt shoulder blade. The occurrence of augury by the use of the burnt shoulder blade of the sheep is likewise reported among the Tungus by Georgi, as quoted by Andree.

The extension westward of this custom is shown in references to the tribes in northeastern Iran. It is noted among the Hazara of the last century by Masson.[12]

It is especially popular in Tartary. The shoulder blade is put in the fire until it cracks in various directions and then a long split lengthwise is reckoned as the way of life, while cross cracks on the right and left stand for different kinds and degrees of good and evil fortune: of if the omen is only taken as to some special event, then lengthwise splits mean going on well, but crosswise ones stand for hindrance; white marks portend much snow and black ones a mild winter.

From the pen of Dr. Berthold Laufer, we have a review of burnt-bone divination in China:

"The ancient Chinese possessed a highly developed and a very elaborate system of divination by cracks in burned tortoise-shells.[13] All together, a hundred and twenty different figures formed by these cracks were counted, and there were twelve hundred answers or oracles.[14]

10. W. Radloff, *Aus Siberien* (Leipzig, 1884), I, 475.

11. Adolf Bastian, *Geographische und Ethnologisch Bilder* (Jena, 1873), p. 405; *Bemerkungen auf einer Reise im Russischen Reiche*, I, 285.

12. Charles Masson, *Narrative of Journeys in Baluchistan, Afghanistan and the Punjab* (London, 1842), III, 334.

13. See John H. Plath, *Die Religion und der Cultus der alten Chinesen*, Part I, "Abhandlungen der Bayerischen Akademie" (München, 1863), pp. 819-27; J. Legge, *The Chinese Classics*, III, 335 ff.

14. Mr. H. Y. Feng kindly adds the following note to the above: "This practice of 'tortoise-shell' divination was greatly clarified by the discovery of the inscribed tortoise shells (known as oracle-bones) in the village of Hsiao-

"In Japan, scapulimantia seems to go back to a very early age and to the so-called proto-historic period, before Chinese and Korean influences were felt. From the oldest work of Japanese literature, the *Kojiki*, written A. D. 712, we learn that divination by means of the shoulder blade of a stag was a favorite way of ascertaining the will of the gods.[15] By means of the Chinese annals, which furnish the oldest accounts of Japan, we are enabled to trace this custom back almost to the beginning of our era. In the books of the later Han dynasty it is said of the Japanese that they divine by scorched bones, and by this means ascertain whether their luck will be good or bad.[16] The 'Wei Chi,' a part of the *San Kuo Chi*, relating to the period A. D. 220-280, states that the Japanese have a custom, when entering upon a proposed undertaking, of scorching a bone and divining, in order to ascertain the auspiciousness or untowardness of the event; they first declare what they wish to divine, in language similar to that used in the tortoise-shell divination, and discern the augury through the cracks made by the fire.[17] The lamas of Tibet, as do other nations of Northern Asia according to Rockhill, divine[18] by counting on their prayer beads, by lines which the inquiring person traces on the ground, by burning sheep's bones, or by gazing into a bowl of water."[19]

Scapulimancy is also found among the Lolo, a barbarous, somewhat independent people scattered in the mountains of southern and western China. Their seers divine the future by observing parts of the sacrificed animals—the cracks that develop in the heated shoulder blade.[20]

The extension of scapulimacy westward into Europe takes us into regions which have undoubtedly been influenced by the diffusion of sheep domestication. Andree's extensive references again serve

---

t'un, An-Yang, Honan province in 1899 and subsequent excavation in 1928-30. The finding of these thousands of tortoise shells actually used in divination by the Shang-Yiu dynasty people (1766-1122 B. C.) gives us an idea of the extensive use of this practice and the details of how it was actually practiced. [See the *Preliminary Reports of Excavations at An-Yang*, Parts I-III, 1920-31.] The study of these inscribed tortoise shells has already become a new field in China. The tortoise shell found is the part known as the plastron, while the ox bones are the scapulae or shoulder blades. On the under side of the bone or shell, small holes are drilled, but not completely through. Burning charcoal was then applied to these cavities, causing slight surface cracks from which the oracles would read to the questions asked. The questions and answers are written on the surface, and deal chiefly with simple queries as to whether the sun would shine next day, whether it would be opportune to take a journey, and so on" (*Illustrated London News*, June 21, 1930, p. 1142).

15. B. H. Chamberlain, "Ko-ji-ki, or Records of Ancient Matters," in *Transactions of the Asiatic Society of Japan* (Yokohama, 1883), X, Supplement, lix; K. Florenz, *Japanische Mythologie* (Tokyo, 1901), pp. 21, 197.
16. E. H. Parker, "Early Japanese History," in *China Review*, XVIII (1890), 219b.
17. *Ibid.*, p. 223a.
18. W. W. Rockhill, *Journal Royal Asiatic Society*, XXIII (1891), 235. He quotes E. Quatremère, *Histoire des Mongols de la Perse*, n. d. p. 267.
19. R. Andree, *Boas Anniversary Volume* (New York, 1906), p. 164.
20. A. L. Kroeber, *Anthropology* (1924), p. 469.

generously. In the lower Indus it appears among the Mohammedans, Sindhi and Baludchi, which are of so-called Aryan affinity. While the process of scapulimancy is here fundamentally analagous to that of the peoples of Mongolia, a new element enters, namely, astrology. Considerable attention was given to the interpretation of the signs by Burton.[21] Here the shoulder blade is divided into twelve surface areas which correspond to the signs of the zodiac. Andree reasonably conceives this case to be a later development by which astrology has become associated with the more primitive form of augury. Farther westward in the Caucasus, the practice is recorded among the Cherkess.[22] Among the Arabs also scapulimancy is known.[23] For the tribes of Oman, Wellsted is the reference. Here they burn the bone to obtain portentous information by means of certain mystical characters which appear after partial calcination. The camel or sheep scapula is used for the novel purpose. Islam has been responsible for the spread of this augury into Morocco. Dr. Lenz while traveling in south Morocco through the Sahara saw his servant burn the shoulder blade of a sheep to discover what fortune they would have on the journey.[24] The late entrance into Europe of this interesting rite is indicated by its distribution in a culture level later than that of the early Hebrews and the people of classical antiquity. Indeed, though the shoulder blade played a rôle among the Hebrews, being concerned with the ritual of Moses and Aaron in connection with the dietary laws and sacrifice, it did not serve the purpose of augury as we see it operating in Asia.[25] The same seems true concerning the Hellenes, the Etruscans and the Romans.[26] The shoulder blade in classical archaeology, often appeared as an important talisman, nevertheless. Pliny refers to it, among the Romans, as the seat of power. Andree thinks that probably not earlier than the eighth century B. C. did shoulder blade divination find a place in Europe, due to the introduction by the Scythians. The latter shared the custom by the first century after Christ. The practice is thought to have become general among the Avars, Alani, and Turks. By the sixteenth century the Russians in eastern Europe had become influenced by the Tartars to the extent of having adopted Asiatic

21. R. F. Burton, *Sindh and the Races that Inhabit the Valley of the Indus*, (London, 1851), pp. 189-92.
22. Haxthausen, *Transkaukasia* (1856), II, 172.
23. Von Wreder, *Travels in Arabia* (1838), I, 344, quoted in Haxthausen, *op. cit.*, I, 35.
24. O. Lenz, *Timbuktu* (Leipzig, 1889), I, 329
25. 3 Moses, 9, 21; 7, 32.
26. J. Pervanoglu, *Culturebilder aus Greichenland* (Leipzig, 1880), p. 51.

mantic practices, according to the records preserved in Erman's *Archiv für Wissenschaftliche Kunde von Russland* (1842).[27] The shoulder blade oracle was found among the Byzantines in the eleventh century. A manuscript by Michael Psellos, published by Politis, deals with shoulder-blade divination as a means of foretelling events and answering questions. The shoulder blade of a lamb was consulted. The practice differs somewhat from its Asiatic cognate in that the bone was not scorched; the augury was observed in the lines and colors appearing on the bone. In the ninth century a reference leaves the question unclear whether the bone was set before the fire or not.[28] Scapulimancy still serves in Greece of today,[29] at the feast of St. George, for example; and among the Macedonian bandits, to determine whether they shall offer for ransom or slay their captives. The use of the shoulder blade of a lamb or kid is a relic of the ancient haruspicy which has survived in Greece and in many other countries.[30] In the seventeenth and eighteenth centuries the outlawed Clephts in Greece still used the shoulder blade to divine the future, and nowadays Greek peasants use it to tell the success of their crops, the advisability of marriage and many other ventures. The bone is cleansed and held to the light, and its color, veins, spots, are all full of meaning. And among the Rumanians of the Balkan peninsula it is still a surviving practice. Among the South Slavs it is mentioned, and in Bosnia.[31]

It also survives in Corsica[32] and enters into the practices mentioned in connection with the early life of Napoleon. It is possible to trace it in modern Germany, in the Tyrol, for France and Spain, and among the Lithuanians.[33] We may even trace the shoulder-blade oracle to Great Britain where it is recorded in the sixteenth century, functioning to furnish proof of a wife's fidelity, the same as among the Cherkess, previously noted. There are several references to the rite, which is known as "reading the spealbone" (from the French *épaule*, shoulder). From this time on in England there are a number of

27. II, 122.
28. Pervanoglu, *op. cit.*, p. 49.
29. *Folk-lore Journal*, II (1884), 369.
30. W. W. Hyde, *Greek Religion and Its Survivals* (Boston, 1923), pp. 128-29; G. Weigand, *Die Olympo-Walachen*, p. 16.
31. Luka Grgjic-Bjelokovic, *Wissenschaftliche Mitteilungen aus Bosnien und der Hercegovina*, IV, 462-64; F. S. Krauss, *Volksglaube und Religiöser Brauch der Südslaven* (1890), p. 166.
32. F. Gregorovius, *Corsica*, I, 272.
33. J. von Zingerle, *Sitten, Brauche und Meinungen des Tirole Volkes* (1857), p. 192; F. Michel, *Folklore Record*, I (1878), 176; Grimm, *op. cit.*, p. 322.

references to the shoulder-blade augury. One is as late as 1850. It did not fail to reach even the Scotch Highlands.

Palaeo-Asiatics.—Turning back again to northeastern Asia we find it among the palaeo-Siberians, the method of procedure deviating in but few details from the method noted among the cattle-nomads of inner Asia. But we are struck here with the impression that the practice descends to a lower culture level, to that of reindeer-nomadism, and finally to the exclusively hunting and fishing cultures, whereas the European rites ascend to modern times with the intensification of animal domestication. Here in the Far East, pursuit of the topic leads us to understratification. In the northeast of Asia the sheep is no longer concerned, for it is neither indigenous fauna nor has it become a culture acquisition. Yet scapulimancy flourishes, through the employment of seal and reindeer shoulder blades.

Several references by W. Bogoras establish the occurrence of scapulimancy among the Chukchi and Koryak.[34] Bogoras, in his study of Chukchi religion gives sufficient detail to deserve quotation.[35]

Among the Chukchi, divination with the shoulder blade is almost as much in use as the divining stone. The center of the shoulder blade is held over a small fire until it is partly carbonized and cracks in all directions. The detail of the cracks determines the meaning of the answer. Among the reindeer Chukchi its chief use is for determining the direction of the next movement of the camp. It is also employed to foretell the success of a hunt or of a journey, the approach of the wind, the imminent danger of a contagious disease, or of an attack on the herds by wolves. The shoulder blade of the domesticated reindeer is the only bone used for this purpose.

During the fall the shoulder blade of the left side is used for divination in personal or family affairs, while that of the right side is called "alien" and used for the affairs of other people. During this period, divination is employed first, when changing camp after the first snow, then again about two months afterward, when moving into winter quarters.

In the wintertime, divination is seldom used, but it is resumed in the spring when moving from the winter pastures to the summer abode. This moving is considered as "returning"—mainly to the

34. *American Anthropologist*, III, 96.
35. *The Chukchee Religion*, Vol. VII, No. 2, pp. 487-90, figs. 298, 299.

tundra. During this time divination is used for every new move, but now the bone of the right side is used for the affairs of the family, while that of the left side is considered as "alien." For all journeys made without reference to the moving of the herd, how-ever, such as trading trips or hunting expeditions, the left shoulder blade is used throughout the year.

In explaining the lines of the cracks the shoulder blade must be kept with the broad part up. The ridge in the middle is called "mountain" and is considered to represent the mountains and in-lands generally. All the lower part of the blade beneath the burned spot is called "bottom of bone" and is considered to represent the underground countries. The outer edge, all around the broad part and down to the very bottom, is called "sea" and is considered to represent the seacoast.

Usually one vertical crack is formed with various ramifications above and below. The following principles are applied for the ex-planation:

Everything that comes from the sea is good, even though it be from under the supposed level of the ground. Indications from the "bottom of the bone" are of evil character. From the mountain above the level, there may appear indications of either kind, good or evil.

If only one vertical line is produced, it is a favorable indication; but if this line is short or if it reaches the very edge of the bone, the indications are unfavorable. The small crosslines not reaching up to the principal crack when in the upper region foretell only news of something; while the longer lines, crossing the principal crack, foretell the arrival of the thing. A large cross zigzag line fore-tells the greatness of the thing which will come. For instance, a detached crossline from the "mountain" may signify news about the wild reindeer; a lower line, the coming of wild reindeer, and a zigzag line, an abundance of the reindeer. A crossline from the "bottom of the bone" foretells an attack by wolves or the "arrival of the spirit of disease," or even death.

A line formed on the top of the original crack signifies a snowstorm; a semicircular line on the same place signifies unexpected death; a detached line in the region of the sea, some unexpected news.

In performing divination regarding the direction of moving, a direction must first be selected to inquire about. If the indications are unfavorable the proposed direction is abandoned. In this case the shoulder blade itself is immersed in a mass of stuff emptied from the reindeer paunch, which is generally considered as highly effective for ceremonial cleansing. While immersing the bone, the questioner says: "This is not my shoulder blade; this is an alien shoulder blade." After reading, the bone is left sticking in the stuff. On the next day another reindeer is killed and the divination resumed for a changed direction of the route. This is watched with the keenest attention, lest through some carelessness the true meaning be misunderstood.

The maritime people use the shoulder blade of the seal for purposes of divination, but this is done less frequently, chiefly because there are no questions to decide regarding the choice direction for moving.

The Chuvanzi and the Lamut of the Anadyr country have also adopted this way of foretelling the future. The Lamut probably imitated it from their Chukchi neighbors.

Another eyewitness describes the Chukchi practice.[36]

"Meanwhile, the old woman made a fire, and each Chooktcha threw into it a driftwood log. One old man, who was dancing to the sound of a drum, threw into the fire the shoulder blade of a deer and each person present threw in a piece of fat. When the thick smoke had cleared, the old man took out the shoulder blade, and, after carefully examining the cracks caused by the fire, announced that the dead woman would be favourably received by the Great Spirit."

Practically the same procedure is reported among the Koryak. Seal hunting is here a vital activity; hence, the shoulder blade of the seal is burned to ascertain whether the chase, in particular that of the whale, is to be successful. The details of treatment of the shoulder blade as given by Jochelson[37] are much the same as among the Chukchi.

One purpose of treatment here is to show the distribution of this interesting concept in the lower strata of Asiatic and American hunting and nomadic cultures. It hardly seems necessary to follow it upward into the realm of modern folklore in western Europe. To do so would lead us into the history of its development in recent superstition, but would draw attention away from the contemplation of its antiquity and origin in the East.

36. I. W. Shklovsky, *In Far Northeast Siberia*, trans. by L. Edwards and Z. Shklovsky (London, 1916), p. 143.
37. W. Jochelson, *The Koriak* (Leiden, 1905), IV, 73, 74.

Turning back to the survey of scapulimancy among the tribes of northeastern Siberia, we find that most authors regard the Pacific to be its distribution terminus on the east. Andree, in his study of divination remarks upon its absence in America. He was followed, apparently, by Kroeber, who expresses a similar opinion on its Eurasiatic occurrence to the exclusion of the New World.[38] The latter author agrees with Andree in ascribing the origin of the rite to a culture level beginning with the domestication of the sheep and spreading southward and westward with this culture complex. I intend to show evidence of its nativity in the hunting life of the Algonkian, and possibly among some of the Athapascan of the northern fringe of North America as a proximity prototype. Here no domestic animals were known, but in the hunting practices of these early Neolithic cultures shoulder blade divination appears to be still as important as among the culture groups of Asia; and moreover, as we shall see, some of the details of procedure show close correspondence, constituting a religious complex—one that could hardly have developed independently and retained such uniformity.

Mention of the rite in published accounts dealing with American aborigines is by no means as frequent as we find it for the Old World. One reference for the Athapascan is all that I have found, but it serves its purpose, while Dr. C. B. Osgood is oral authority for its occurrence among the Kutchin of Alaska. In traveling through the Barren Grounds of northwestern Canada, Caspar Whitney relates the following, presumably referring to the Dog Ribs.

"I was very much interested in watching the development, out of a caribou shoulder blade, of an Indian hunting talisman. The shoulder blade when finished becomes at once talisman and prophet. It is scraped clean of its flesh, and then with a piece of burned wood the Indian pictures upon it, first, the points of the compass, and then one or more hunters, with caribou in the distance. When his drawing is complete the blade is held over the fire, and the dark spots that appear in the bone indicate the direction in which game will be found. Where several hunters are represented in the drawing, that one nearest the spots is hailed the lucky individual."[39]

38. A. L. Kroeber, *Anthropology* (New York, 1924), pp. 210-11.
39. Caspar Whitney, *On Snowshoes to the Barren Grounds* (New York, 1896), p. 262.

The consultation of oracles is to the Montagnais-Naskapi the embodiment of religious practice. We find them continually trying to learn from friendly animal spirits acting as oracles, when and where to go to secure game. Of equal interest with their desire to know when and where to hunt, are other circumstances, those of impending fortune in respect to weather, sickness, and personal concerns. In the pursuit of such knowledge their zeal is unbounded. Accordingly, animal oracles assume a dominant place in religious performance. So fundamental are they that divination is the one motive of religious ceremony that strikes our attention in the whole area to the exclusion of almost everything else. Divination is the sequel in action to dream revelations and promptings coming from the soul or Great Man of the individual. Dreaming, wishing, intention, and exercise of will form the theory of religion; the consultation of animal oracles forms the practice. To my mind these characteristics are so dominant in the religious thought of this region that later the ethnologist may proceed to test out its relationship with other areas in North America as well as in Asia, where we have hints of similar rites. It should serve as a worthy criterion in the problem of diffusion. In the history of human thought divination would seem to occupy a rather primitive place. Until the topic has been more definitely investigated in northern and northwestern America, however, progress toward a conclusion as to its position faces a temporary impasse. My treatment in this chapter is offered as a challenge to attention for what appears a most interesting and important topic in subarctic American and Asiatic ethnology— one which I hope I may not be accused of overestimating at this early time.

The Indians of the Labrador peninsula are given most intensively to the performance of divination in connection with their pursuit of game. The general practice is fairly uniform, both in act and theory, but considerable differentiation marks the procedure of different local bands and even of individuals. This will become clear as we compare the observations that have been recorded from the populations on the eastern portion with those of the southern and southwestern territories of the peninsula. Besides, many inhabited districts are not represented by information.

The use of the shoulder blades of game and fur-bearing animals is the outstanding phenomenon in divination here. In the rite of consultation this tablet-like bone is subjected to heat, and the burnings, in the form of blackened spots, cracks and breaks, are then interpreted by the cunning and ingeniousness of the practitioner. Imagination suggests the likeness of the marks produced by the heat, to rivers, lakes, mountains, trails, camps and various animals—the latter either single or in groups. The direction of the burnt marks and their respective locations are also significant. Persons are also believed to be represented by the spots or outlines. Abstract ideas may be represented: life, death, success, failure, plenty, famine, sickness, chicanery, time periods, warnings, encouragement; and general good or bad luck are likewise indicated by the cabalistic figures.

It would seem, from what will appear later, that there is some idea of force by fire in extorting from the animals' bones the revelations which they are able to give to men whose soul power is sufficiently strong and who are in good standing with the world of animal spirits.

In the following pages I have arranged the available instances of this interesting rite that I have collected during exploration and research in the region, grouping them under two areas: the western and southern, or the so-called Montagnais; and the eastern and northern, the Naskapi. At the conclusion of the account, I have arranged a summary of shoulder-blade oracle phenomena from my own notes and from various authorities who refer to the practice in the Old World, among whom Andree stands forth pre-eminently.

Investigating shoulder-blade divination among the natives of the southwestern confines of the peninsula, we encounter the following cases of oracular method and interpretation from the Lake St. John Indians.

Aside from the individual opinions on the interpretation of the ever-varying burnings and crackings on the divining-bones, there seem to be some general rules for interpreting them. At Lake St. John, for example, one of the most favorable indications is when the bone cracks clean across the middle, or when it refuses to burn. "If it does not wish to burn or does hardly burn, that is the sign of good luck" and "if it breaks like that (fig. 9 A, which shows the informant's idea as sketched on a piece of paper), perhaps in two days he is going to find large game, maybe a bear, moose or caribou."

FIGURE 9

A   B

Burnt shoulder-blade omens (Lake St. John band): (A) Native sketch to illustrate
a favorable omen in bone divination; (B) an unfavorable one.

On the other hand, if the burning takes the form of little spots or
holes, the sign is bad— "sickness, death in the camp, perhaps, at any
rate bad luck!" The omen in one case will refer not only to the securing of game, but it may prognosticate the weather; in itself a condition tantamount to success or failure in the hunt. Figure 9 B is typically unfavorable, from a native sketch. On several occasions I recall
seeing hare shoulder bones used to foretell weather conditions; a burning away of the edge being unfavorable, of the center favorable (fig. 10).

The pelvic bone on one occasion was laid upon the coals in align-
ment with the shape of the hunter's trapping grounds. In this case

FIGURE 10

A   B

Hare shoulder-bone divination: (A), unfavorable sign; (B), favorable.

— 143 —

the hunter was Cimon, and the bone was that of a beaver. He said that he wished to learn which river in his district he should follow to have success in obtaining big game. The direction in which the cracks would run, should any appear, was to be his answer. After a few seconds the bone began to blacken and then a bifurcated crack (fig. 12 A) showed which he interpreted as representing the two principal rivers of his "road," to the left Ashuapmouchouan, to the right the river leading to Lac Brochet, upon which was located one of his hunting stations. The sign told him that up the rivers he would meet with success in his quest for game. As he left some three or four days after this experiment and as I did not meet him for over a year afterward, I did not succeed in learning from him what the outcome had been.

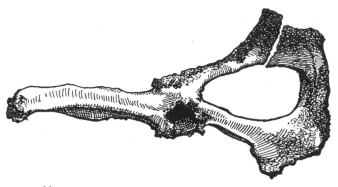

FIGURE 11

Montagnais divination device (Lake St. John band): Pelvis of beaver, burnt to determine prospects of the hunt. The clean break is a favorable sign.

By multiplying instances we can gain a deeper insight into the thought and method of operation of the individual rites. Before leaving the village on a recent occasion I repaired to the cabin of one of the hunters who had frequently divined before, and asked him to get something and go to work. In the afternoon he produced a beaver pelvic bone. This he heated in the usual way in front of the fire, and suddenly it cracked clean across. The crack ran straight for half the distance; then finished in a couple of zigzags. "Aha!" he said, "you will go part way all right, but at the end you will encounter difficulties." Having just bought a dog from him I alluded to the possession of the animal as the probable cause of the expected

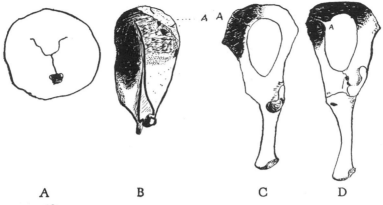

A   B   C   D

FIGURE 12

Bone divination devices: (A) Scapular divination by burning. Native sketch showing instructions to hunter, which branch of river to follow to find game (Lake St. John); (B) burnt beaver shoulder blade showing favorable divination by presence of roundish spots at A (Lake St. John Montagnais); (C) burnt beaver pelvic bone divination. Burning away at A on outer margin is unfavorable sign (Lake St. John Montagnais); (D) burnt beaver pelvis divination. Burning away of inner margin of orifice at A is a favorable sign (Lake St. John Montagnais).

trouble—but this he laughingly waved aside lest I change my mind about the purchase. To satisfy any curiosity that may be aroused, I may add that after a few days I did have all the bother I cared for on account of that dog.

Several cases in which the shoulder blades of the northern hare were employed in divination illustrate the method of procedure.

In the winter of 1923, early in January, a woman at Lake St. John named Sapi [Sophie] performed divination for me to learn whether my homeward trip would be a safe one. Sapi and her mother, old Tcikwe'menu, who had died the year before at a very advanced age, were both given to the practice of divining with hare shoulder blades. This time the bone was placed on an ember before her fire. The burnt space soon showed up (as in fig. 13 A), a larger black area and a smaller one beside it. The larger one, she said, smiling, represented me, the smaller one my home. All would be well and I would arrive safely, she declared. (I did.) She then took the other shoulder blade and placed it on the coal. A brown burn overspread the surface and inside this a crackled black center (fig. 13 B). This augury was not favorable. "Someone is coming down from the woods with bad

FIGURE 13   A   B

Montagnais divination device (Lake St. John)—shoulder blades of northern hare
burnt to ascertain nature of impending events.

news," she declared. Several of the members of her sister's family,
standing by absorbed in the performance, now broke into conversation trying to guess who it might be, who had been sick in July when
the families started back to their hunting grounds, and so on. The
sequel to this prediction I learned the next winter in the village.
A few days following my departure, news came that a young man
named Napoleon, who had borrowed a hundred dollars from various
Indians on a pretext of need of provisions, had bought a gallon of
whisky with it and taken it to the bush to satisfy his appetite—but,
as we would say, to dissipate. This indeed was bad news to the
village and was remembered a year afterward when I could inquire
what had happened either to prove or disprove Sapi's ability. I
usually gave Sapi twenty-five cents for her services, and she was
always pleased—the tobacco she bought with it was always acceptable to her *mista'beo*. Her success in this line of *mətənca'wan* is
widely known in the Montagnais village at Pointe Bleue. Here are
some of her records:

She is reputed proficient in being able to extort information from
the shoulder blade regarding the arrival of families expected from the
more remote interior districts. Many of her divinations seem to have
proved correct. On one well-remembered occasion she employed the
bone and announced that Cimon was coming down to the post
from his hunting grounds. She further announced that he was coming
down with three dogs and would arrive in two days. This seemed
like important news because he was not expected so soon and besides
he had only two dogs when he left. In two days, then, he did arrive

with three dogs. He had bought an extra one in the bush!"The *nič̌tu′t* of Sapi again told her what was true," they said.

Three additional examples of shoulder-blade reading from Lake St. John (fig. 14 A, B, C) carry out the general idea of interpretation. The circumstances under which they were obtained are interesting. I selected one of the hunters of this band, who on account of lameness was unable to go to his winter trapping grounds, giving him one hog and three sheep shoulder blades with which I had provided myself before entering the country. Looking over the bones when I gave them to him to "read" for me, he examined them to see if they were fit for the purpose. One of them, the old hog's scapula, he discarded with the exclamation *k̩oķo′c!* "pig!" That settled the bone for him as he declared that the operation required the *utli·gǝn,* "scapula," of a wild animal. I wondered what conclusion he would reach in regard to the others from the sheep. They passed his scrutiny—*pi·ji·u′!* "lynx!" he exclaimed and accepted them, without observing my smile. Later he raked some glowing embers from the cooking fire and before an admiring group of some five children, his wife and sister-in-law, he heated them until they blackened in the usual places. He did them one after another. The first showed black on both sides of the spine of the bone. "You will have trouble somewhere" (fig. 14 A). Soon he burned the second. During the heating it cracked at the top with a sharp "chink" (14 B). "Aha! he speaks. That means better luck. It will come out all right." And he examined it close to his eyes without saying more. When the third one blackened across the top and down one face (14 C) he was satisfied and said that I would make out well enough for I would have good luck in the form of money. These examples, while not very specific, are typical of the mantic practices which dominate their movements in the bush. Again, for those who may wonder what the outcome of this prognostication was, it may be added that considerable personal "trouble" was experienced by me before reaching home, and that I did receive some money shortly afterward—though the latter was not exceptional in view of the fact that most white men are the recipients of salaries.

The hunter just mentioned burned a beaver pelvic bone on another occasion. His method was the same as that just described. The bone cracked on the upper outer edge, and a small nick broke away (fig. 12 C). This is observed as a bad sign in reference to the undertaking

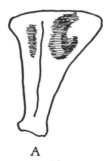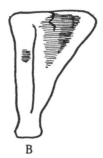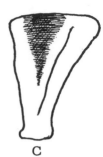

A   B   C

FIGURE 14   FIELD MUSEUM OF NATURAL HISTORY

Burnt shoulder-blade divination: (A) Denoting "trouble coming"; (B) denoting good fortune returning after bad luck of (A); (C) a sign of good luck in form of money gain.

he had in mind. I fail to recall now what this was. He had in his camp two beaver hip bones, large ones, hanging from a nail in the wall. These he was keeping until need should arise to use them in divination. I asked him to burn one for me to find out if possible what the results of my trip would be. The heat caused the bone to crack across the arch (fig. 12 D) and he said "Good!" because the fissure was a straight, even one and ran through to the center. His readings were in general regarded as having a favorable import when the cracking

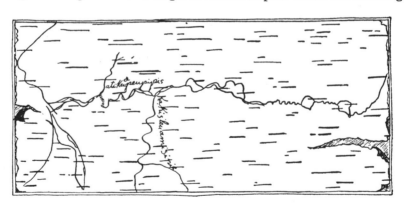

FIGURE 14D

Sketch of a map outlined on birch bark showing the river *Atikwabe'o* and also the manner in which these hunters chart the rivers of their hunting grounds. At the left is the shoreline of Lake St. John, into which this river empties. The stream branching to the right is *Kak^wste'namickcipic*, "Black Beaver River"

did not occur on the outer edge of the bone, the favorable area being near the center of the bone. A hunter at Lake St. John engaged in the act is shown in plate VIII. The same hunter, Cibic, burned a shoulder-blade which showed a river with two forks (fig. 12 A). This represented his hunting territory which he had outlined on a birch-bark chart (fig. 14 D). Scapulimancy is often cartographic, as instances will later show.

Divination by the same means as that just described is mentioned as common among all the bands of Montagnais so far visited.

As an illustration of the manner of operation among men of this group, I will describe what I saw done by one of them, David Basil, whose territory is south of Lake St. John and who has lived considerably with the Têtes de Boule formerly residing at Kokokash on St. Maurice river—in fact is married to one. These Indians, too, he says, practice the shoulder-blade reading in the same way. In January, 1926, he burned a beaver scapula, taking about two minutes for the action, placing it near some wood embers drawn from his cooking fire. The bone turned black on the upper left-hand edge and showed some fine cracks (fig. 12 B). The heat caused it to give forth a cracking sound. "*Paḳ! mičtacḳwe'məgən*" he cried. *Paḳ!* he cries out strong! He will answer." The interpretation of this was explained as a good sign on account of the roundish cracks.

Testimony from individuals in the country around Lake St. John seems to unite in denying that the caribou, moose, or deer scapulas are employed by hunters in general. It is regarded here as belonging to the practice of the experienced conjuror to employ bones of big game. They are regarded as "too strong" for ordinary men. Beaver or hare shoulder blades and partridge breastbones are spoken of as preferred by most hunters. Some have personal preferences for using bones of certain animals, but for children to practice would attract a cannibal (*wi'ndigo*).

It has already been noted that beaver shoulder and hip bones are ordinarily used as oracles testifying on the prospects of the beaver hunt, and caribou bones for the caribou chase; but hare and partridge breastbones are thought to "speak" in reference to any kind of game. This is specific for the Indians about Lake St. John. When asked about burning bear shoulder bones for oracular purposes, Joseph Kurtness expressed disapproval of the idea. His sister, a Mistassini woman versed in divinatory practices, exclaimed, "Sh!

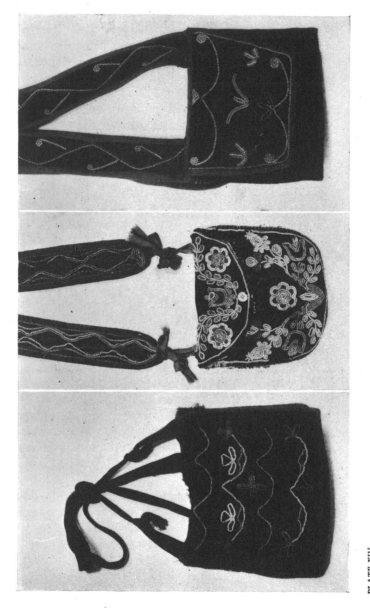

PLATE XIV
Decorated Naskapi cloth shot pouches with symbolical designs. Left and right, pouches of Natasquan band.
Center, Mistassini band.

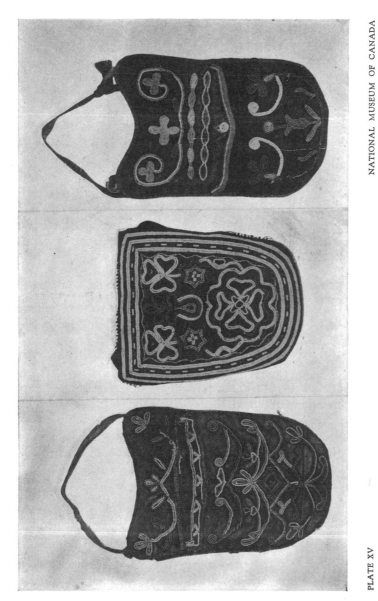

PLATE XV

Decorated shot pouches; those on left and right, Moisie band; center, Michikamau.

Sh! Our grandfather!" and would hear no more of such a suggestion.

The infrequency of scapulimancy in the recorded ethnology of the Athapascan, with the exception of the Dog Rib instance, has been a source of perplexity to Dr. Cooper as well as myself. [40] I have mentioned Dr. Osgood's recent discovery of the practice among the Athapascan Kutchin of Peel River, Alaska. Miss De Laguna does not report the practice among the Eyak of the Copper River delta.

Outside of the immediate area over which the Montagnais-Naskapi are distributed, I found and reported scapulimancy in identical form occurring among the Algonquin proper at River Desert. [41]

The evidences of the practices of shoulder-blade reading among the Wabanaki of former times are furthermore very weak. From the Penobscot we learn, through Roland Nelson, of the consultation of the muskrat's shoulder blade, when taken from the freshly killed animal, to secure information concerning the success of the next attack on the game. If the shoulder blade of the muskrat appears spotted with blood, the sign is favorable.

Scapulimancy Among Northern Labradorean Bands

Among the more easterly divisions of the Indians of the peninsula —those who have generally been referred to as Naskapi by other writers—the modes of procedure in scapulimancy are similar to those among the Montagnais. There are, however, deviations in the scheme of interpretation that should be significant when the practices of divination are finally recorded from other areas in the north, not as yet investigated, which now separate the Labrador tribes from those farther west. The Naskapi, ranging from Seven Islands east and north, practice extensively with the caribou scapula. I have remarked on the aversion to the use of the scapula bones of the caribou and moose among the southwestern bands. This is a geographical variation. And again, the augury chiefly concerns the caribou hunt. It seems, besides, that the burnings on the bone assume more pictographic values in the minds of the sign readers. Practically all the hunters among these bands practice this form of divination as a religious rite of importance throughout that part of the year when they are living upon the caribou in the interior plateau. While sojourning at the missions and trading establishments on the coast

40. John M. Cooper, op. cit., p. 217.
41. F. G. Speck, "Divination by Scapulimancy Among the Algonquin of River Desert," Indian Notes, Museum American Indian (Heye Foundation), Vol. V (1928), No. 2, pp. 167-73.

during the summer, however, the religious practices of the wild life are never seen. In consequence of this circumstance, I was obliged to adopt the plan of letting various men sketch the outline of the caribou scapula and then have them mark out imaginary burnings upon the figure to illustrate their ideas of the meanings of the burnt spots and cracks. This plan worked well, for they all knew what was intended, and they took much interest in comparing their varying individual readings of the signs on one anothers' drawings. This, indeed, brought out the fact, which otherwise might have been passed by, that to different hunters the same burnt figures meant somewhat different things. In all, I obtained in this way about twenty examples of the desired details. In some cases the sketches represented imaginary results of burning the bone, but in about half of the cases illustrated they were reproductions from memory of former experiments which seemed to remain vividly in their recollection. It must be remembered that such doings had every reason to be impressed upon their memory; as much, indeed, as important business transactions would be upon the minds of inhabitants of the white man's world. A similar method of investigation will need to be carried on in other areas, where, for the want of systematic inquiry, we know nothing even of the existence of scapulimancy. It would be a rare thing for an outsider to come accidentally into the presence of a scapulimantic rite, as did the late Napoleon Comeau, the well known *habitant* author in the village of Godbout. We have to thank this writer for a most painstaking and useful account of a divination performance which he observed among the Indians of the Godbout band many years ago. It is the only spontaneous description of the rite that I can find in literature of the region and, coming from one who knew the language, and from an area where the present Indian hunters are badly dispersed, it is a most acceptable piece of evidence.

Among the many superstitious beliefs and practices of our Montagnais Indians I think that what is known as "shoulder-blade reading" is one of the least known and most curious. It is seldom practiced in the presence of a "white brother" unless the latter is held in very high esteem or has lived among them. I suppose this is due to the fear that the secret may be revealed to their prejudice. In the Montagnais dialect the custom is known as *outlickan meskina*, the literal translation of which is "shoulder-blade track."

The bones of various animals are used for this purpose, but the favorite, the most truthful and most far-seeing, in their belief, is that of the caribou. As soon as the animal is cut up the shoulder blade is removed by cutting at the first joint. The meat is then cut away with a sharp knife as close to the bone as possible and the latter is boiled for a few minutes, just sufficiently to allow of all the meat being wiped off. It is then hung up in the wigwam to dry, and in the evening after the children are asleep the bone is read in the following manner:

A small piece of wood is partially split, and into the end of this the joint end of the "blade" is inserted to form a handle. It is then held over red hot coals for a few seconds. The intense heat causes the bone to crack in various directions according of course, to the amount of heat to which the different parts are subjected. As this can seldom or never be exactly alike the reading varies. A long straight crack from end to end means death or starvation. A short zigzag one

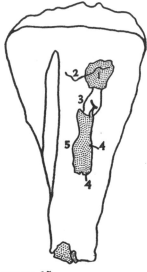

FIGURE 15   FROM N. A. COMEAU

Diagram of caribou shoulder-blade divination, Godbout band, Montagnais. (1) represents the hunter and his wigwam, (2) the useless trail, (3) two trails leading to game, (4) and (5) tracks and location where game is found.

without any branches means much trouble and hardships. Cracks like the branches of a tree with small, roundish burnt spots on the edges indicate plenty. When these spots are close to the stern portion it is a sign that the game they are seeking is close at hand. If they are at the extremities of the branches the game is distant in proportion. It is wonderful what an amount of reading some of the experts can get out of these few cracks and spots. The illustration on the opposite page is from a photograph of a bone actually used by an Indian hunter as above described and shows what is considered a lucky burning. Figure 15 (1) is supposed to represent the hunter and his wigwam—a large dark patch. Figure 15 (2) is a trail in which direction it would be useless to go as there are no markings to represent game.

Figure 15 (3) shows two trails, both of which lead to game, as shown by the brown portion between the two lines. Figure 15 (4) and (5) indicate the tracks and direction in which the game is to be found. The hunter who owned this bone and read its signs assured me that on his first day's hunt after the reading he found and shot four caribou in the direction indicated and added that for miles around in every direction there was no other game. The Indians' faith in this is unbounded.

The largest burnt spot always indicates the camp. If the bone burns very brown before cracking it means a long spell of bad weather and so on. This bone-burning is mostly practiced to find out things pertaining to hunting, although occasionally some of the "wise ones" pretend that it can foretell for them other events. I used to take much interest in watching their solemn faces while this reading was going on, and certainly no gospel truth was ever more firmly believed in than is this peculiar rite or practice. [42]

The same terms as elsewhere in the peninsula are used here to denote shoulder-blade divination, mətənca'wan and its synonym utni''gən meckənu', "shoulder-blade path." The process of augury is, among the Naskapi, governed by a fairly definite idea.

By way of contrast with the preceding, it seems that the populations on the western side of the peninsula do not so consistently wait for the dream as a preliminary requirement. In using the shoulder blades of smaller animals, the western bands employ more varieties and they introduce a wider range of questioning. In the case of the northern and eastern groups, the caribou bone is most prominent, and revelation is more concerned with that animal. Indeed, it would seem from the cases recorded here, and the subjects, which were determined by the free choice of the informants, that caribou interests have eclipsed all others.

In divining with the burnt shoulder blade the procedure is first to dream. This, as we shall see, is induced by a sweat bath and by drumming or shaking a rattle. Then, when a dream of seeing or securing game comes to the hunter, the next thing to do is to find where to go and what circumstances will be encountered. And since the dream is vague, and especially since it is not localized, the hunter-dreamer cannot tell where his route is to lie or what landmarks he will find. So he employs the shoulder blade. As one informant put it, the divination rite cleared up the dream. "We generally use the caribou shoulder blade for caribou hunting divination, the shoulder blade or hip bone of beaver for beaver divination, fish-jaw augury for fishing, and so on." Drumming, singing, and dreaming, next

42. N. A. Comeau, *Life and Sport on the North Shore* (2nd ed.; Quebec, 1923), pp. 264-66.

divination by scapula, then, combine as the *modus operandi* of the life-supporting hunt.

The Indians here follow the custom of shaking the rattle or drum-ming and singing in the evening before going to sleep when they feel that the occasion is right for divination. This is apt to induce a preliminary dream. When burning the shoulder blade they hold the narrow portion of the bone toward the body, the wide portion away from the body, and then as the burnt spots and cracks appear these indicate the directions and locations to be followed and sought (the directions indicated by the burnt spots being intended to rep-resent the actual ones to be followed). The shoulder blade is, then, regarded as a blank chart of the hunting territory.

An interesting condition arises when the hunter, having drummed and sung, having received his dream prompting, and having consulted the burnt scapula, follows the directions given and then fails to find what the revelation promised him. I questioned a number in reference to possible falsification on the part of the shoulder blade augury. The general answer was that the bone never prophesied falsely unless the Great Man of the individual using it was responsible for deceiv-ing the individual on account of some deception or negligence shown toward him. It was also said that occasionally the hunter did not find the caribou promised him, because he did not estimate the dis-tances as they appeared on the bone correctly in the actual territory in which he was seeking his game, or "because the road was too much obstructed by snow for him to cover all the distance required."

It may be added, on the testimony of several of the hunters ques-tioned at Seven Islands, that in the interior when there is a dearth of food, the shoulder-blade oracle is consulted with great frequency; as often as every three or four days.

Let us now turn to the actual specimen drawings and readings offered by hunters of the various bands congregated at Seven Islands. Figure 16 A was first drawn by Jean Pierre, who was born in the Un-gava band. His sketch shows four burnt spots connected by cracks. At A he indicated his camp; B, C, D, as three caribou to which his tracks would lead him as indicated by the connecting lines. This reading he called *epwamia'n nictoti''kʷ*, "I dream three caribou." Philippe Germain of the Moisie band then looked on and offered explanation of the meaning of the burning. He first pointed to D and called it "caribou," then to C and said, "We sing here"; to B and

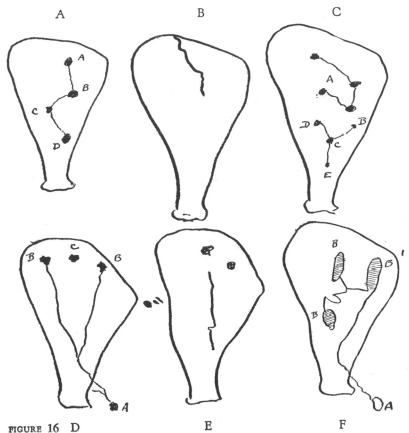

(A) Diagram of a caribou shoulder blade, with burnt markings. The specimen received different interpretations by three informants (Naskapi of Seven Islands). (B) Caribou scapulimancy, favorable sign (Petisigabau band). (C) Caribou scapulimancy. Prognostication of caribou hunt (Petisigabau band). (D) Caribou scapulimancy: Favorable reading; two caribou at end of trail. (E) Caribou scapulimancy: Unfavorable reading, no caribou. (F) Caribou scapulimancy: Favorable augury (Michikamau band).

said, "drum"; and to A as his camp. This he added to and interpreted as "I get caribou and then will dance and drum in my tent to satisfy Caribou Man." Pierre André of the Petesegabau band indicated D as "myself"; C as "Caribou House"; B as "conjuring tent"; and A as "Caribou House." He did not explain it as a prognostication of success as did the others.

Figure 16 B represents the interpretation of a favorable prospect for the caribou hunt by Antoine Dominique (Petisigabau band) for which here marked, *miam mətənca'wan a·ti'ḳ'ᵘ umecḳənu'*, "good divination, deer path."

Figure 16 C is another schematized representation of a burning by the same hunter as sketch B. This is rather complex. The four upper spots A represent four caribou, B, the hunter himself, C and D, big family camps, and E the hunter's camp where he will finally stop without having connected with the trail of the caribou at A. The reading is then an unfavorable one. The informant's words were, "Caribou! And here were four caribou! The hunter sees the caribou and turns his track toward a big camp, women's camp, and beyond is the hunter's trail and here his camp—all for nothing!"

Figure 16 D is one in which the hunter, represented at A, dreams of seeing two trails which lead him to two caribou at B, but there is another at C which he will miss. He said, "In my tent [A] I dream I see this trail appearing on that shoulder-blade, which will bring me to those caribou."

Figure 16 E is by the same hunter. His tent is also at A and by taking the trails indicated he will make three camps without ever coming upon the trail of caribou—a hopeless prospect for the proposed hunting excursion.

Figure 16 F is another by Chief Mackenzie of the Michikamau band. His words were "I dream of my trail. Caribou are there—two of them together. A good divination, so it tells me."

Figure 17 A is the recollection of a burning again by Antoine. It outlines the direction and the turns in the trail he was admonished to follow by his dream mentor, his "great man." At A is the hunter's camp, his starting point, at B are the herds of caribou in and around a lake, and at C is the hunter's camp and feasting place after the kill.

Figure 17 B is a schematized shoulder-blade burning by a hunter named *Miċtənabe'o*, "Big Man," of the Michikamau band. He had recently gotten this figure as the result of a dream and scapula-burning, and said that it represented a porcupine, A, and a man, B; namely, himself, and "the man ate the porcupine."

Figure 17 C is another by the same man. "I dreamed it," he said. "Fox track A, a bear B, it not being winter. The man's camp C— the man ate the bear!"

Figure 17 D is a drawing by a boy whose father hunted on the

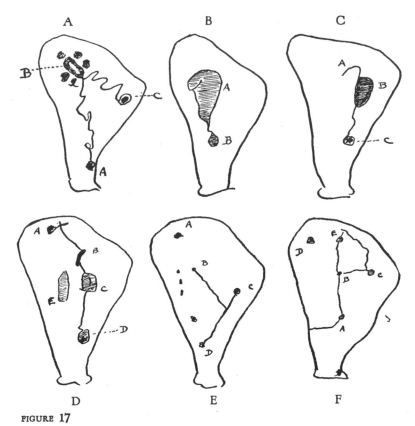

FIGURE 17

Caribou scapulimancy: (A) Burning denoting a hunter's camp and trail leading to herd of caribou on a lake. (B) Caribou scapulimancy: Omen of killing a porcupine, at A (Michikamau). (C) Omen of finding a bear at B, when following a fox track, A. (D) Caribou scapulimancy: Specimen burning by a boy showing camps, caribou and mountains (Moisie band). (E) Reproduction of a burning by a former conjuror, representing his vision of a tragedy in the interior, the starvation of three people in a camp (Petisigabau band). (F) Burning showing the route of a hunter who kills game at C (Northwest River band).

upper Moisie River. He was just beginning to hunt in the capacity of a man, and so his testimony is interesting as representing a stage in native scapulimantic education. He said that A denoted his camp. He follows the trail and reaches a lake half-way B, where there is a caribou. He kills and eats the animal at C. Then he travels on to D where he sleeps, with plenty of food. E marks the location of a range of mountains which helps him to identify the location where he was to find the lake and caribou, *B* and *C*.

Figure 17 E. An extensive narrative, that is in comparison with those accompanying other scapula readings, was given as the explanation of the figures on this burnt caribou shoulder blade by Antoine, who has been referred to before. His own words are sufficiently explanatory and convey the best idea of the type of thought associated with the scapula readings. "An Indian camp, a Petisigabau man's camp by divination! *A*, Caribou House. Already a man is dead there —he had nothing. He did not eat food, he did not eat meat. He could not kill any caribou. He was as good as dead before he could find food. Not a beast he saw for him to eat. Not a beast could he kill. And for four moons he was already dead. So said the divination! And with him [in his camp] were two others dead; one woman, a man and a boy baby. Even the little dogs were dead. His name was Ocku'n, 'Bone' [that dead man]."

The burnt spots show at *A*, the camp, and at *B*, *C*, *D*, the three starved people. There are no burnt spots representing food near them.

It was explained how this revelation was brought out by a conjuror when Antoine was a boy, and how by his use of the scapula divination the conjuror at the time learned of the sad event. The tragedy seemed to be quite generally known among the hunters who stood near when Antoine gave the story and explained the figures. I regard it as a good example of a second-hand specimen of the conjuror's scapula oracle.

Figure 17 F was made and explained by a hunter of the Northwest River band named Mictəben, "Big Ben." It reproduced a burning which he had performed the winter before. At *A* he indicated the location of his camp at the time the divination was undertaken. Here he took a sweat-bath to prepare for his hunt. The line to *B* pointed out the route to the next night's shelter at *B*. The divination foretold that if he took the trail to *B* from *C* he would expect to find caribou. He did so but did not encounter the game and returned to his previous camp at *B* and slept there. He had a camp at *D* but did not go there because the divination did not show a line connecting it with his route. He then went as directed to *E* but found no game. Here he sang and drummed for better luck [at *E*]. The next day he took up the remaining line to *C* and there he found the caribou and made a kill—thus fulfilling the prognostication. His own curt summary of his experience was: "At *A*, the hunter's camp, for his sweat-bath, afterward his divination in the cabin. I go, I miss the caribou, I do not find them. I sleep. Then I send myself down there [to *E*] the next day. I am exceedingly hungry. I do not use my divination, but I take my drum (this time at *E*) and use it that night. The next day I really find the caribou [at *C*]."

Figure 18 A is another specimen sketched by the hunter who did the foregoing one. His camp is at *A*. He followed the trail indicated to *B* where he camped again and then went on to *C* where he found caribou—a successful augury. The burnings on the right were not favorable. It shows the road from *D*, but it also shows, by the absence of the right kind of spots, that on this trail [*D-E*] he will not find game.

Figure 18 B. A hunter from the Ungava band, Peta'banu ["Brings the Day"], who has married and settled down with the Michikamau Indians who come out in the summer to the post at Seven Islands, produced this and the following specimen sketches of his experiences in divination. He is reputed to be a mixed Eskimo-Naskapi. He began by indicating his hunting route to have begun at his camp *A*, and leading to *B*. The prognostication on this occasion was unfavorable, because the scapula showed him that the caribou were far away at *C* and *D* and that his trail would not connect with their route.

Figure 18 C is another product of the same man. In this he showed how the augury would appear if it were favorable, since the burnt cracks in the bone connect the lower spots [*A*, *B*] with the upper [*C*, *D*].

Figure 18 D. Peta'banu was also the author of this sketch of divination. Its interpretation is as follows: *A*, the camp of the hunter who had the dream. He is directed to go in the direction of *B* and build a camp. From here he sends one party of his companions to *C*, another to *D* in search of caribou. The bone burns out by a crack to the edge at *E*, which is an unfavorable sign, so they will get nothing.

Figure 18 E. The same hunter did one more with this interpretation: At *A* is the camp of the hunters who have had the dream of game. The three spots, *B*, *C*, *D*, are herds of caribou which lie in that direction, the other spots being lakes. The hunters are instructed to go to those places, build camps there, and kill the caribou. The lines

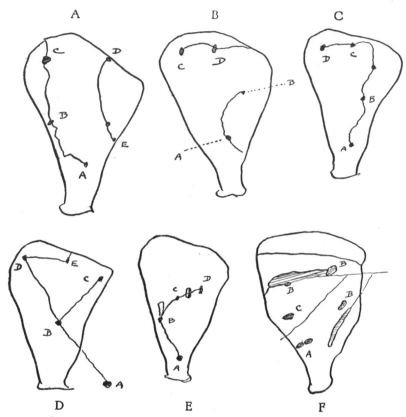

FIGURE 18

Caribou scapulimancy: (A) A favorable divination on the left; unfavorable on the right side (Northwest River band). (B) An unfavorable prognostication, since hunter's trail, A-B, does not join that for caribou, C-D. (C) A modification of figure (B), showing a favorable augury (Ungava band). (D) An unfavorable divination, due to burning of crack to edge at E (Ungava band). (E) Burning showing location of three groups of caribou, B, C, D, and successful hunt (Ungava band). (F) Native sketch of burnt shoulder-blade divination. Spots show lakes, rivers and caribou, B, which the hunter will kill (Michikamau band).

joining all the spots indicate success in finding and killing the animals.

In Peta'banu's readings we see the procedure of a Naskapi who is regarded as being a conjuror among his people. He does not practice openly, so I had no opportunity of learning more about the matter.

It will be noticed, however, that in the last two readings the diviner is sending forth companies of hunters and not going over the route himself. This has the characteristics of the professional performer who has been employed to practice for the community of hunters to find out where they may go for game, what luck they will have.

Figure 18 F. A free-hand sketch by Alexander Mackenzie, a hunter of Lake Michikamau. A represents the camp of the hunter who had the dream. The lines and enclosed spots are rivers and lakes, except for those marked B. These are caribou to be found at the corresponding situations about the lakes. The divination declares that he will kill them if he proceeds thither, but that there are caribou at C which he will not reach.

Discussion of Distribution

Now to glance at the wide area over which scapulimancy is extended in Asia and Europe. The Central Asiatic nomads are regarded by Andree and others as the original possessors of the rite. One of the assigned reasons for associating it intimately with sheep culture as they do is that the shoulder blade of a sheep is invariably employed by those practising it. Among these tribes the characteristics of scapula divination run in unison. The scapula is submitted to drastic heat. The appearance of the scorched areas, the cracks and breaks, form the omens. The scope of the augury, strikingly uniform throughout the area, is the foretelling of death, sickness, famine, plenty, the arrival of visitors, news of absent persons, and even answers to questions of a personal nature. When we realize that the characteristics just mentioned apply equally to scapulimancy among the hunters of northern North America, the reason for an inclination to regard it as a custom inherent in early cultures of the northern regions becomes more evident. With these the shoulder blade oracle is an important and prominent rite. The Central and Northeastern Asiatic areas seem to differ only from the American in that the shoulder blade is divided into imaginary zones, sometimes into two halves divided by the "spine," or longitudinal ridge of the bone; the zones having definite answer-values. It is here in this stage of its growth that we encounter the earliest chronological reference to it among the Mongols of the thirteenth century.

Throughout America the characteristics of scapulimancy are much the same as among the Asiatic tribes, and since they occur as culture features harmoniously adjusted to the hunting nomadism of America and since this is a primitive one, we are evidently penetrating into an earlier rather than a later phase of its evolutionary history. An exception to this line of reasoning, however, may be conceived if we assume that with the origin of the custom in a sheep-raising environment it spread by direct diffusion to non-sheep-raising tribes and that here it became functional with shoulder blades of various game animals prominent in their economic life.

The study thus briefly offered has a bearing on the diffusionist theories. For without affecting our attitude of deliberate caution in regard to the absolute single source of diffusion of human culture traits, it would seem that from the American data a view has at least been opened in new directions. Apart from the possibility of trait diffusion from Asia across the North Pacific in relatively recent times, another supposition arises; namely, the retention of a very early common-origin hunting rite by peoples both in Asia and North America, a survival unobliterated by continental separation. The North American cases would seem indeed to throw the rite back into the primitive setting of a simple circumpolar hunting culture instead of leaving its origin to be assigned to the relatively late stratum of Neolithic animal husbandry.

That scapula augury should not have been recorded with greater prominence in journals of American travel and exploration is somewhat strange. And it is still more strange that it seems to have been generally overlooked even by ethnologists among the northern hunting tribes where it assumes prominence. Lack of intimate association and knowledge of native tongues may be assignable as a reason.

Divination by Gazing

Wabənatca'kwoma'n, "soul seeing," is a most interesting and widespread practice, and one of great importance among the bands under discussion. It is simply the practice of gazing upon a decorated object, or a mirror, or into a pool of water until, through concentration upon the subject upon which information is desired, an image (atca'kʷ, also "soul") appears providing the response. In the case of a beaded object (a shot pouch, or a cap pouch, or even a needle bag is mentioned as an article to be used), the gaze penetrates through it and

— 164 —

the object-answer shows forth, though the actual design is invisible. It has been mentioned that this procedure should be carried on in the dark with the head covered to exclude any possible entry of light.

A story illustrates the picturesque details (Mistassini). An old hunter related how he once discovered the footprints of a bear in the snow in early winter. The traces were lost in the deep barrier of a drift. The hunter, desiring to locate the bear, took his shot pouch and, covering his head with his blanket, concentrated his gaze upon the object in the dense darkness beneath. Soon the footprints came before his spiritual vision (*wabənatca'kʷoma'n*, "he sees the soul-image!") leading in a certain direction. He removed his head covering and proceeded in the direction revealed. Soon after he found the bear and killed it.

Beaver Pelvis Oracle

The pelvic bone of the beaver, besides being scorched as previously described, also serves in divination by touch. The process was witnessed among the Naskapi from various bands gathered at the Seven Islands post. There it is called *opətce'sigən ami'ckʷ*, "hip-bone beaver." The procedure is simple. The pelvis is passed over the head in one hand and with the index finger of the other hand extended, the two are brought together. If the extended finger enters the hole in the bone it is a sign of the affirmative in answer to the question, "Will I kill a beaver?" The Indians sometimes closed their eyes when doing this. They said the answer would also apply to weather, wind, and luck in general, though the chief concern was with the beaver hunt. The beaver pelvis was the only one used by these people. Frederick Johnson learned from some of them from Michikamau (1925) that if the finger entered the hole it was a sign of getting a male beaver; if it struck into the socket (acetabulum), the hunter would get a female. An identical interpretation was given by the Têtes de Boule on St. Maurice River to Dr. Davidson later in the year when he inquired about it. A wide distribution to the westward is shown by Dr. J. M. Cooper, who informs me of learning of it at Rupert's House, Kesagami, Moose Factory, Waswanipi, Obidjuan, and Abitibi. [43]

The use to which the pelvis of a beaver is put among the Lake

43. Correspondence, December 9, 1927.

— 165 —

St. John hunters is illustrated by an incident that took place in the winter of 1926 at that post. There a specimen of the pelvis was obtained from a hunter, David Basil, who used it in the following manner. He first asked, according to his desire and need at the time, for a "lake containing beaver." Then he swung the bone over his head in one hand and pushed the finger of the other hand toward it. If the finger entered the large orifice the answer was favorable. If, however, the finger touched the edge of the bone or the socket cavity the answer was unfavorable. The bone, in his method, was divided into three areas each with a meaning, the central orifice being the lake, the margin a female beaver, and the socket a "beaver house." He first expressed his desire for one of the three, then tried the trick and if the finger came to the corresponding part of the pelvis, the answer was favorable; otherwise not. The wish and answer had to coincide for a sign of success. It was the only case of such a variation in reading-divination that I know of.

The pelvic bone divination is reported from the Abenaki of St. Francis and from the Penobscot and the Malecite of the Wabanaki group. The details are essentially the same as those just recorded in describing the Montagnais-Naskapi practice. (The St. Francis Abenaki speak of the pelvis as *utəli·gə'n*, Montagnais, *utli'gən.* "shoulder blade.") It may be worth adding that a Malecite (New Brunswick) whom I saw perform the trick asked the bone, *Ta'ma kwosəbe'msisiyu'*, "Where is a little lake?" meaning a lake containing beaver. And he added that the muskrat bone was equally serviceable. The detail and phraseology are noticeably close to those recorded above.

Beaver Tibia Oracle

The tibia of a beaver is another source of revelation to be consulted before starting to hunt. It refers particularly to the prospects concerning the beaver. The bone is taken in the two hands, a piece of skin or rags wrapped around its ends to protect the skin of the palms. Then by a violent effort the diviner will try to break it. While straining to do so, he fastens his thought upon the desire to get beaver. If the bone cannot be broken, it is taken as a sign that his Great Man will not give him anything. But if he does break it, the sign indicates that he will kill beaver. And the manner of breaking is a further indication of details as to how many and the like. The specimen figured (fig. 19) was consulted one evening by Malek, the grown son of Tsebic, who broke the bone in two after a brief but strenuous effort. The result he interpreted was that two beaver cabins would be successfully attacked by him, as fore-told by the two severed flakes of surface bone appearing at the edge of the fracture.

FIGURE 19

Montagnais divination device (Lake St. John): Beaver tibia broken by wrist twist to determine prospects of the hunt. The break denotes that beaver will be gotten; the two chips broken at point of fracture denote that it will be two beaver.

Moving Oracle (Bear Patella)

The knee bone of the bear, the patella, is also employed for the services of divination in the whole region.[44] Specimens have been gotten among the Montagnais of Lake St. John, but the more frequent finding of the bones in the possession of hunters of the Seven Islands and Moisie bands seems to show its prevalence as a favorite means among the easterly Naskapi bands. This insignificant bone is often seen among the paraphernalia of the hunters, in their tool bags, for instance. To put it into operation the bone is warmed a little, then placed upon a heated flat rock if the place happens to be in the bush, or on the top of a stove if one is near. It is placed with the rounded side down. As soon as it is affected by the heat it will respond according to its "disposition," under the control of the hunter's soul-spirit. This divination is performed to find out whether any game will be gotten in the next hunting excursion. A choking motion is affirmative.

An instance of this type of divination I observed among the Seven Islands Indians. One of the men, named Tcenish, produced from his repository, amid bags and the like, two of these knee bones. He scraped one of them a little with his knife, then put

44. Dr. John M. Cooper has kindly called my attention to the mention of the bear patella divination among the Hare (Athapascan) by E. Petitot, *Exploration de la Région du Grand Lac des Ours*, p. 14.

it on the top of his stove. It trembled a trifle, after which he said there would be only small success upon his next venture. His remarks on the act, which I took down, were as follows: "The bear's knee bone there is burned on a stove. It [is supposed to] move. If it does not move—nothing, but if it moves then I will find something [game]. In place of a stove, a stone will serve. The stone then moves the knee bone."

At Lake St. John I learned of the beaver patella being put to the same service in answering questions relating to the beaver hunt.

Divination by Tossing Fish Bones

Divination by tossing is practiced with certain bones from the fish. We are told that the fish spirits, when under the control of a hunter who has been "good" in the native sense by having observed the taboos against wastefulness (see p. 118), will vouchsafe answers to questions pertaining to the securing of game. Divination with fish bones is naturally considered more effective in matters concerning fishing, for the fish are able to "speak" for their own kind.

The mandibles of large fish (*utabǝsi'gǝn nǝme'c*) are commonly used among the eastern Naskapi (fig. 20). When divination is desired

FIGURE 20

Divination device: Mandibles of codfish tossed up for divination (Ste. Marguerite and Michikamau bands).

the mandible is tossed in the air a foot or so and the question simultaneously called out. If the mandible falls with the teeth upward it is affirmative, teeth downward, negative. At Seven Islands I observed several times some young hunters of the Petisigabau band engaged in tossing the jaws of codfish taken in the bay. The questions and the answers I recorded as follows: "What [kind of fish] is going to bite on the hook? Is he going to be big?" The mandible fell on its end. "He does not say so directly!" Meanwhile, he threw it again while saying, "It will be so indeed, large like this one (meaning the mandible he was tossing), as large as this and that will be big enough!" as it came down teeth up. The performer was young Tcenish, a hunter of the Ste. Marguerite Naskapi. Another hunter took the jawbone and tossed it asking, "North wind to-morrow?" "Yes, it says," as the mandible settled teeth up. Again, "Will I see caribou?" "This time 'no' it says," as it fell reversed. Another in the company tried it. "Will I have a child?" and a fourth, "Will I marry [in the native sense] tonight?" In the laughter that ran around among the half dozen who had gathered, I did not succeed in recording the answers to the last two questions, but the loss is small.

The clavicles of fish (*utətci·'gən nəme'c*, fig. 21) are employed in exactly the same manner. When the concave side remains upward

FIGURE 21
Divination device: Clavicle of codfish tossed up for divination
(Ste. Marguerite band).

after being tossed, the answer is "yes," when down, "no." Specimen questions from occasions overheard among Ste. Marguerite and Michikamau men are: "Will he have nice hair, Sylvestre?" [meaning an expected child] and "Will he have luck in fishing?" as the clavicle was tossed; "No! he [the fish] says," as it came down convex side up.

It is worthy of note here that the fish-jaw divination is not prac-ticed at Lake St. John for the reason that these Indians do not in-dulge extensively in eating the salt-water salmon and so do not con-sult its parts for information as to their luck.

Divination by Tossing up Muskrat Skull

The tossing-up divination game known to the Lake St. John band as *wətcə'ck učtəgwa'n me·towagə'n*, "muskrat head play," is one now indulged in for amusement, but which may possibly have had in former times a more serious tone. [45] A cleaned muskrat or woodchuck skull is used, a sharpened stick having been pushed into the nasal orifice to serve as a pointer (pl. VIII right). The men of a group desiring to play the game are all seated about the fire, whether it be in a house or in the open. One plays the part of thrower. A question is asked and up goes the skull into the air from his hand. When the skull falls to the ground, the person toward whom the stick in the nose of the skull points is the one denoted as concerned with the answer. Questions of a personal nature are, for instance: *awe'n me'tcit*, "who is homely?"; *awe'n me'locit*, "Who is good looking?"; *awe'n tse'ʺtə-mət*, "Who is a coward?"; *awe'n tceni·bu't*, "Who is to be married?"; *awe'n ne'tauba'lət*, "Who is comical?" But questions as to the outcome of the next hunt are the rule in winter. The individual in whose direction the stick points next becomes the thrower. The play is productive of much simple enjoyment. The questions often run deeply into personal affairs, and the victims of the mirthful exposure sometimes become irritated. Great amusement is caused when the skull points to the thrower or to one who proposed the question; the joke being turned upon its author. Because the muskrat is a liar in the stories, they say, his head is employed to reveal their affairs for amusement—the Montagnais way of expressing the old saying, "There's many a true word spoken in jest." I asked if other skulls were used, but was told that only the muskrat or woodchuck served the purpose at Lake St. John, where the game was found.

Otter-Paw Oracle

The Lake St. John Montagnais use otter paws (pl. VIII, lower left) in tossing-up divination. [46] They grow two paws, held facing each other palm to palm, up in the air. The individual taking the action first combs out his hair with the toes of the paw as though he were to appear before his sweetheart. If both paws come down palms up, it is good. If both come down palms down, it is not good. If one comes one way and the other the opposite way it is only

45. Dr. Cooper writes me that his notes on divination contain reference to this practice among the bands at Rupert House and some adjacent regions, the bear skull being employed for a similar purpose; in this instance, the skull being dropped from the man's head. He writes that he also learned of it from the Waswanipi.
46. The bands at Rupert House, Harricanaw River, Kesagami, Moose Factory, Waswanipi, Obidjuan and Abitibi observe a similar rite, as I have been informed by Dr. Cooper. Dr. Davidson records the similar use of a pair of bear paws among the Têtes de Boule of St. Maurice River, and my own notes describe the same for the band at Montachéne.

half luck. The operator of this device will address the otter by euphemisms: *ni·təmu'ciatsu'ḳ,* "my sweetheart-otter," if the animal is a female. *Ni·c̆ta'yatsuḳ,* "my brother-in-law otter," if it is a male. He will imitate the otter call by a grunt, "*uh,*" as the otter cries when he starts to run. The otter is "conjured into giving an answer."

Ni·təmu'c tsəgənto' naḳəhotananu', "My sweetheart, are we going to meet anything as we travel [in the canoe]?" (or *nic̆ta'u,* "my brother-in-law, etc." for a male animal), is a usual form of questioning.

Perhaps these incidents are even better. A Lake St. John hunter, taking the otter paws in his hands, combs his hair with the claws, throws the paws into the air, grunting in imitation of the animal's voice, *e'! tsəntu'nəḳ·hot·ena'nu ah! a'! nis̆ta'yatsuḳ,* "You see what we shall meet with," *ah! a'!* "My brother-in-law otter," or *ni·'təmucaya'tsuḳ,* "my sweetheart otter," in case of the animal's being a female.

Again, he asks, *tsəgəntaḳ·uməltə'n,* "You see what will be found [in my trap]." He throws the paws. When they fall on the ground he grunts, *a'!* This time the paws do not augur favorably. He picks them up, dashes them violently to the ground, and abuses his "brother" or "sweetheart," as the case may be, crying *matci·'oc̆tene'te! Pegwu'n tceite'ltaman eḳa nəpi·'ta'n!* "Go off there into the wilderness! It is the same to me, even if I do not kill you!"

A variation by a Mistassini hunter may be added. He tossed a beaver foot, asking it *awe'n ḳamatc̆to'tən?* "Who has done evil?" The foot pointed to no one standing by.

The preceding types of divination are described as *ota'meotcəgə'n,* "he leaves (*ota'meo*) scratching [with his paws]," meaning that the otter-spirit is leaving to examine the future after he has scratched his captor's hair (Lake St. John band).

Among the forms of divination by "tossing-up" should be mentioned that of throwing a bear's vertebra into the air to judge of coming fortune by the position in which it falls. I have no further particulars to offer since the procedure was only described to me by a Lake St. John hunter.

Divination by Skinning Otter Tail

One of the Lake St. John hunters recalled seeing his father, when skinning an otter, foretell the number of pelts he would take on his next hunt by observing the number of hairs adhering to the meat of the tail after the hide had come off.

A similar rite was recorded among the Naskapi of Davis Inlet, Labrador, by F. W. Waugh in 1921. His notes, placed at my disposal by Mr. Jenness, state that the father of Cänic in skinning a marten pulled the bone out of the tail, looking to see if hairs remained attached to the tip. He saw two hairs there, meaning that he would catch two more martens. He believed he would catch as many more as he found hairs.

Other Forms of Bone Divination

Penetration of the divination concept into the very fundamentals of northeastern Algonkian religion is shown by instances of the practice among neighboring bands on the margins of the Montagnais-Naskapi. In some of the contiguous bands of Algonquin and Ojibwa casual mention of bone divination shows some deviation in these groups from the more general practices just described. For instance, the substitution of a grouse breastbone for the scapula in burning divination is recorded by Dr. Cooper from Rupert's House, Waswanipi and Obidjuan. [47] Among the Algonquin of Lake Temiskaming the same is reported. [48]

Throwing into the fire the "flat bones of the porcupine," so as to judge by the appearance of the flame whether the beaver or porcupine hunt would be successful, is mentioned by Hind. [49] While the Micmac have been deficiently reported in matters of religion and magic, it seems that one instance of bone-burning divination has come to light in the Newfoundland group of this tribe. [50] We have, moreover, a reference to Penobscot divination in Maine showing that the luck of a future hunt may be foretold by the presence or absence of blood clots on the scapula of a slain muskrat. Divination, however,

47. Correspondence, 1927.
48. F. G. Speck, *Myths and Folk-Lore of the Temiskaming Algonquin and Timagami Ojibwa,* "Anthopological Series," Memoir 71, No. 9, *Geological Survey of Canada* (Ottawa, 1915), p. 24.
49. H. Y. Hind, op. cit., I, 185.
50. F. G. Speck, "Beothuk and Micmac," *Indian Notes and Monographs, Museum American Indian* (1922), pp. 126-27.

seems to have had less prominence in general in areas marginal to the typical Cree-Montagnais-Naskapi, and where it does appear it is in forms modified from the typical developments of the north.

The Mohegan of Connecticut, near the southern margin of the hunting-divination areas, so far as positive information goes, believed that a staff stood on end and allowed to fall would point in the direction to be taken by the hunter for a successful expedition. [51]

The Iroquois, who, it would seem, were less imbued with a passion for the animal hunt than the man hunt, are not characterized by numerous or important hunting-divination practices. [52]

51. G. Tantaquidgeon, *Forty-Third Annual Report, Bureau American Ethnology* (1928), p. 275.

52. Illustrative of the more practical turn of mind characteristic of this group when confronted with folk-practices of the Algonkian, a Cayuga of the Six Nations, after being asked if he knew of such a custom as the Mohegan divination mentioned, commented upon its futility and said that the only observance preparatory to hunting he had heard of was to observe the direction of the wind and embark on his excursion toward the direction whence it blew—the common sense of which any hunter will at once recognize.

MAGIC PRACTICES

Chapter Seven

Invoking the Soul-Spirit by Singing, Drumming and Rattling

AS ADJUNCTS to the execution of the will in matters directed toward securing a successful hunt, or in concerns of a more personal nature, the influence of the human voice and the tympanic vibrations of the drum and rattle are considered indispensable. The ordinary process is this: When an individual has begun to concentrate his thoughts upon securing animals, or upon some other objective he desires to accomplish, he will sing and at the same time, if an instrument is available, accompany himself with the drum or rattle. It depends upon the occasion. The more frequently a hunter has occasion to resort to the power of sound in arousing his soul-spirit to activity in his behalf, the more likely he is to make for himself a drum. The size of the instrument is often a handicap on the arduous voyages he is called upon to make, and besides, the materials called for in the construction of a drum are often likely to be wanting. In lieu of a drum, then, he may depend simply upon the exercise of the hand rattle which is similar in function yet much less cumbersome and less fragile. Musical action is, in short, regarded as a means of strengthening the Great Man of the individual. There is really little to say objectively about drumming and rattling, but I will describe and illustrate both instruments. As for the rest, since the singing is the major part of the performance, more will be said later.

The drums of the Labrador Indians show an interesting tendency toward what appears to be the diffusion of a type common in the north from the shamanistic tribes of northern Asia. The specimens that I have obtained, about a dozen in all, show the development of one simple idea no matter in what bands they may be found in use (pls. ix, x). There is little variation in either size or form except in one important feature, namely, that the people east of the Ste. Marguerite use a drum with only one head, while west of this longitude the drums are made with two heads. This distinction seems to hold true through to the northern frontier of the Naskapi; as illustrations in Turner's report on the ethnology of Ungava, showing a drum from the Little Whale River band, and as specimens from the Mistassini to Lake St. John and Escoumains which I have collected, as well as those from the Têtes de Boule (D. S. Davidson), seem to show. Aside from this peculiarity, the drums are the same in pattern. Ranging from fourteen inches (in one specimen) to twenty-four inches, they are built upon a hoop from three to six inches wide made of birch or poplar. The caribou-skin head, in parchment form, is stretched taut over a wooden ring to fit outside of the hoop forming the barrel of the drum. When there are two heads, they are laced tight over the end of the central portion by means of rawhide thongs, very strong and thin and sometimes dyed red. When there is but one, the head is laced through the wood of this portion and so attached.

Montagnais-Naskapi drums all have the "snare" attachment— a length of sinew stretched tightly across the parchment, to which four to six, and even eight, sections of caribou bone or goose quill are tied by a clove hitch. The small bones taken from the legs of an unborn caribou are most in favor for this purpose. They have slight knob formations at the ends. The device produces a buzzing sound sustained as an undertone as long as the drum is being struck. In the words of the natives, this sound is "singing." In the single-headed drums there are likewise two snares, one being stretched above and the other below the head at right angles to each other. In all the specimens I have seen, the snares are a constant feature. It is generally believed, as I learned from a Mistassini drummer, that the singer addresses these bones and that they obey his commands. This completes the technical description of the Labrador drum, which deserves considerable thought by the comparative ethnologist, in view of the fact that there is no other form of the instrument in existence in the area. It is worth noting that the drum of this type is restricted to the northern regions, where its constructional resemblance to Eskimo and Asiatic forms is striking.

A word as to the drum beater. Among the more remote hunters of the interior the proper thing is a tine of caribou antler cut off so that the base nodule forms the striking end. But in many specimens the material is wood—simply a stick with a widened end. I might add that neither drums nor beaters commonly show any attempt at decoration beyond the application of a coating of vermilion. Some of them made of antler, are, however, carved, and treasured as conjurors' heirlooms.

When in use the drum is supended from one of the poles or cross poles of the tent or from the rafter of the wooden domicile, swinging to a distance level with the drummer's head. A loop of rawhide serves for supension and another at the lower end of the drum becomes a grip for the hand, enabling the drummer to hold the instrument obliquely near his face in order that its volume of sound may mingle with and smother the tones of his voice. This is a noteworthy mannerism of the Naskapi singer (and one to which he confesses only in confidence), prompted by a desire that his song be not clearly enough heard by the audience for them to learn it. It is part of the process by which he casts his voice abroad to rouse the emotions of his hearers.

Everywhere throughout the peninsula the drum is known under the name of *tewe'higən*, a term which offers us again the repetition of a radical (*tewe-*) associated with the idea of magic and sound.

That the drum is more than a mere object, that it has the form of a living entity, is shown by the statement of a Mistassini informant who spoke of it as having a head and a tail; one side being the head, the hoop being the body, the other side, the tail. In this case the Mistassini drum has two heads. Life symbolism in form may be of common distribution throughout the peninsula, but it has not been mentioned to me elsewhere. The informant, in the instance noted, compared the drum to the pack string or *ni·ma'ban* in having its parts correspond to head, body and tail. In speaking further of the drum and its spirit personification I shall use the expressions as they were given to me. "It can speak to him who understands its language when it is beaten. It talks, but all do not understand. When it is beaten by one whose soul is strong, it reveals what is going to happen. Sometimes during sleep the drum will address itself to the soul of a man and urge him to rouse himself and consult its meaning by attacking it with his drumstick. Whereupon it utters forth its message, to be grasped, if possible, by the imagination of the operator." Joseph Kurtness remembers seeing old men rouse themselves in the night and fall to drumming and singing to learn what the drum wanted to say. There was something, he said, that troubled them in a dream, or some fear that seized them during sleep. The following story will serve as an example.

"The father of a woman now living at Lake St. John, Madeline, whose name was old Gabriel Apəci'c, and his brother, were one time camping in the bush at Rivière au Rat. The old man went outside the camp upon this occasion and suddenly felt fear. He turned about and went back into the camp, saying, 'Take your drum and beat it.' His brother did so. After about fifteen minutes he declared, 'Yes! He is coming. I know it." He sang and drummed a while longer. Then he went out and built a conjuror's lodge and discovered by his inner power that a cannibal giant was coming in their direction to kill them. He directed his power against this demon and killed it, as it was afterwards found when a man who had been suspected of cannibalism was later found dead. His drum spoke the truth."

This same drum remained in the hands of his offspring for several generations. It was acquired for the Museum of the American Indian in 1924 and is illustrated herewith (pl. ix). In commenting on this story, Basil, of Lake St. John, added his own views by saying, "But I don't believe in that now. It all belongs to the olden times. It is what we are taught to call the devil, perhaps. The times have changed. With the coming of the whites and Christianity the demons of the bush have been pushed back to the north where there is no Christianity. And the conjuror does not exist any more with us, for there is no need of one. Nor is there need for the drum." Nevertheless, my good friend had a lone drumstick in his own camp, where I spied it by accident. Then he had his wife bring it to me when I asked for it, and he laughed when I accused him of being a drummer himself. He confessed to sometimes using a rattle made of a small tin box, the kind in which gun caps are sold to these Indians for their muzzle loading rifles, containing a few shot, with a stick inserted through its ends. This is the modernized form of the original disc-like rattle (cici·kwu'n) made of skin. He sometimes uses this when singing and walking back and forth in his camp, which I should say is his way, a Christianized one perhaps, of securing an oracular revelation. It is a matter of general information in the peninsula that both the drum and the rattle are made in response to prompting received in a dream. [1]

Every Tête de Boule, or White Fish Indian, according to James Buteux (Jesuit, 1641), had a sorcerer's drum, which was everything to him, giving it to a priest being considered unconditional surrender to the faith. Father Buteux was busy burning in bonfires drums which had been given to him. But we are told that the Têtes de Boule were uncompromising converts when baptized. He says even that one day that a zealous convert found a French drum in his cabin and with fervor kicked it to pieces, for it looked so much like a conjuror's drum. Yet the same Indians could not have found complete solace in rosaries and religious pictures given them by the fathers, for they still have drums and know how to use them in the bush.

The only occasion that I have had to observe the use of the drum in spiritual machination took place among the Naskapi at Seven Islands several years ago, when a young man of the Michikamau band, who had had at one time some native religious training in the bush, but who professed Christianity, demonstrated the method which he said was proper in attacking the drum for one of its declarations: The conjuror smears grease upon his forehead. Then he drums and sings at intervals for about an hour, using a short, rapid beat with occasional pauses. At the termination of this period, when he is ready to sink into his subconscious state, he snaps the head of the drum violently with his second finger. He hits the center of the drum and the four cardinal points at the right, the left, above, and below. Then he falls into a stupor and in about two hours assumes again his normal condition, though weakened and exhausted through sweating. The conjuror does this, he said, to make his Great Man strong—the result of the singing and drumming—to increase his heart action where, as we have learned before, the Great Man dwells.

I might add that here on the drum we encounter one of the explanations of the five red dots (four orientated about the central one) which serve so often in this region as shaman symbols. And next, the snapping of the fingers on the drumhead calls to mind the punishment in the cup-and-ball game. It is a snap of the finger on the part of the winner against the forehead of the loser; suggestive of defeat on the part of the drum and its submission to the overmastery

1. Campbell, *op. cit.*, p. 52.

of the spirit of the drummer. That this is an old symbol appears from the fact that the distant Penobscot and Malecite of Maine and New Brunswick employ the same trick as a sign of defeat in their form of the cup-and-ball game. Occasional specimens of drums from northern Canada show five red dots painted on the head and arranged in the manner described (see p. 186).

The service of the drum in social dances should not be overlooked. In this capacity, we are told, the song leader and drummer is employing his spiritual means to influence the soul-spirits of those taking part in the dance to make them strong, by the exercise of their endurance in the dance, and to cause them to perspire for the same idea which, we are to understand, is the sign of mounting strength. In all the dances which I have seen among the Naskapi of the eastern peninsula, the sweating effect is admirably achieved, but as much by the abundance of clothing worn by the dancers as by the violence of the singing and drumming, in which of course they do not take part.

Turner tersely summarizes the function of the drum among the Naskapi of Ungava. "If a person is ill the drum is beaten. If a person is well the drum is beaten. If prosperous in the chase the drum is beaten; and if death has snatched a member of the community, the drum is beaten to prevent his spirit from returning to torment the living. The drum beat is often accompanied with singing, which is the most discordant of all sounds supposed to be harmonious."[2]

Drum Speech

Having already mentioned the idea that the drum is capable of speech when it is "beaten," a most important fact remains to be presented. The vibrations of the drum are carried through the air to distant parts, challenging the sensitive ears of distant conjurors and even of animals. In the case of conjurors the challenge may be accepted and the contest be begun, the one against the other. This is, to the Indians, drum "broadcasting"— no wonder they regard the radio-machine with so little awe. They are of old acquainted with the vibration principle which their conjurors employed through the medium of sending by drumming and receiving through sense response.

2. "Ethnology of the Ungava Territory," *11th Annual Report, Bureau American Ethnology*, p. 325.

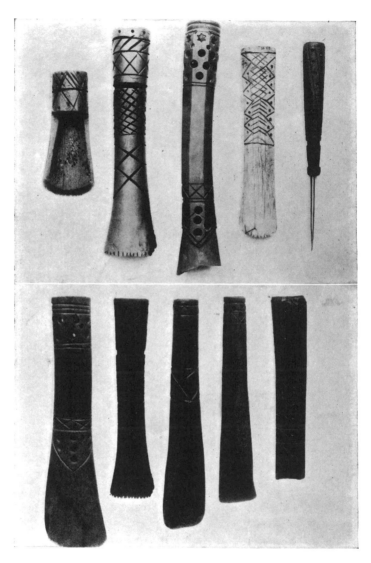

Montagnais-Naskapi bone skinning tools decorated to comply with dream instructions. (Michikamau, Ungava, and Moisie bands.)

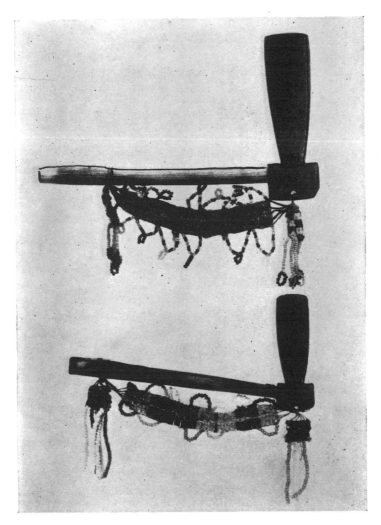

Stone pipes used by hunters in smoking at feasts in honor of game killed, from Michikamau and Moisie bands.

As regards the use of the drum by women, I have once seen a woman take a drum and sing to its accompaniment. At Lake St. John, a very old Tête de Boule woman Tcikwe′menu, who died in 1924, had the habit of singing with the drum at times. Michelson gives a very definite opinion on the impropriety of women drumming among the central Algonkian.

The rattles of which I have spoken are throughout the peninsula as uniform in construction as they are in the name (cici′gwu′n) they bear. A circular hoop of maple one-half an inch in width and about six inches in diameter is the foundation. A double covering of caribou-skin parchment is sewed tightly over the hoop. A handle is formed by allowing an extension of the hoop to project straight out. Sometimes the handle is carved on its margins, sometimes painted red, sometimes decorated with ribbons. Specimens are shown in plate x.

The service of the rattle is similar to that of the drum, it being a substitute at times for the drum. Occasionally, one sees the rattle itself used as a drumbeater in the performance of dances. It is considered a toy for children but as such I have never seen one used.

Singing

The following songs belong to that class of compositions known among the various bands of the region as *nana″ḳau ni″ḳəmənа′nuts awe′cicəts*, "different songs for animals" (Lake St. John). They are also spoken of as *eni‵minа′nuts eməlo′tagənts*, "songs of rejoicing," meaning that the hunters exult over their success in obtaining meat and furs.

At Seven Islands, Tcibas St. Onge, a hunter of the Shelter Bay band, revealed to me the origin of a song that he uses with the drum when invited to furnish the music for the round dance. He said that years ago he dreamed the words and refrain of the theme and woke up from his sleep with the song at his tongue's end. Thereupon, he adopted it as a property. I have heard him produce it upon a number of occasions when—once for five evenings in succession—the assembled families coming to trade at the Seven Islands station from distant parts of the peninsula would hold their vigorous round dances. The words, taken down from a whisper after I made him a little present, are as follows:—

ni·milowe·te'n	"I am contented
ni·pi·tatci·a'n	When I have killed something ⟦game⟧
pemotaya'n	Traveling along."

The melody spans only two notes, starting on a high one for the first syllable of each line and dropping one tone for the other syllables. The last tone of each line is sustained for several beats. Without apparent variation he was accustomed to sing it for a period varying from five to thirty minutes or more for the company to dance to. He accompanied himself with the single-headed dance drum, striking in alternating long and short beats in rapid succession.

Several examples of hunters' songs were obtained from Lake St. John. Some have been transcribed from phonograph records that I made in 1909 during the summer when the men had finished their annual trading with Mr. Hamilton, who was then the factor of the Hudson's Bay Company post there.[3] One of the hunters was from Lake Mistassini, but my notes fail to show his name. His song seemed to contain but one verse, which was translated by Joseph Kurtness, who induced him to sing at the time, as meaning, "I wait for the otter when he comes out." It bears frequent repetition of the word *ntsu'k*, "otter," and alludes to a method of still-hunting the otter in which the hunter stations himself near the lake during a rain waiting for the animal to come out, as is its habit in rainy weather.

From one of the hunters of the Petisigabau band, Antoine André, the following phrases of one of his *ati·k*ᵂ*nakama'n*, "caribou songs," were recorded.

> *nicta'm nika'kwotcistamu'wan*
> *aisime'wo sit tcuna'ga*
> *tcewitci·'metutcemu'yan*

> "First time I try ⟦to⟧ eat
> In Eskimo land, (*tcuna'ga*, no meaning given)
> You come with me to play and dance."

He explained its origin in a dream, in which he encountered an Eskimo hunter with whom he danced and sang and afterward killed plen-

---

3. The cylinders were included in a collection made for the Museum of the University of Pennsylvania bearing the original numbers 98 and 99. They were transcribed by the late Jacob D. Sapir.

ty of caribou. With his song he beat the drum rapidly and evenly, striking about four times to the second. He sang in a loud high shouting voice. A peculiar mannerism he had, in cupping his right hand behind his ear. I asked him why he did that, whereupon he laughed and said he could hear it better that way. The singer in this case did as most of the Naskapi do, in the ending of his words, increasing the enunciation by lengthening the vowels and adding vowels to the closed final syllables, a practice that is done for its emotional effect, they declare. So the word ending *mu'wan* becomes *mu wa'n·a*, or a form may be shortened from *metu'wetci* to *metu'tci*. I observed that his musical affectations were variable in his repetitions.

From Joseph Mackenzie, also of the Michikamau band, comes another, an otter song (*ntcu'k· nəkəmə'n*), the phrasing of which is in the general tone that may be expected from the foregoing.

> *ekwute' tabwe' ni·mi·'nowa'teti·'*
> *katci·' busta'bi· tcecku'k*
> *muko' neci·'kako' ni· pa'nit·*

> "And here enough I am satisfied
> When put [my *nima'ban*] on my back;
> Only [the otter] runs plunging in and out of the snow."

The burden of the song refers to the satisfaction the hunter feels when he carries the otter he has killed back to camp by means of his pack strap (*nima'ban*). The last phrase portrays the animal in his headlong dash of flight through the snow drifts. The drumming of this song was hard and fast.

An interesting example of a song dedicated to the caribou, and at the same time a very old one, was sung for me by Alexandre Mackenzie, nephew of the chief of the Michikamau band. He had learned it from his grandfather, who in turn had acquired it from his father, old Jérome Antoine. The phrase of the composition is

> *uca'm kabe'tc mino'nagonəwa'*
> "Because of him who comes, it looks fine."

The reference to "him" is to the caribou, the coming of which is a vision of joy in the dream of the hunter. The melody was most complicated and wild. The words as given above were embellished with vowel endings so that, as actually sung, the syllables were *uca'* *uca'm* *ḳabetci'* *eminona'gonewatega'*. The singer beat the drum rapidly and sang the phases twice over to cover the song.

A bear song (*macḳ⁰* *uʒnʒḳʒmʒ'n*, "bear his song") may be added from the repertoire of a hunter of the Mingan band, named Tci·na'-bem. The words were:

> *ḳene'yape'wut* *tcina'pema'*
> A chicane is your man (singer's name).

The meaning is obscure, but it was explained as accusing the bear of being a "chicane," a clown. The actual syllables sung were lengthened for lyric effect, being *ḳa* *na'ya* *pewi·'yit* *tcinai·'ya* *pema'ya*. The result was to render the theme almost unintelligible to one not accustomed to the process. The musical phrase was so complicated as to amount to gliding almost through an octave, fast and loud with numerous modulations and variations.

From the examples given a partial idea may be formed of some features of Montagnais-Naskapi hunting songs. They come from seven bands of the peninsula, from widely different quarters (Mistassini, Lake St. John, Bersimis, Shelter Bay, Mingan, Petisigabau, Michikamau). The songs are the property of individuals, and like other property may be inherited from generation to generation. The songs do not appear in the repertory of singing groups, nor are they disseminated through instruction by their owners. They do not seem to be firmly standardized in melody or syllables by the individual singers, although I must make this statement solely upon my own musical judgment. They are, accordingly, proportionately individual in character and conception, the wording forced out of linguistic form. I have never heard two men sing the same song together, and after hearing several attempts of some of them at Seven Islands to learn the songs of others, I doubt if they could reproduce them accurately without living as intimately together as father and son or uncle and nephew. They emanate, according to native belief, from dream suggestions which are carried over from sleep to the waking hour and remembered. They exert an influence upon the game animals as part of the hunter's working equipment. A feature worth mentioning is an attempt to rhyme the word endings in some of the phrases. The padding of song texts by adding syllables and by transforming grammatical phrases is char-acteristic of Algonkian ritualistic songs in general. Even the same syllabic increments (-yat, -yet) appear in Fox and Ojibwa song recitative, as we may observe in the collections by Michelson.[4] The musical qualities themselves, however, cannot be treated until extensive phonographic collections have been made and studied by a musical technician.[5]

Dancing

Religious ceremonial dances cannot be shown to exist among the native populations of the peninsula. Nevertheless, dance performan-ces appear in which spiritual influences are invoked, though they seem to concern only the individual. The dance is called ni'mi'. It is indulged in at times when families come together in the bush, but more especially when they gather at the various rendezvous at the lakes of the interior and at the post and missions along the coast. This, however, is somewhat against the wishes of the missionaries, who do not seem to understand how essential such emotional outlets are to the native's mental balance, or how much better adapted to native mentality these are than the but half-comprehended Mass.

Aside from the social benefits, which they fully appreciate, the Indians recognize a certain physical stimulus in the dance which they interpret as an awakening of the soul-spirit and a development of strength. Sweating is one of the objects of dance exertion. It tends to cultivate strength and bring good luck, for "dancing is a remedy, it lies in the sweating."

A scientific discussion of the dancing is hardly possible for here the art as well as the religion of dancing is not a regulated one. The

4. T. Michelson, *Fortieth Report, Bureau American Ethnology*, p. 112 *et passim;* and W. Jones, *Transactions American Ethnological Society, passim.*

5. The importance of the dream motive in religious music of the whole northern and central Algonkian area is shown by the following quotation concerning the Ojibwa of Minnesota.

"It is said that in the old days all the important songs were 'composed in dreams,' and it is readily understood that the man who sought a dream desired power superior to that he possessed. A song usually came to a man in his 'dream'; he sang this song in the time of danger or necessity in the belief that by so doing he made more potent the supernatural aid vouchsafed to him in the dream." F. Densmore, *Chippewa Music*, Bulletin 53, *Bureau of American Ethnology* (1913), II, 16.

Review of the sacred bundle, or pack, rituals of the central Algonkian area, worked out by Michelson, Har-rington, Radin and Skinner shows dream experience to be their source of origin.

The musical scores of the above series will be published as a separate article after examination by Dr. G. Herzog.

FIGURE 22

Native drawing of two Naskapi hunters of the Ungava band in a canoe, spearing a herd of caribou crossing a lake. One of them after drumming and singing the caribou song, had a dream instructing him to undertake the hunt; then, employing the caribou shoulder-blade means of divination, he discovered the location of the herd. They will now surround and spear all the animals one by one and tow them ashore. After this they will return to their camp and move with their families, erecting a new camp at the locality, to butcher, skin and preserve the flesh of the animals. (Drawn by Shushepish Peta'banu, Ungava band, at Seven Islands, 1925.)

steps are of one form, for men an alternate shuffling with the foot brought down heavily and a shake of the whole body; for both sexes the arms, hanging loosely at the sides, and chest are given a violent jolt at each step.

Dreaming

To dream (*pwamu'*)[6] is a religious process of these peoples. The hunting dream is the major object of focus—*kantó· pwa'men*, "he hunt-dreams" (*nto·'pwata'm mack*ᵂ, "I hunt-dream a bear," *kan-tó·han*, "I hunt"). It is part of the process of revelation by which the individual acquires the knowledge of life. It is the main channel through which he keeps in communication with the unseen world. His soul-spirit speaks to him in dreams. Therefore, dreaming is very

FIGURE 23   FIELD MUSEUM OF NATURAL HISTORY

Bladder-sac of otter containing bear's grease (*opitcipma'nᶜ*). Used by hunters to supply grease for food and in practice of magic and to keep it sweet

6. This element may bear a relation to *bao·*, *buo·*, common to many Algonkian dialects denoting magical transfer of power. F. G. Speck, "Penobscot Shamanism," *Memoirs American Anthropological Association* (1920), Vol. VI, No. 3, p. 249.

FIGURE 24

Sketch of caribou made on a birch-bark comb case by Naskapi hunter to give satisfaction to animal after a dream and successful hunt.

important. We have seen how, when the soul-spirit of man is strong and active, he believes that he may expect from it continual direction and guidance in all affairs. [7] Accordingly, frequency of dreams is a blessing. Anything that will induce dreaming is a religious advantage: fasting, dancing, singing, drumming, rattling, the sweat bath, seclusion, meditation, eating certain foods, as well as drinking animal grease (fig. 23), various kinds of medicine, both alcoholic drinks and drugs, when such things (now forbidden by a paternal government) can be gotten. Then when dreams are obtained, interpretation is required, for who can localize and rationalize without some help even the clearest of these fleeting revelations, even when it becomes habitual to pay close attention to them and to remember as much as possible of them for interpretation during the waking hours? The means of interpreting are by divination. With only a few exceptions, the parts of slain animals, mostly the bones, serve for divination. This engrossing topic in the religious life of the Labrador Indians has received treatment in a previous chapter. A native's sketch of a dream experience and what goes with it is shown in figure 22.

Finally, the dreams obtained and interpreted remain to be paid for; satisfaction to be rendered to the dream source and to the animals whose lives fall victims to its power. The means of compensation are to be found in the respect paid to the animal remains, in the observance of the animal post-mortem rites which we have already discussed, and in the execution of symbolic and decorative art

7. It may not be going too far into the historical perspective to note that Miss M. A. Czaplicka notes for the Gilyak that everyone has a lesser soul residing in the head of the principal soul, and "all that a man sees in dreams is the work of this lesser soul." *Aboriginal Siberia* (Oxford, 1914), p. 272.

designs which serve as memorials to the slain, furnishing them with a kind of satisfaction (pl. xi, lower and fig. 24). The significance and character of Montagnais-Naskapi art is, then, something still remaining to be considered. As for what has just been said in general concerning the theory of dreaming, I have arranged the explanation to present the substance of extended conversations on the subject with members of different bands: Mistassini, Lake St. John, Moisie, Ste. Marguerite, Nichikun, Michikamau. There is evidently still much more to be understood, as one might imagine to be true of a matter so personal and so subjective. A few short dream narratives being available, I will let the natives speak for themselves to illustrate their thoughts. These were voluntary expressions which I hurriedly recorded in my notebook.

One of the dream significances recorded from a Michikamau hunter is that it is a very favorable omen to dream of a good friend, or a "gentleman" (otcima'u, "chief"), and when this occurs the procedure is to take a drink of whisky, even if it is only a spoonful, to cause the dream to be realized. In place of whisky, if none is available, tea may be drunk to secure this benefit. The underlying theory is that the soul-spirit, being gratified and strengthened by the alcohol, will do the necessary work leading the dreamer to success in his next venture. Mackenzie also averred that it was an omen of coming good luck in the hunt for a man to dream that his wife was having intercourse with one of his friends. A gift of some article of clothing or an ornament is believed to act as a superinducement to such dreams. After giving the informant just mentioned one of my red neckties that he admired, he told several of us that later during the winter, when he was short of food, he would wear it about his neck and would then have one of these dreams, which should be followed by a good hunt. To dream of women in general they regard as an omen of happy portent, which makes one think of interesting possibilities in a Freudian investigation of Naskapi dream experiences.

A narrative by Napani' relates how once he had a dream of a tree that had been mauled and bitten by a bear. He was able, it seems, to identify the tree of his dream with one that he knew of. The next day he went to the place and found the tree in the condition as he had dreamed of it. He called upon his friend, David Basil, and they went to the place again and found the bear there hibernating.

According to an opinion generally entertained among these men, to eat much meat is a means of stimulating dreams. Aside from its purely pathological plausibility, this belief is one intimately associated with the influence of animal spirits upon the spirit of the eater. "To eat that which is alive [meat], is certain to bring on animal visitors in dreams" is the substance of a remark I noted by a hunter at Lake St. John.

To dream of an old woman is bad luck—"something unpleasant coming" (Lake St. John).

David Basil never heard of anyone dreaming of seeing himself face to face. The human face seldom appears as a carving or portrayal in Montagnais-Naskapi decoration prompted through dreams. On only one specimen, a carved bone skinning tool, have I observed it. The figures of animals and, in several cases, boats or canoes, dreamed of by the hunter are, however, accepted as devices in birch-bark ornamentation and beadwork.

"Dreams take the place of prophecy, inspiration, laws, commandment, and govern their enterprises in war and peace, in trade, fishing, and hunting. It is, indeed, a kind of oracle. You would say that they are of the sort of the Illuminati. This idea impresses on them a kind of necessity, believing that it is a universal spirit that commands them, so far even that if it orders them to kill a man or commit any other bad action they execute it at once. Parents dream for their children, captains for villages. They have also men who interpret and explain their dreams." [8]

And finally, the statement by Hind aptly summarizes the importance of dreaming in the lives of these people. He says they "follow their dreams with utmost precision, wholly regardless of any consequences other than those to which the fulfillment of a dream may lead." [9]

A close analogy exists between the dream beliefs of the Huron, as recorded by the missionaries to this people, and those of the Montagnais-Naskapi. Like the latter, the Huron interpreted dreams as expressions of the desires of the soul. The relationship of the two culture groups is a subject to be seriously looked into, considering the proximity of their respective domains three centuries ago.

8. *Memoirs of Father Joseph Le Caron*, 1624, quoted by J. D. G. Shea, in *First Establishment of the Faith in New France* (New York, 1881), I, 216.
9. H. Y. Hind, *op. cit.*, I, 190.

Wish Power

An important force at the disposal of an individual through the agency of his Great Man, is one known by the term *mɔtonɔltcigɔ'n* (Lake St. John). Variants for the terms are *mɔtone'itcigɔn* (Mistassini), and *mɔtone'ntcigɔn* (eastern Naskapi). This term is another difficult one to render in English, probably the nearest equivalent being "power of thought." One of its manifestations is the wish. This, we may add, is one of the emanations of *mɔntu'*. So the designation *mɔntu' elte'ltɑk̚*, "spirit-power thinking," is another mode of expressing the process (*elte'ltamɔn*, "he thinks" [Lake St. John]). Wishing, for the accomplishment of one's desires, becomes an important phase of magic, and we hear much, both in verbal discussion and in tales, of hunters, conjurors and legendary heroes attaining their objects by this method. It is practiced in one form by silent communion, in which the individual concentrates upon his desires and waits for his Great Man to make it a reality for him. The Great Man is stimulated, in this case also, by singing, drumming, and rattling on the part of the individual. A most interesting element of the process may be contemplation, the while, of art designs in beadwork, embroidery, or other processes of decoration. This is one of the religious functions of art. While the practice of accomplishment by wish is known in many parts of the world and enters into modern religious thought, we must remember that among these Indians the desire is addressed to the soul-spirit. Hence, while the outward appearance of the practice might suggest a similarity with some aspects of Buddhism, it has certain differences, and while in contrast with the modern theory of desire-power, we may note that Montagnais-Naskapi wishing-thought is not so much connative as supplicative.

The practice of this abstract subjective magic so underlies the spirit of religion here that it is felt to be present in practically all of it, but I will present a few anecdotes illustrating its deliberate employment by hunters as a magical result. The wishing power is accredited with the accomplishment of wonders, knowledge of some of which are first hand to informants, others described by those who heard of them through comment.

The father-in-law of Cimon, a hunter at Lake St. John, had a powerful soul-spirit (*nictu't*). "He once found himself with his family on the north side of Ashuapmouchouan River in the spring just as the ice was breaking up. They arrived too late to cross over and no canoe was available. That night, when they camped, he devoted himself to singing and wishing, and in a short time the floating ice lodged and an ice bridge took form six or eight feet wide from one side of the river to the other. It was just wide enough for them to cross over. Below and above was foaming water. Immediately, when they reached the desired point on the south shore, the ice bridge broke."

Another narrative relates to Napani', also of Lake St. John, who has been referred to as having been a shaman in his younger days. Napani', it is said, once came to a river with his family. Having no canoe he told them to sit in a circle and close their eyes. This they did, and he proceeded to wish and commune with his *nictu't*. When he was finished he told them to open their eyes—and behold—they were all across on the other side!

A story relating to an event that took place among the Montagnais at Escoumains illustrates another phase of the power of divination by wishing.

"An old man one winter had nothing to feed his family with. Then he told his wife and children to go to sleep. When they slept he commenced drumming and singing. Then he spread a sheet of birch bark on the snow in front of the door of the camp, and went to sleep himself. In the morning there were many tracks of hares on the fresh-fallen snow on the bark, leading in several directions. The old man then went in the directions indicated by the tracks and found hares in abundance. Upon another occasion he did the same in respect to caribou."

In this case we may assume that he incited his soul-spirit, by drumming and singing, to induce the hares to betray their whereabouts to him.

Sunbeam Revelation

One of the most interesting and illuminating sidelights on the poetic concepts of the region is to be found in the information coming in some detail from the Mistassini band, but of general distribution from here northward wherever native beliefs have not been forced into the background by the invasion of the crass materialism of the whites. This concept teaches us that the revelations that come from

Tcemɘntu', "Great Spirit," to the devout hunter often take the form of sunbeams falling obliquely from the sky through rifts in a heavy cloud mass, illuminating certain tracts of country while the rest lies in obscurity.[10] The idea as caught by an artist is portrayed in the sketch in plate XII. The revelation in such an instance is that fortune in the form of game lies waiting for the hunter in the districts so shown. The belief applies not only to such a scene in reality, but equally when visioned in a dream. Could anything be more inspiring than the feeling that the areas spread before the eyes of an eager hunter, spotted here and there with the slanting sunbeams over the expanse of the snowclad plateau, are intended as a blessing from the supreme deity revealing life's most needed support. Such phenomena are common in the North, perhaps more so than elsewhere in the forested regions, unless where cloud formations accumulate and the air remains clear, permitting distant vistas over the land. To the eyes of the European such scenes are beautiful and moving, but to the Naskapi they are the response to his prayer—singing, rattling, and drumming. He calls them *tceƙa'cɘƙo pi·cɘma'*, "spottings of the sun." Several tales recorded from one of the Mistassini headmen will define the mental process by which the hunter, when he beholds a sunlit area in a clouded landscape, either in a dream or in his waking moments, knows it for a revelation to him or to the group that sees it, where they may go with full confidence of securing game, or other blessings.

Before turning to the tales of illustration, however, mention should be made of the manner in which the "sun illuminations" are symbolized in art. Upon many specimens of household utensils and the like, obtained from the Mistassini, and other Naskapi bands to the northward and eastward, groups of little spots of red paint are frequently observed. They often take the position of four dots outlining a diamond, with a fifth one in the center (·:·). The dot-figure occurs chiefly upon drums, rattles and dishes which are used for food obtained subsequent to a dream of revelation. These red paint spots are nothing less than symbols of the sun-ray illumination and are placed upon objects in response to the feeling of gratitude for the game that may be killed following a dream. (See pp. 173-74). This reason for employing the red spot figures is given definitely among the Mis-

10. The informant attributing this blessing to the Great Spirit did not conform to the usual belief that it should come from the individual's Great Man. It may have been due to missionary teaching that he referred it to the Supreme Deity.

tassini, and we may infer that where the design occurs in adjacent bands who have become more influenced in their art and religion by association with the whites, the reason formerly prevailed there, too. A similar interpretation also applies to the holes made in bone and wooden utensils (pls. xi, xvi, and fig. 25). When the spot or hole designs, however, are not associated with dream motives, they are called simply "partridge tracks" and pass for implicit magical symbols. We find that the red dots are painted small in size when produced by a young man and larger in size for older men, the size increasing with the age and spirit power of the makers. The same rule of age distinction applies to the number of the spots painted upon drums, rattles, or other objects of utility. (Plate x shows a prayer rattle from the Barren Ground band with a single medium-sized spot in its middle space.) We learn in this connection that, should a young man make the spots large, it would fail in its purpose of bringing him luck. We are told, also, that some men make a single spot for each dream of successful hunting, adding a new spot on drum, rattle, or bark dish each time such a dream works out. One informant, in discussing the sun-spot symbols, pointed to the sunbeams cast upon the walls of his tent as the afternoon rays fell obliquely above the forest. And another indicated the sunbeams shining upon the floor of his house as signs of anticipated blessing in some line of endeavor. [11]

The several tales following in order show the application in life of this most picturesque interpretation of nature's phenomena.

A Hunter Dreams of Sun Illumination and of Killing a Herd of Caribou [12]

The story of the father of Charley Metowe'cic's wife is an instance of the power of a dream of sun illumination as a source of revelation as to where luck awaits the hunter. The man in question had a very clear dream of one of his large lakes thrown into clear illumination by the sun shining through a rift in the clouds. He accepted it as a sign from his Great Man to go there and receive his luck. So to celebrate his fortune in having such a good dream when the food supply had gotten low and the people were dreading a famine, he

11. Mention of this belief was made in a paper by the author, "Mistassini Notes," *Indian Notes, Museum American Indian*, VII, No. 4 (1930), 439-41, from which pl. vi herewith is reproduced showing one of the bark dishes.

12. Generalized Mistassini version from narrative of Charley Metowe'cic, 1930.

called them together to his camp and announced a feast (ma'ḳocan), in which they were to eat all the food that remained before starting out to go to the lake he saw revealed in his dream. He took his drum and sang all his hunting songs for the various animals while the company danced. Soon, however, he stopped drumming and asked the men present if any of them had an eagle feather—the white tail feather with a black tip.[13] But none had one, so he continued singing and drumming.

After the dance and feast were over, the man who was dreamer and host equipped himself for the caribou hunt and assembled the men to embark on the excursion to the lake he had seen in his dream. As they were going forward in single file, the strongest man breaking the trail ahead for the snowshoes, the dreamer called for them to stop and then said that he wanted to go first and head trail. So he marched some distance in advance of the others and, although an old man, he seemed tireless as he led them on. Before long he was observed by those following, to stoop down and pick up something from the snow. Then he held it up for the others to see, and behold it was a white eagle tail feather with black tip, the same as he had called for during the feast. He put it in his hat and proceeded. The occurrence was all the more remarkable since this was still when the ground was covered with snow and the lakes with ice; long before any eagles would come north to nest, and at a time, indeed, when no eagles had been seen by anyone, so there could not have been one in the vicinity at the time. As they went on soon the lake of the vision came in sight and they could see far out from the shore a large group of caribou moving slowly. The party became excited over the prospect of a kill, and the dreamer and leader arranged for them to cut off the band of caribou at the foot of the lake, posting some of the most expert hunters at the point where the animals would reach the shore. Then the dreamer took some of the experts with him and started to run the caribou and shoot them down before they reached the shore. So successful was he that by the time the animals got clear of the ice and the last were about to escape, he himself had shot twelve or fourteen of them. And the men at the edge of the woods killed the rest. They killed the entire herd, but the remarkable part of the event was that they were all large fat bucks except for two

13.   It was explained later that it had come to his mind that he needed an eagle feather to complete the power of his vision.

— 195 —

females. To take care of the mass of meat and skins obtained by the lucky turn, the whole band was moved to the spot, and there they camped for the rest of the season.

The Hunter Dreams of a Fishing Place[14]

The experience of Wisketcani·'c, alias "Little Blacksmith," shows that the hunter may dream of illumination of fishing grounds, as well as hunting grounds, as revealed by the sun. On his hunting grounds was a widening of the river where the current was slack. Here his father had been accustomed to set nets and to take an abundance of fish. But Wisketcani·'c himself had never had any luck there and so had given up trying the place since his father's death. Whenever he passed that way, he always went by without either camping or stopping.

One time in winter, however, he dreamed of this place on his river and saw it revealed by a flood of sunlight while the country round about was in shadow. He dreamed on, seeing himself on the ice at that place in the act of picking up a quantity of chips, as though he had been cutting wood there, and throwing them into a big pile on the bank. To dream of the place was a surprise to him. So not long after he went there and thought he might as well try his luck, and he set his nets there in the ice. The next time, when he hauled net, he got a great many fish, so many that he had them piled on the bank just as he had dreamed of himself throwing chips there. The place turned out to be such a good place for fish for some time after that he moved and built himself a camp there.

Magic in Decorative Art

Aside from its ethnological significance, something should be said of the purely religious aspects of art among these tribes.[15]

Designs painted, embroidered in silk or in beadwork, or worked in cloth or skin appliqué upon garments, and ornaments, incised lines, and dots and patterns upon bone and wooden utensils, constitute their objects of art. It may be observed that tools, also, are often decorated with engraved figures. And that the tools so ornamented are mostly the finer ones made of bone is an indication of antiquity for

14. Narrated by Charley Metowecic, 1930.
15. See reference to connections between art and magic mentioned in the Introduction.

both the objects themselves and the designs. This furnishes a symbolical background out of which practically all decorative devices in art in this area function as spiritual aids.

We thus meet with a scheme of pictorial symbolism which not only establishes beyond further doubt the native origin of the flower and tree patterns, but also their functional application to dream life and spiritual control. This disclosure is not only a new one in the investigation of native American art in a number of its details, but one which, in addition, must alter somewhat our attitude toward floral art representation in America. In respect to religious associations, which are the object of interest at present, it works out that the soul-spirit requires that objects, figures, creatures, colors, and materials revealed to the individual in dreams be represented graphically or by symbols in order that their power (*məntu'*) may be employed to secure success for the individual in his undertakings. If the dream commands and visions should be ignored, the soul-spirit is thought to be ignored. Hence, it would seem that the seat of aesthetic appreciation reposes within the soul. Individualism in symbolic art is accordingly most emphatic, there being little occasion for *motifs* to become standardized beyond what limitations are, of course, determined by local technique and traditional art stock— that is, what the individual artist-dreamer has already seen among the decorated properties of his group.

Among the Montagnais at Lake St. John the techniques of silk- and beadwork, on cloth and skin, of ribbon, cloth, skin and fur appliqué, and birch-bark etching, show wide variation around a few characteristic design properties representing tree, plant, animal, occasionally human, and celestial phenomena. Specimens in museums[16] are now abundant enough to make an interpretative summary much more than a mere tentation.

The pictorial or symbolic representation of the plant or animal whose aid is to be secured, or has been secured, is equivalent to the creature or object itself. Hence, we may say, to put it roughly, that there is an analogy in far northern Algonkian philosophy between symbol or picture and control-power, in bringing the objects portrayed under the dominance of the individual human spirit for the accomplishment of its needs. Work toward this end is generally done

16. A manuscript by the author of this volume is awaiting publication by the Bureau of American Ethnology, giving details of techniques and symbolism in the art of the northern Indians.

under the suggestion of dreams bestowed by the inner spirit residing in the individual. And the spirit, we are told, it strengthened by being afforded the satisfaction of seeing its promptings obeyed, whether it be in the active pursuit of game or in the field of art work, in depicting animal life and nature.

No material, ornament, or design is too insignificant to be recognized as a force in the exploitation of spiritual agencies. It would, of course, be folly not to realize that there has been degeneration from the spiritual level in art and ornamentation where contact with the whites has taken place. Indeed, development in the decorative arts from dream or magic associations is apparent, especially where purely aesthetic interests have to be considered as operating in the evolution of tribal art. Thus we may conceive of specimens of embroidery coming from these areas in which there may have been no deeper motive than the desire to make something pretty with an appeal to the eye. But this is not true of the majority of specimens of the art products of the more remote bands, those which are made for themselves to use in the strenuous life in the bush. Most of the actual products of decorative industry used among the conservatives of these tribes the makers can explain as to design, interpretation, and symbolism if they choose to do so. In northeastern America, however, we find an exception to the general conditions prevailing on the continent, for here there can be little doubt of an aboriginal setting for the fundamental curve designs with tree, flower and foliage values. Whether this development is unique in the art of the northern American regions or whether it is a congener or a descendant of some phase of North Asiatic motivation still remains to be seen. But the correspondences of forms are not to be ignored.

I have previously discussed the magical motives underlying the art in beadwork, braid, or silk embroidery, carving on bone utensils, and etching on birch bark. The motive of decoration arising from the need to satisfy the personal spirit of the hunter or the spirit of the animal encountered in a dream comes from the man. But the execution of the design itself is a matter left to the technical realm of the women. Here the art tradition of the band or group determines the character of the pattern and the choice of outline and colors. The women, it should be understood, seem to have only a general idea of the symbolism involved. It is not necessary for them to interpret their decorations, nor to accommodate them in detail to the revelation of their husbands' dreams. They produce when requested. Hence, their functioning is art in its real sense. The quality depends upon their gifts; and these appear limited or stimulated in degree of excellence or crudeness according to their technical and decorative traditions. The range of variation is quite wide among the different bands. Those of the north and east seem to excel in respect to taste and in the technique of their patterns.

We learn from the bands in the northern portion of the peninsula (Ungava), who employ the technique of painting for the decoration of their caribou-skin coats and leggings, that these designs are worn to help them subdue the game; in short, that animals prefer to be killed by hunters whose clothing is decorated with designs. This explains much in the religious life of the people. Then we learn (Ungava, Mistassini, Natashquan, Michikamau) that the souls of the hunters also like to see them dressed and decorated in colors. And that explains still more.

The purposes of presentation will, I believe, best be served by offering some specific examples of design with some facts regarding motives of their creators and the objectives arrived at in their creation.

When a man dreams he meets another man, it is a sign that some animal is visiting him in spirit form, and so he has to employ divination to interpret the revelation further. Or he may dream of an animal in its proper form. The incident is accepted as an expression of the animal's wish that he be given something; in short, the animal of the dream asks the hunter for something. So the hunter having the dream accepts the charge to satisfy both himself and the animal by having some article, of apparel or use, decorated with a design to bring about this form of satisfaction, *nahe'itam* (Mistassini). At Lake St. John the corresponding term is *mi'lowe'ltam*, "good thought." Therefore, he asks his wife to take some beads or other material used in embroidery and make something to satisfy the animal and his own spirit. Hence, the name given to beads, *mɔnto' mínu'cits*, "spirit berries" (diminutive). This interesting term again involves the stem, *mɔntu'*. Among the Mistassini beads are called *mi'tcɔts*, a term having apparently some relation to the verb "to eat," (*mi'tcu*). A local explanation suggesting itself for this circumstantial correspondence is an assumption that the beads in this instance are symbolical food. Another and a more plausible view is that the latter term is a simple corruption and borrowing of the English "beads" arising from the habit we observe among the bands residing about Hudson Bay of naming things brought in by the Hudson's Bay Company traders. The termination, -ats, would in such a case denote the animate plural. The foregoing is a rendition of the statements of explanation given by Joseph Kurtness.

The Montagnais-Naskapi regard the forest itself as a complex organism; whence the appeal made to trees and flowers through the medium of the representative patterns in their art—the convention-alized tree figures. The shaman also appeals to the "heart of the tree" to obey him.

Games as Magic Devices

The practices of magic also include certain devices which would be regarded as existing purely for amusement were it not for a native attitude that, even though they can hardly be called religious, they nevertheless involve the exertion of magic influence over animals. In such a sense these games (me'towa'gɔn) are quasi-ritualistic. In the first place, native opinion regards them as acting upon animal spirits in contribution to their satisfaction through imitation of their acts. But in a deeper sense the plays or games satisfy the soul-spirit of the individual who indulges in them. The resulting exercises serve in developing a sharpness which we would consider as tactually advantageous, but which the native considers as spiritually strength-ening, by affording pleasure to his Great Man. The function of games is comparable to that of decorative art, since the emotional pleasures of the arts stand forth as nourishment to the soul. Here, indeed, is a semblance of rational psychological theory. I might be accused, possibly, of interpreting the idea in Naskapi thought my-self. But I have had it many times, and by different informants of the old régime, so explained that there is no difficulty in picturing the ease with which it would come forth under the pressure of dis-cussion with any of these Indians who have not been for some time under the materializing influence of the whites in the country. The function of the games also resembles that of wish-power, previously mentioned. Wishing to achieve success in the "hunting-play" is a wish aimed at the killing of animals.

It might easily be shown that the theory of magical motivation could be overrated in considering the acts of ordinary life, as though everything done by the individual must necessarily have a magico-religious or at least some spiritual background. For, once the idea of spiritual interpretation of certain acts connected with subsistence is imbibed, there might be the temptation to read the motive into every performance, no matter how spontaneous it might be. For instance, to be specific, seeing children, as at Lake St. John, playing with pieces of birch bark folded and cut like little canoes tied to a stick might be conceived by the overzealous theoretical convert as having the implication of a prayer rite for a safe voyage in the canoe for the father who is away on the hunt—a natural line of thought if insisted upon. But in reality there is not the shadow of evidence to support the interpretation in this instance.

It would be difficult to decide which of the several types of games is the most serious in the respect just outlined. String figures and a form of cup-and-ball game might claim priority.

String figures (*metowagɔniabï·'*, "play-string"), produced by the manipulation of a loop of string between the fingers, ordinarily known as cat's cradle, are of considerable importance in this region. And while they are played at all times by both old and young, we are told very frankly that they are directed toward the representation of snaring the animals whose likenesses in outline are produced by the really skillful manipulation of the cords. Collaboration in the field has resulted in a study of Naskapi cat's cradles by Dr. Dorothy Kern Hallowell, undertaken in 1924, at the Seven Islands post. She has furnished the accompanying abstract of her cat's cradle material.

Ring-and-pin divining game.—The Naskapi possess a form of the almost ubiquitous cup-and-ball game. This game is the perfection of the scheme by which the play-performance of killing animals becomes influential in the real act. By constantly playing at killing, one will say, the killing is finally accomplished through sympathetic magic. Great Man, too, likes amusement and gets it in games. The ring-and-pin game among these hunters is of but one type—a series of metacarpal bones of the caribou, usually ten, hollowed and shaped to telescope into one another. These are strung on a line of leather and attached at the far end to a marten or caribou tail, at the near end to a pointed bone pin. The latter is often ornamented. A specimen of this important and really characteristic game is shown (pl. IX). It is called *tapi·'gɔn* (eastern Naskapi), *ta'bɔgwan* (Moisie), *nɔkwa-*

ni·abi·' (Seven Islands), *tapəha'n* (Lake St. John), and *ta·panəgi'* (Barren Ground band). [17]

It symbolizes the spearing of game, particularly the caribou, though among the Indians one would hardly suspect this seriousness of purpose amid the hilarity with which it is enjoyed. And I imagine that to many of the younger generation it has lost its significance. At Seven Islands it has the influence of "calling the caribou." Wagering also goes with it. Among the different bands there is no variation in the manner of playing, but some irregularity in the counting values. I will give a few of the local differences in this respect.

The system of scoring in this game seems to be irregular in the values of impaling the holes on the skewer, depending upon the number of bones on the thong. There is general agreement in assigning a value of either one hundred, or ten, for catching the tail on the bone. Some will count this as a win no matter what the value is. Then, for catching all the bones on the bone, a count of ten; for the little holes at the base of the last bone some say ten, some twenty. For other catches some allow a count of one, and others will allow the number corresponding to that of the bone caught, counting from the end.

When the game is played by a number of persons it is passed on to the one sitting next when a player fails to score a count. He who loses the game by failing to reach the count of his opponent must submit to having the winner snap his second finger smartly against his forehead—a mild piece of effrontery. The game and its peculiar forfeit for losing have been met with from the Escoumains Indians eastward and northward. The term employed to denote the forfeit is *pelckwama'gən* (*pestco'*, "to snap the forehead" [Escoumains]). Waugh mentions the game among the members of the Barren Ground band of Naskapi, in the same form as described by me. He gives the following counts: the whole string of bones, fifty; the outermost bone (there being five of them), ten, the next nearest the pin, twenty, and so on. A marten's tail forms the termination. Specimens of the game from the same band, obtained through Mr. White, have the termination of a caribou-hair tail tuft.

From the same source have come three specimens of another form of this game in which a hare skull, a porcupine skull, and another skull replace the hollowed metacarpal bones, the object being to

17. Notes of F. W. Waugh.

catch the skull, on the point of the bone or wooden pin, in one of its orifices—identical among the Labrador Eskimo.

We shall have to include, also, the twirling buzzer in the category of minor magical playing devices; for, while it is operated for the amusement of children as well as adults, the buzzer in its original function "calls the winds to come." The buzzer is made of a single caribou astragalus attached by sinew to the two sticks serving as grips. It is called *tawa'bətsigən* (Michikamau, Ste. Marguerite), *tewe'bətsigən* (Lake St. John).

Another amusement having a hidden serious motive associated with it is shooting with arrows at a target set up in the form of a caribou. Turner mentions this for the Ungava band. The Mistassini enact a similar pantomimic game-hunt, making figures of the caribou from birch splints.

The spinning top is frequently seen. It, too, is a divination game in a light sense. The top is most often made of the end of a cotton spool. It is spun with the fingers. Sometimes it will be asked in which direction meat will be found, and when its motion ceases, the direction in which the stem points will be accepted as an indicator (Lake St. John, Mistassini, Barren Ground). Other questions put to it are, "whose mother can dance best?" "who will be married first?" and so on.

The similarity of some of these minor games of divination with those of Europe is noteworthy in respect to the tossing-up devices and top, suggesting imitation on the part of the Indians. This may not, however, be the case. Both areas may partake of the properties of an old northern culture stratum. The same game, with its divination use, is met with among the Wabanaki. [18]

From a recent article in which were published some remarks concerning games as exerting spiritual influence over game animals in the belief of the Mistassini Indians, I take occasion to quote the following:

"*Game of caribou hunt* —For children to show a desire to play games in the fall before the main winter hunt, either purely for pastime or for divination, is a lucky sign. On the other hand, if

18. A variant of the ring-and-pin game among the Abenaki of St. Francis, employed in hunting divination, is interesting enough to mention here. The information is given by William Watso, ex-chief of this tribe. To a sharpened stick about twelve inches in length, seven rabbit skulls were attached by a thong. In divining by this means, if an odd number of the skulls were caught on the stick, the sign was pronounced unfavorable. Even numbers were, however, favorable; four being more lucky than two, and six more lucky than four. The device was called *soha'* and was used in connection with all kinds of game.

children do not seek pastime with games or toys, it is a bad sign for the coming season. Little girls, for instance, who make dolls of wood and dress them with pieces of cast-off skin, rags, or fur, are prognosticating for themselves a happy and fruitful future as mothers. Again, if the boys make bows and arrows and seem eager to play at hunting, the sign is favorable for a lucky winter. And so the game of caribou hunt may be mentioned as one of particular import. In this a toy herd of small caribou is made, each figure about eight inches in length. The caribou are made from a splint of birch to form the body, neck, head, tail, and antlers from the one piece by splitting, bending, and shaving until by the clever use of eye and knife a remarkably suggestive creation results: one which, while out of proportion, is unmistakable for the great game animal of the North. A series of these figures represents the game to be looked for. Instead, however, of using a toy bow and arrow with which to shoot them, the child players use a snapping stick of spruce by which they propel tiny shot formed by biting off the end of a flat sliver of the same wood.

"The snap-stick is bent back with the forefinger and thumb of the left hand, which at the same time hold the wooden bullet against the snap-stick. The missile is then violently snapped at the figures. To knock some down portends well for the boy's father during the caribou hunting season, and at the same time is thought to develop the boy's hunting power while he is growing up. This play is called *taci'packwu'ni'gan,* 'pulling and letting go.'

"*Hare-hunt game.*—Again we learn of a children's pastime by which an effect is produced on the hares, inducing them to come to the snares set for their capture. This game is the 'hare hunt,' *wapuco'kana'n.* I learned from the second chief of the Mistassini that this magic pastime is usually reserved for that precarious time of the year, toward the end of winter usually, when other game has become scarce and when the remote families are reduced to a diet of hare meat, the least nourishing food and the last to be resorted to when famine is imminent. The father of the family then makes the articles needed for the game and the children are encouraged to play it, to bring the hares as victims to the snares that the starving time may be tided over until better meat may be procured. The articles called for are a series of split birch sticks, called 'snares,' and an equal number of 'hares' whittled out of cedar sharpened at both ends, with a circle of 'curls' made by shavings turned back near the bottom of the sticks. Now the sticks to serve as snares, one intended for each child who is to play, are set up in the ground in a circle outside the tent. The diameter of this circle is usually about twelve or fourteen inches. Inside the circle of snares, the sticks called hares are set in a tight cluster, the parts with shavings at the bottom near the ground. One of the hares in this group is meant to be game for each child playing, the number being the same as that of the snares. Next a small piece of meat, or bread if no meat is to be had, is impaled on the pointed upper end of each hare stick. And now with a few shreds of birch bark as kindling, the shavings at the bottom of the hare sticks are lighted and the fun commences. With a puff and a flare the shavings burn, the hare sticks burn through, and one after another fall with their tiny burdens of meat or bread on their points. Each time that one falls afoul of one of the branched sticks called snares in the encircling fence, it is a catch for the child opposite it, and with a yelp the always hungry urchin snatches the piece of meat or bread from its point and eats it. That is his hare. Those hares which, when their bases are burned through, fall clear of the snares, have to be played again, and so on until the children are satisfied with their luck, or the tidbits of meat or bread are exhausted.

"*Otter-hunt game.* The otter hunt is another divination game learned of among the Mistassini. The procedure is for the hunter to make four bundles, each about five inches long, of cedar 'twigs tied with babiche or thread which he calls 'otters.' Setting these side by side as targets, he stands about six feet away and, with a small bow (about twelve inches long) and arrows, attempts to hit one after the other of the otters. The number of otters hit is the answer to the question, 'How many will I kill on my next hunt?' Should he hit one of them with an arrow, he uses the same arrow for the next shot—this being the lucky arrow. The Mistassini call this *papi· matckwa'n*, 'shooting otter.' The arrow release for the toy bow is the primary but in shooting with a large bow it is the Mediterranean.

"*Cedar-bundle game.*—Catching the bundle of cedar twigs on the end of a sharpened stick attached to the bundle by a string is a game noted for every tribe and band of northern Algonkian, as one associated with the idea of increasing one's luck in hunting. Beneath the idea of luck may lay that of giving practice to the eye and hand

— 205 —

in the manipulation of the thrusting spear in attacking animals. The Mistassini, as well as all the Naskapi and Montagnais bands, play the cedar bundle as a substitute for the more elaborate device in which caribou metacarpal bones hollowed to articulate into one another and strung on a thong, are the objects to be impaled by the sharpened stick or bone—a form of cup-and-pin. The Mistassini call this game *tap'hatəwa'n.* . . . .

"*Drawing lots with sticks.*—A device employed by the young for determining the identity of one who has been guilty of this or that action, whether serious or not, is the following, which might even assume the dimensions of a minor ordeal by drawing lots. A bundle of ten small smooth sticks about an inch and a half in length, among which is one of twice the usual length, is provided. The long stick is called *mahi'kan,* 'wolf.' The sticks are grouped so that they all appear equal as from above, the long one projecting underneath. These sticks are held in the hand of the person applying the test. When the sticks are drawn from the bundle by those accused, that in-dividual drawing the long stick is declared guilty. Drawing lots is called *ma'hikana'tuk*ʷ, 'wolf sticks.'

"*Heart sticking.*—Another method of play, leading at the same time to the determination of luck, is 'heart sticking.' When the carcass of a hare or a marten is being spitted whole before the fire, children take sharp sticks and try to spear the heart of the animal to see who will have luck, those who strike its heart being con-sidered 'chancy,' as the northern voyageurs term it."[19]

The Game Feast

In discussing the manner of treating the remains of various game animals—the bear, caribou, and beaver—there has been occasion several times to mention the somewhat formal feasts which occur when quantities of meat are secured during times when the people chance to be assembled at some gathering place. I shall not repeat what has been said in previously describing them, but shall merely recall them again for attention in a separate aspect, and add some general remarks to point out how this joyous festival is the nearest approach to what might be called a ceremonial religious assembly.

19. F. G. Speck, "Mistassini Notes," *Indian Notes, Museum American Indian* (Heye Foundation), (New York, 1930), Vol. VII, No. 4, pp. 425-32.

Such a festival is known throughout the area by the term, *cabəto-wa'n.*[20] It is the game feast. Several illustrative cases will recall the event. A typical one was witnessed and recorded by Turner some forty years ago among the Naskapi of Ungava.

Feasts are given now and then to celebrate success in hunting and similar achievements.

In 1883 I was invited to attend a feast of furs to be given by one of the most energetic of the Indians. We repaired to the tents spread on the top of a high wall of rock a few rods from my house. As I approached the scene I observed a tent of different construction. It was nearly oval at its base and had a diameter of about eighteen feet and a length of about twenty-five feet. The top was drawn to an apex resembling the common roof of a house. The entrance to the structure faced southeast. On a pole, supported with one end on the apex of the tent and the other resting on a post, were numbers of skins of various animals—wolves, wolverine, beaver, otter, foxes, and muskrat, together with a number of the finest reindeer skins. The sound of the drum was heard within the structure, and as I approached the door the noise ceased. I paused and was invited to enter. Immediately two old men next the drummer moved to one side and motioned me to sit down on the pile of deerskins reserved for me. It was evident that the feast had been in progress for some time. Around the interior of the structure groups of men were idly disposed, some reclining and others standing. Not a word was spoken for some time and this gave me opportunity to look around. The floor was covered with boughs from the neighboring spruce trees, arranged with unusual care, forming a soft carpeting for those seated within. I saw a number of piles of deerskins and several small heaps covered with cloth. To break the silence I inquired if the drum was tired. A smile greeted the inquiry. Immediately an old man came forward, tightened the snare of the drum, and arranged the string, suspending it from one of the tent poles at the proper height for use. He then dipped his fingers into a vessel of water and sprinkled a few drops on the membrane of the drumhead to prevent it from breaking under the blows to be delivered. The performer then seized the drum-stick with the right hand and gave the membrane a few taps; the transverse cord of twisted sinew, holding the small cylinders of wood attached to it, repeated the vibration with increased emphasis. A song was begun and the drum beaten in rhythm to the monotonous chant of *o-ho, o-ho,* etc. Three songs with tympanic accompaniment followed. The songs appeared alike and were easily learned. In the meanwhile, the guests were treated to a strange looking compound which had lain hidden beneath one of the cloths and is known as "pemmican." I was solicited to accept a piece. The previously assembled guests had either brought their own bowls and saucers to eat from or else appropriated those available. Not to be at a loss, one of the young men remarked that he would find one. From among the accumulated filth around one of the center poles supporting the structure a bowl was produced. The man cooly took the handkerchief which was tied around his

20.   The term denotes a dwelling which one "passes through" in entering and leaving, not doing so by the same doorway. That is made by combining several tents to form a long tent in which there may be several fires; the covering is supported by a ridge pole stretched between the ordinary round-tent frameworks.

forehead to keep his matted hair from his face and wiped out the interior of the bowl, and placing a piece of the pemmican within it, handed it to the attendant whose duty it was to offer it to me.

I, however, found it quite inedible. Other guests constantly arrived and some departed, made happy by their share of this compound of rancid tallow and marrow with a due admixture of pounded dry meat of the reindeer. I soon departed, and attempted to take the remnant of the pemmican with me. This was instantly forbidden, and information given me that by so doing I should cause all the deer to desert the vicinity, and thus make the people starve. I explained that such was not my desire, and after wishing continued prosperity and enjoyment, I made my way out. I was then informed that the feast would continue for a time, and wind up with an invitation to the women, who had been hitherto excluded, to come and eat the remnants left by the men. At the end of two days thereafter the feast concluded and a dance took place. In this performance there was nothing remarkable. The men sang songs and kicked up their heels, while the women shrugged their shoulders as they swayed their bodies from right to left, and assumed various other postures, although their limbs were apparently kept in a rigid position, occasionally uttering their plaudits as the men made humorous compliments to their generous host.

The feast was given by one who had been unusually successful in the capture of fur-bearing animals, and, to prove his wealth, displayed it before the assemblage and gave a feast in consideration of his ability. Other feasts of a similar character occur, and differ from this in no special feature. [21]

McKenzie, in 1808, describes the game feast occurring in the fall and in the spring at the time when the hunters left for their winter hunting grounds and again when they returned.

As the fall of the leaves is the beginning of the hunting season, they meet at a sumptuous feast so as to bid each other adieu, communicate what they mean to do, etc. They have another feast in the spring, in order to congratulate one another on their different successes and exploits in the chase, on which occasions their tents, which are generally made small and in the shape of a sugar loaf for the accommodation of a family or two, are now made capacious enough to contain the people of a whole tribe, and in the form of a roof of a house placed on the ground.

In this spacious hall those good folks eat and drink, caper and grunt, until tired, but what affords the greatest fund of merriment and loud peals of laughter is the unexpected, though not unwelcome, report from a *leather gun*, and the wit of the company is displayed in the different construction put upon the purport of the messenger's visit.

They all dance together, the women on one side and the men on the other side of the wigwam, while the greatest man beats the drum and sings, to which they keep time, a very easy matter, as the musician keeps continually repeating the same note, the dancers hopping the same step and grunting at every jerk like so many hungry pigs. [22]

21. Turner, *op. cit.*, pp. 322-23.
22. McKenzie, in Masson, *op. cit.*, pp. 416-17.

Another account, this time a description of a former caribou feast among the Mistassini people, obtained from one of the chiefs of the band, mentions that quantities of caribou fat hardened and formed in squares and bear's grease contained in birch-bark baskets, together with dried caribou and bear meat were piled up in the middle of the large double tent, *cabatowa'n*. Men, women, and children, all were welcome, but not the dogs. The Mistassini generally held the meat feast in spring, sometimes twice a year, but not in winter.

At the feast all the holes in the covering of the lodge, whether it was of bark, skin or canvas, were carefully closed, so that the spirits of the beasts whose flesh was being consumed would not go out and, in consequence, fail to return to life in the others of their kind to be born. Only after all the meat had been eaten would the lodge be opened. The entire quantity of meat secured for the feast had to be distributed to the guests. Should it be impossible to have all consumed it could be left in the "lodge" and eaten later there, but it could not be taken to the dwelling tents. For this occasion the men had their individual stone pipes about which I shall have something to say under a separate heading.

As I have previously remarked, this is the only festival gathering indulged in by these hunters. In its general aspects the feast is one in which the participants are obliged to eat all the meat brought together; a special lodge is erected for the occasion, a large oval in its ground plan; the openings are all kept closed lest the animal spirits who are thronging outside enter or obtain a glimpse of the procedures inside; dogs are excluded from eating the viands or bones; the bones are all pounded and burned; and there is dancing and singing and recitation of dreams by special speakers who volunteer to address the gathering (Mistassini).

The ceremony, none other than the widespread "eat-all feast," is clearly related to the almost universal game feast and entertainment among other Algonkian groups, among some of whom it takes a more serious form as part of the festival known as the Grand Medicine Lodge (Mide'win). It is, possibly, the undeveloped forerunner of certain elements of this important festival in the central regions and about the Great Lakes.

It is hard to see what the main religious aim of this feast may be. Whether intended to placate spirits of slain aimals or whether it is a breaking forth of indulgence in carnal appetite—since we observe

that measures of deceit are taken to include animal spirits from wit-
nessing it—it is certainly an orgy of repletion.

A diagram showing the arrangement of the interior of the feast
lodge is drawn in figure 6. The lodge is composed of several tents
combined, connected by a ridge pole to make a long tent with two
fires. There are entrances at opposite ends of the lodge, and in front
of each entrance a large flat slab of stone, upon which burns a fire.
Here the meat is cooked. The bear skull, in case the feast celebrates
the killing of a bear, is placed facing inward before one of the fires.
The singers of the occasion sit at one side of the lodge at the end
where the skull lies, and here hangs the skin drum ready to be beaten
for accompaniment by the performing singer. When a song is commenced, those who desire to dance do so, all in single file, turning
their steps so as to outline a figure eight in the center of the lodge
between the two fires, going clockwise and contraclockwise. (See
also chap. v, p. 104, fig. 6).

The Ceremonial Game Carrying String (Ni·ma'ban)

In the religious equipment of the hunter throughout this whole
area, a most significant object is the sling or pack strap for bringing
in freshly killed game. This object is called ni·maba'n (ni·mawia·'ban,
Natasquan), a term which might seem to include ni·mi·, "dance,"
and -abi·, "string, cord," though such an etymology cannot be ap-
proved as a positive one. The article is made of moose or caribou
skin. While it occurs with much the same significance throughout the
peninsula, the forms differ in the eastern and western areas. In the
west it is a broad single sling, like the ordinary pack strap but smaller, and often bearing animal figures embroidered in silk. In the east
and north it is a finer braided babiche or tanned leather line having
bead, silk, or ribbon attachments as symbolic ornaments.

To introduce the idea involved, I quote some words of Lake St.
John and Mistassini informants.

"After the pieces of freshly gotten meat had been eaten, especially
if the people had passed through a period of famine or want, the
whole family would build up the fire and someone would beat the
drum. Then all would dance around the fire in rejoicing. That was
to make them forget their suffering of before. When a boy was about
to embark on a hunt, someone would make a ni·ma'ban for him, a

small one, and, when he could go out for small game, give it to him. And he would lay it on the first game he killed, and then carry the carcass back to camp with it. Then as he killed bigger animals he would get new and larger ones.

"Some hunters made a different string each time they went out for big game. Some of the strings had only ribbons or beads as symbols of different animals, while others [Lake St. John] had actual animal figures embroidered on the strap. As the hunter gets older he has larger and larger pack strings and has attached to them the symbols of various animals he would need. They were mostly kept for time of need. In ancient times, having no trade goods, nor trade food, they needed the ni·ma'ban more than they do now.

"When game was killed, the hunter stretched an animal out on its back and put the ni·ma'ban on its neck, the ends running down the body. Then he sat down nearby and smoked his pipe for about an hour. He put tobacco on the bear's heart or in its mouth. The ni·ma'ban can be used only by the man who makes or orders it made, and who owns it. A man cannot say, 'Here, take my ni·ma'ban and go on a hunt.' It would be valueless to another, but if one buys it then he can expect it to be of value. It is done to make the bear or other animal contented when he is attacked by the hunter, so that others will come to him, as he shows himself to be a respectful hunter. If a man starts on a hunt and forgets his ni·ma'ban, he will have no luck, but if next day he takes it, he will get his game."

We see from the above generalized declaration that the game-carrying, or portage string is an object of ceremonial significance.

I have dealt briefly with the ni·ma'ban in a previous paper,[23] from which I propose to quote in part. The three specimens described below are classified as the type of the Pikwa'gami ("Flat Lake," Lake St. John) Indians.

The ni·ma'ban used for a bear hunt is made of well-tanned moose skin. In form it closely imitates the ordinary pack strap, and in fact it symbolizes one. The wide part is bound on the upper edge with a red silk ribbon, and on the lower one with a similar ribbon of green. The scene is embroidered in red, yellow, and light blue sewing silks. This magical object is worn by the hunter who has had a revelation about getting game in the near future. He carries this

23. F. G. Speck and G. G. Heye, "Hunting Charms of the Montagnais and the Mistassini," *Indian Notes and Monographs, Museum American Indian* (1921), pp. 1-19.

decorated strap with him on the trail, and when, true to the revelation, he gets his game, he ties the meat in this strap and brings it home on his back or dragging it on the snow. The hunter keeps the strap more or less in secret, and does not show it lest it lose its power to function as a safeguard against starvation. The figures show trees at each end, the trail and canoe, the hunter with his ax, and the bear trying to cross to a lake which has a cross trail. When the hunter finds and kills the bear, he sits down near it and smokes. After having laid the bear out on its back with crossed paws, he puts black tobacco in its mouth and places the *ni˙ma'ban* on its breast or about the neck. Sometimes, before this is done the hunter places the *ni˙ma'ban* across his head, allowing the ends to fall over his shoulders. He then dances around the fallen game, at the same time singing, thus expressing the hope that he will have to utilize such a pack strap often in bringing back game, and at the same time voicing his joy at the success of his hunt. The length of this specimen is one hundred fifty-eight and a half inches, and its extreme width at the embroidered part is two and seven-eighths inches.

Another example is of tanned moose skin and was made by Napani', one of the oldest Montagnais hunters of the Lake St. John band. He said he used this after returning from a hunt in which he was under necessity to avert famine. When the needed animal was killed, he put this *ni˙ma'ban* on his forehead, dancing around it once or twice singing, rejoicing for luck and success. Old Napani' illustrated how he danced around the fire and sang with the strap on his head—after drinking two bottles of porter and two of strawberry soda which he had me buy at the trader's to refresh his soul-spirit. *Ta'kana'ka' ka'naye*, he repeated many times and with laughter. It was a recompense to the spirit of the beast. This specimen, also, represents a pack strap, and as in the former one just described, symbolizes the desire to use a full-sized one in bringing home a quantity of meat. There are four tufts of red and black ribbons attached; the red ones represent small game and the black ones, bear. This specimen is fifty-five inches long and one and one-eighth inches at its widest point.

Another specimen was intended for a youth going on his first caribou hunt with his father; it was made for Awani'c, son of Simon Rafaël (Lake St. John). This specimen also symbolizes a pack strap and is of soft tanned caribou skin. The broad part is bound with a lavender colored cloth, attached to which are red and green silk ribbons, and a small piece of green ribbon is attached also to the narrow ends, but to the wide part. The red ribbons signify small game, the green ones large game. The scene is embroidered in red, yellow, pink, and green sewing silk, and represents in the center the hunter on snowshoes in the act of shooting a caribou. Behind him is a tree on which is perched a loon; while farther to the right is a lake containing figures of a duck and a beaver. On the left of the caribou figure is depicted another tree, and also a lake in which is a figure of a gull. The curved figures above and below both the "lakes" represent trails. This example is seventy-one inches long and two and a half inches wide.

Two more of the broad moose-skin pack straps for small game, from the family of David Basil (Lake St. John), show figures of animals embroidered in silk. One represents the desire for beaver and otter as indicated by the outlines of these animals, the other has rabbit and bear likenesses, which expresses the wish for large and small game on the part of Basil's son, Joseph.

An example of the flat, pack-strap-like *ni·ma'ban* of the south-western bands is a recent specimen from Kiskisink, in the Lake St. John territory, obtained by Frederick Johnson from an old woman there, Thérèse Clairée. It is eighty-two and a half inches in length, of tanned moose skin one inch wide on the middle portion. There are six red and blue braid ornaments at intervals. The explanation of the specimen given by Mr. Johnson coincides with that of others from this region, and is as follows:

"I was told that there was only one kind of *ni·ma'ban*. This form was used for all animals large and small which were killed by the Montagnais. It was used in the following manner. The animal, after being killed, was laid upon its back with the forepaws crossed upon its chest. The *ni·ma'ban* was then folded in the middle and the fold placed upon the neck of the animal; the rest of the string was laid upon the chest and stomach of the animal, stretching towards the rear as far as the length of the string would allow. After doing this, the hunter sat near the animal and smoked, thinking all the while of the animal which he had killed. At the completion of the smoke the hunter would carry all or a part of the game to his camp waving the *ni·ma'ban*. The old lady said, 'The *mista'beo* of the animal likes that.' She refused to say any more concerning this custom."

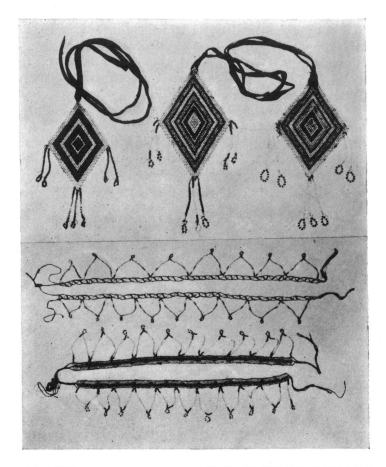

Upper photograph: Beaded neck charms worn by hunters (Barren Ground band), symbols of the forms of game animals. (Center figure, 4.75 inches in length.) Lower photograph: Bead-woven strips worn as charms tied as garters about knee of hunter (Barren Ground band). (Length, 14.25 inches.)

The pack strings of the Mistassini Indians are even more highly conventionalized than are those of the Montagnais. Here they do not take the form of pack straps, but are woven cords.

A large, white tanned caribou-skin *ni·ma'ban* of four strands was obtained from Mia'nckem. The *ni·ma'ban* is Mia'nckem himself, the loop seen at the lower right-hand corner is his head, the loose ends, his legs. He explained the white coloring as symbolic of the caribou, which he needed for his sustenance. The first ribbons symbolize: green, small game; dark blue, bear; red wool, beaver; pink silk, lynx. In the middle the two strings of blue and white glass beads are the legs of the *ni·ma'ban*, and they symbolize caribou. The final pair of strings of beads are the hind legs of the *ni·ma'ban*, and the loose string ends are the tails of the *ni·ma'ban* and symbolize "trails of game." Mia'nckem said that he did not display his *ni·ma'ban* often, because it weakened its power. He carried it in his game pouch and, when approaching his victim, often wound it about his shoulders. If he took small game, he tied the carcass in it suspended thus over his shoulder, the head of the *ni·ma'ban* (the loop) cleated over a stick piercing the nostrils of the animal, like a toggle (resembling the Eskimo method of dragging home seals), the "tails" of the *ni·ma'ban* tied to the animal's right hind leg. In the case of large game, he left the carcass with his *ni·ma'ban* stretched on the animal's chest, its head to the animal's head. Mia'nckem could sell the power of his *ni·ma'ban*, but if he gave it away or lent it, it would not thereafter function.

The length of the string is proportionate to the age of the owner, and in this case is exactly fifteen feet. Young men have small ones, which are replaced by longer ones as they grow stronger and kill more animals.

Mia'nckem was about forty years of age. There was more to learn from him regarding this specimen, but the absence of a competent interpreter prevented the obtaining of further information.

Another example was a small, smoked, caribou-skin string belonging to Metowe'cic's son, who is about twelve years of age. His mother had made this for the boy, who was about to accompany his father on one of his first more serious hunts. The symbolism is as usual; a loop, the hunter's head; the tuft of ribbon and braid representing: blue ribbon, bear; red braid, beaver; and red silk, small game, these being the animals especially desired in this case. The boy is taught the individual symbolism by his father and instructed in the ceremonial procedure when he has killed a beast.

The tail is four-ply, and the two long pieces tie the whole string together for carrying purposes. When a beaver is killed, the hunter pierces the septum of the animal's nose, inserts a stick as a cleat, puts the loop, or head, of the string about the cleat, and ties the two longest strings of the tail around the right hind leg. He then smokes over the beaver and carries it home, slung over his shoulder on the *ni·ma'ban*. If he should get a bear, being unable to carry it alone, he would smoke first, then leave his *ni·ma'ban* on the bear's chest, rolling the animal on its back; the string doubled with its head toward the bear's head. When an animal has been left, to enable the hunter to return to camp for help, it is believed no beasts of prey will eat the carcass while the *ni·ma'ban* is resting on its chest. Possibly the man-smell on the cord may be a safeguard.

Every Mistassini hunter owns and carries a *ni·ma'ban* on his excursions and renews it from time to time according to some religious prompting. Metowe'cic himself had a string ten feet in length, of two-ply, red-dyed babiche. At the end is a loop, the head of the string, in which the cleat of wood is placed when attached to the nose of the slain animal. There were a number of ribbon attachments and flannel tassels which the owner said were rivers and lakes. A larger tassel of ribbons denoted, to his imagination, a bear of which he was accustomed to dream. This part of the *ni·ma'ban* represented the summer hunt. The other portion of the string represented the winter hunt, the white tassels along its length symbolized snow; and the caribou tail at the end symbolized the owner's winter game, the caribou. He summarized the interpretation of this most interesting specimen by saying that it was his road, "*meckənu'*," showing the various kinds of game he secured, and different districts of his country, in summer and in winter. He carried the *ni·ma'ban* with him everywhere he went, keeping it clean inside a pouch. Like the other men, he was reluctant to show it, and added that he would be buried with one when he died. In an apologetic tone, he added in my ear, "The *ni·ma'ban* is not intended to harm anyone. It is not directed against anyone's welfare." I agreed with him.

Another example of the color symbolism associated with various game animals in the carrying string, appears in a specimen seen in the possession of a hunter now living with the Mistassini band, but born at Lake Nichikun. His string was a braided babiche one, colored red. Green ribbons attached to it denoted a desire for luck in finding beaver, as did also a quantity of red silk tassels; pink ribbons for caribou; blue for bear; pink silk tassels for lynx; and yellow silk tassels for red fox.

Among some twenty or more specimens which have been collected from the eastern bands, the following may be noted as illustrative of the forms and decorations of the ni·ma'ban.

One (Ungava band) is made of three-ply braided caribou babiche eighty-seven inches in length, used for carrying otter in wintertime. At the head are three beaded tassels with loops. The colors are mixed; at the other end, fifteen inches from the termination, are two single bead tassels with loops which symbolize "legs," and at the extreme end a bead tassel with two loops. (Made by Mani.)

Another (Ungava band) is made as the preceding, also for otter. At the ends are tassels of blue and green silk symbolizing the otter, with the same repeated at intervals along its length. (Made by Margaret.)

Yet another (Ungava band) is made of three-ply twisted babiche dyed red, twenty-five feet in length, used in winter for dragging otter. This specimen has no tassels nor beads, the color symbolism being that of game in general. At the head is a large loop to go over the hunter's shoulders.

Plate XIII, F (Michikamau band). Made of two-ply twisted babiche dyed dark red, tassels of blue thread and green ribbon at both ends and near middle, which symbolize otter. Length, ninety inches doubled. (Made by wife of Chief Sylvestre Mackenzie.)

Plate XIII, G (Michikamau band). Made of single strand twisted babiche dyed red and intended for transportation of otter on snow and ice. The specimen is undecorated and explained as being of the type used by a shaman. No ribbons or beads were needed in this case because his power was considered sufficient without them. (Made by Chief Alexander Mackenzie.)

Plate XIII, C (Ungava band). Made of three-ply braided babiche in natural color. Length, seventy-eight inches doubled. This contains four beaded tassels with loops at intervals of eighteen inches apart, ten inches from end where small wooden toggle is fastened. At intervals of eighteen inches are three pairs of beaded tassels, blue and yellow. The informant stated that these represented the hunter, whose quest in this case was for beaver. (Made by Pien Wapistan.)

Plate XIII, D (Ungava band). Made of three-ply babiche in natural color, sixty-four inches in length. Used for dragging otter in winter-time. Large loop at end has bead tassels with loops in mixed colors. (Obtained from Pien Wapistan.)

Plate XIII, A (Nichikun band). Made of quarter-inch strip of tanned caribou leather in natural color. Toward ends cut into short fringe, with heavy wool red fringe tassels at extremities. This is intended for a little boy in his excursions about camp in pursuit of hares. Length, forty inches doubled. (Made by Clara Hestor.)

Another (Ste. Marguerite band) is made of three-ply caribou skin in natural color, red and pale blue with three bunched wool tassels, one at each end and one in the middle. Intended for beaver, as indicated by blue yarn and tassels, or for otter, as indicated by green. Made for summer use. (Obtained from Ely Fontaine.)

Yet another (Michikamau band) is made of strong three-ply caribou babiche in natural color and with no embellishments. This was intended for use in dragging caribou over lake ice. The long loop was to be attached to the main branch of the right antler, the two men to drag the animal by pulling on the branching lengths of the *ni·ma'-ban*. Length, forty inches doubled. (Obtained from Alexander Mackenzie.)

Plate XIII, E is a short string made of three-ply black, red, and white hide braided, and is intended for use in connection with caribou, as shown by a blue tassel as the end, and for game of any character, as is shown by the red tassel with it. (Obtained from Batiste Picard, Seven Islands.)

Another specimen (François Fontaine, Seven Islands) is a ply-cord of babiche dyed red, with a portion of its end forming a loop going over the head and shoulders of the hunter, who is to drag his game behind him on the snow. The red portion drags on the snow for some distance where it is attached to the head of the slain animal. The red ribbons tied to it symbolize beaver; the green, otter.

It strikes me as probable that something related to the ceremonial game-carrying string may exist among the Athapascan of the Northwest. Only one reference to its occurrence, however, has come to my attention. Tappan Adney, in *Harper's Magazine*, writing on "Moose Hunting with the Tro-chu-tin" [or "Klondike Indians"], observes, "After cutting off a chunk of ten to fifteen pounds of meat for each person present, the rest of the meat was covered with snow, and the smaller pieces were wrapped in spruce boughs and made into a pack, *a braided rawhide cord which each carried* being used as a string." [24] Unfortunately we cannot speak of the distribution of this practice until it has been systematically inquired into in the surrounding areas.

From the Barren Ground band of Naskapi we have a series of fourteen pack strings obtained for me by Mr. Richard White, Jr., in 1928. The following list gives a brief description of each one and its use. They form a set of ceremonial articles used by an individual named Sasakwa, originally of the Ungava band, now affiliated with the Barren Ground people.

No. 1. For otter hauling on snow, twenty-one feet long. Tanned caribou skin, three-ply braid. Sixteen inches red at each end. No. 1A. For otter hauling on snow, twenty feet, four and a half inches long, three ply, one end sixteen inches red, opposite end fifteen inches red. Tanned caribou skin.

No. 2. For porcupine hauling on snow. Seventeen feet long. Tanned caribou skin, three ply. Alternating red and plain with spaces varying from six inches to twenty-nine inches. No. 2A. For porcupine hauling on snow. Thirteen feet, nine inches long. Tanned caribou skin. Single string, twenty inches red at each end. About twenty inches in middle of string slightly reddish in color.

No. 3. For carrying otter on shoulder. Eight feet, eight inches long. Tanned caribou skin, three ply. Eleven inches red at each end. No. 3A. For carrying otter on shoulder. Ten feet, eight and a half inches long. Tanned caribou skin, three ply. Twenty-five and one-half inches red at each end.

No. 4. For carrying porcupine on shoulder. Tanned caribou skin, three ply. Ten feet, one and a half inches. Alternately plain and dyed red for about six-inch spaces varying between. No. 4A. For carrying porcupine on shoulder. Eighteen feet, nine inches Tanned caribou skin, three ply. Twenty inches red at each end. Some red in middle of string unevenly dyed.

No. 5. For carrying mink on shoulder. Seven feet, eight inches. Tanned caribou skin, three ply. Six inches red at each end. No.

5A. For carrying mink on shoulder. Eight feet long. Tanned caribou skin, three ply. Eight inches red at one end; opposite end, seven inches red.

No. 6. For carrying marten on shoulder. Eight feet, one inch long. Tanned caribou skin, three ply. Six inches red at each end. Sixteen and one-half inches red in middle of string. No. 6A. For carrying marten on shoulder. Three feet long. Tanned caribou skin, three ply. Nine inches red at each end. Seventeen inches red in middle of string.

No. 7. For carrying beaver on shoulder. Six feet, one inch long. Tanned caribou skin, three ply. All red. No. 7A. For carrying beaver on shoulder. Five feet, ten inches long. Tanned caribou skin, three ply. All red.

The Sweat Lodge

To the Montagnais-Naskapi the sweat bath is a means of strengthening the body and reinforcing the soul-spirit of the individual. It is regarded as the means by which the Great Man may be enabled to reveal the whereabouts of game through the medium of dreams, and at the same time as a means of weakening the resistance of the animal. The actual procedure is the usual one in North America. The lodge is a low, dome-shaped one. Stones are heated and passed inside where the hunter crouches, sprinkling them with water, remaining within until the heat is out of the stones. He may sing or rattle during the process. An interesting opinion was expressed by a Mistassini hunter, namely, that the water extorts pain from the stones which causes them to cry out and finally give forth their power for his service.

The Montagnais-Naskapi do not plunge into a stream or lake after the sweat bath. They cool off gradually. Waugh records the same fact for the Indians at Davis Inlet. He states that they take the bath to alleviate pains in the body. After the sudatory which, he says, is continued until the person urinates, the urine is applied to the wound. One is left to infer that the process is employed, accordingly, to heal wounds.

The sweat lodge is called mədətca′n, mətətsɑ′n, without much variation among all the bands.[25] The word contains the element,

25. Waugh's notes on the Barren Ground band at Davis Inlet give the term as məd·icăn. He apparently wavered somewhat in his decision of its meaning, for on the margin of his notebook it is entered that the word must be wrong.

mɔd[ə], which has the indications of relationship with other terms concerned with the practice of shamanism.

While I have singled out the topic of the sweat lodge as a separate one, it scarcely seems necessary to assemble the information already given. Most of it may be found under the treatment of rites concerning the bear, for it would seem that in this particular region the sweat bath has developed into a means of control over that animal.

Mr. William Cabot informs me[26] that in the summer of 1920 he made a trip overland with the chief of the St. Augustin band of Naskapi and a group of twenty-one individuals. During the journey of thirty-two days, the men of the party "put up" ten sweat baths.

The Shot Pouches

Before the general acquisition of rifles of the modern type the Indians of the whole northern region used the muzzle-loading guns discharged by means of the cap lock. This required carrying with them in the field the pouch containers for shot, percussion caps and powder (pls. xiv, xv). The shot pouch, which is the larger of the two, is known everywhere among the bands as *pi·tɔcɔna'n*, the cap bag as *ma'tɔcɔnan*, "match bag," or *ka'pmiuc*, "cap container," The size of the shot pouch is determined by the size of the hunter's fist, usually about five or six inches. The cap pouch is large enough for two fingers. For the percussion caps and leaden shot, pouches were made to hang suspended on the front of the body held by a cord or bandolier passing around the neck. A generation ago these pouches were an indispensable part of every hunter's equipment. Their position on the body was such that the caps and shot could be handled with the celerity required in loading and reloading while running, if necessary. I might add that, although the muzzle-loading cap-lock rifle has now largely passed out of serious use, there are still some of the men among the remote bands who find these weapons valuable through the easiness with which they may be repaired when occasion arises, and the cheapness with which they may be ammunitioned. In the age of the cap-lock rifle the shot and cap sacks reached the peak of their development, for the same period marked the economic supremacy of the Hudson's Bay Company, from whose stock of trade goods an abundance of beautiful beads, red and black

26. Correspondence, February 14, 1921.

cloth, and silk thread could be supplied. These commodities combined to enable the Indian women to express their deepest artistic sentiments, so the pouches flourished as the most ornate product of native art. The anterior history of the breast ammunition pouches does now, however, terminate in this period, for they may be understood to have existed before the era of firearms as the carrier for fire-making instruments and other equipment in constant demand among the hunters when they were on the track of game. In the several capacities mentioned, as firebag or as shot and cap pouch, the breast pouch, as I have already remarked, is universal from the Montagnais-Naskapi across the North among the Cree, northern Ojibwa, and the Athapascan tribes from Hudson Bay to Alaska. This appears from pictorial representations and specimens in various museum collections.

The wearing of a pouch suspended on the breast suggests reference to the former practice of carrying the knife in a like manner. We get an occasional glimpse of this when mention of the ancient bone dagger is made. Tradition says that the long knife of the dagger type shaped from the tibia of the moose, as we learn of it at Lake St. John where I have had specimens made by those who knew of them, was carried in a leather scabbard hung by a cord or band about the neck. The moose-skin scabbards were decorated with curve designs. Thus we have two symbolically ornamented carrying sacks worn on the chest, the fire-bag with its successor the shot-pouch and the dagger sheath. Both these articles seem to have acquired significance also, in the Plains culture-area and in the eastern woodlands, where they are in evidence in old accounts and drawings. Their extent takes in the Hudson Bay region to Alaska, the northwest coast tribes, practically all the Athapascan, and the northern Plains tribes. [27] So much for the distribution of the article which we see is a fundamentally ancient one in the region.

The next step in our quest is to consider the magical significance attached to the decorations with which shoulder pouches are invariably provided. They are one of the instrumentalities of individual religious life. Everywhere throughout the peninsula speci-

27. We learn from the records of King Philip's war that the Wampanoag of Massachusetts wore their scalping knives hung in scabbards about the neck; suspended at the back ordinarily, but worn in front during time of war. The beaded shot pouch worn at the breast was also a Mohegan-Pequot article, and likewise old pictorial representations of the Delawares show the firebag and pipe bag of skin decorated with wampum worn on the chest. Examples of the breast knife sheath are also shown on men of the Central Algonkian tribes in paintings reproduced in *The Aboriginal Port Folio*, by J. O. Lewis (Philadelphia, 1835), *passim*.

mens were obtained, those shown in the illustrations indicating their wide range and varied form. In every case I found them held in high esteem by their owners as elements in their hunting equipment. The designs appearing on their facings were in many cases deliberately described as representations of trees and flowers (Lake St. John, and Mistassini), or trees and leaves (Ste. Marguerite, Moisie); as celestial symbols (Nichikun); as geographical symbols, rivers, hunting trails, mountains (Natasquan); and as "soul," "heart," or "Great Man" (Barren Ground and Ungava). A more intensive inquiry is undoubtedly called for concerning these pouches. So while the accompanying interpretations are based upon fewer than two dozen specimens at the present time, there is something valid in what is indicated in the first step of investigation. In short, the designs are talismanic; functioning, according to the belief of their owners, as means by which their individual spirits acquire mastery over those of the game animals.

Here again, we encounter the usual concept of soul-spirit control over nature in another of its many expressions, thoroughly consistent with other manifestations. The portrayal of geographical features and the botanic realm of nature carries us to the same field of magical art that we find underlying the painted designs on the skin coats of the people of the Ungava and Barren Ground bands.

Geographical symbols seem to stand out in the pouch designs of the Natasquan band, floral and arboreal figures in those of the bands from the southwestern portion of the peninsula, especially about Lake St. John. In the northern and northeastern bands, however, the specific symbol of the "soul-spirit," "great man" or "heart," demands attention. And here the pattern of the four, or the six-lobed flower-like figure is the paramount design (fig. 2, and pls. xiv, xv). From the Mistassini band northward to Ungava, the shot pouches show this as the central figure of the decoration, and it is given the interpretation mista'beo by the hunters who will disclose their inner sentiments during moments of candor. I might mention that I chanced to learn these interesting facts only lately in my investigation (1924), in connection with the design in specimen plate xv, which was obtained from Pien Wapistan of the Michikamau environs. He parted with this pouch reluctantly and at an exorbitant price. He claimed that it was made by a woman from Ungava. Upon being questioned as to the symbolism of its beadwork designs, he said that the wavy lines near the border were paths (*meckenu'*) and that some of the smaller patterns were flowers (*wepəgwu'n*). When I pressed him for the meaning of the flower-like central figure, he talked fast in an undertone with his wife and turned toward me, without moving his body from its reclining pose, without replying. After a pause I pressed him again for its meaning before producing my payment. Laconically he broke the tension by replying, "That, indeed, is my Great Man!" Then he enveloped the pouch in a rag, handed it to me, and asked me to take it to my quarters and show it to no one else.

A scrutiny of other shot pouches in my own and in museum collections from the northern part of the peninsula, and indeed westward about James Bay to the Cree of Manitoba as we see them represented in the few publications illustrating such material, show the provenience of a similar central figure (rosette) in the same place. It may be inferred with some likelihood of reason, I believe, that close investigation of symbolism among the latter groups would discover a similar value adherent to this pattern on the shot pouches there.

An observation may also be made regarding the outline form of the pouches, namely, that those of the southwestern bands of the peninsula have a rounded lower margin and a straight top; those of the extreme easterly bands are rectangular, while those of the bands from the intermediate territories have the rounded lower edge but a curved heart-shaped top, with the opening halfway down the front. These distinctions of form are indicated geographically in the series illustrated.

The Bone Skinning Tool (Mitsəkwu'n)

Another object of special utility having religious associations is the bone skinning tool known among all the bands as *mitsəkwu'n*. A representation is shown in figure 25 A and in plate xvi. Ordinarily, they are made from the leg bone of the bear, though occasionally caribou, moose, even lynx leg bones for work on small pelts, are used. The bone is cut cleanly at one end and obliquely at the other near where it broadens, thus forming the blade. Frequently, six to ten or twelve fine notches are filed in the blade to improve its value as a scraper—a secondary function. It is a definite teaching among these hunters that the slain beaver feels satisfaction in having its pelt re-

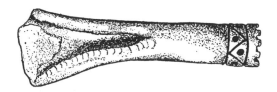

FIGURE 25 A
Bear-bone skinning tool decorated with carving to satisfy the
spirit of the slain animal.

moved with the leg-bone skinning tool. And so it becomes a religious
obligation for the righteous-minded hunter to skin the beaver with
such a tool. The bear, too, out of whose leg bone it is commonly
made, reacts favorably to this procedure, according to some process
of native reasoning. Some hunters at Lake St. John will use only the
bear bone for this purpose, and only use it in skinning beaver. Nevertheless, many specimens made of leg bones of other animals, and
used in skinning them, have been collected, as appears in the figures.

Here we find, as in other cases where decorative designs are
placed upon objects of utility, that a stimulus comes to the hunter
in one of his dreams to try his luck for beaver. Should he succeed
in his excursion, he then "pays for" the admonition by decorating
one of the tools used in preparing the flesh or hide of the animals so
obtained. The bone skinning tool comes in for a large share of such
treatment. Almost half of those I have collected from various hunters
have geometrical figures filed upon their handles, and in a few the
ornamentation is carried further by blackened dots and holes drilled
through the walls of the bone.

Smoking as a Rite

That the smoking of tobacco is an instrumentality of magic among
the Montagnais-Naskapi is apparent from several sources. And
yet tobacco smoking has come into their life only since the advent of
Europeans into the north. No tobacco was raised by them nor was
the fashioning of stone pipes possible without metal tools. The
Hudson's Bay Company in the eighteenth century may be logically

regarded as the source of introduction, this being apparently the only avenue of barter through which the weed could have reached their hands in the quantities demanded. Tobacco now forms one of the most important materials with which the hunters throughout the peninsula supply themselves from the trader's stock. An average amount required by a family during the winter in the Lake St. John environs would be no less than ten pounds. The earlier trade pipes were evidently of clay, whereas they are nowadays nearly all of briar wood. While we cannot readily conclude what were the forms of the original smoking pipes supplied to these Indians, it seems apparent that among the different bands of the peninsula distinctive shapes and proportions came into vogue when they began to make them for themselves. Thus we meet with the deep tapering bowls (pl. xvii) with small "keel-shaped" bases among the northern divisions from Lake Mistassini north and east, the smaller bowls with larger keeled bases between the Mistassini band and Hudson Bay, and a similar shaped bowl with a smaller base from the Lake St. John Indians south and southeast. The latter outline seems also to prevail in the stone pipes of the Wabanaki divisions, Penobscot especially. They are all made of the handsome native banded slate of the region. Constructional characteristics and distribution of type are not our concern at present, so we next turn to their function as spiritual media.

In the various dialects of the peninsula to smoke is termed *pi''-tua'n*, the pipe is *(u)cpwa'gən*, when of stone specifically designated as *acini'' ucpwa'gən*, "stone pipe," and tobacco, *tc'stema'u*.

The beaded ornaments appearing in some form on practically all ceremonial pipes attaching the stem to the bowl, are an illustration of the *mʌntu'* power in beads reinforcing the power of the act of smoking.

Approaching the topic from a generalized viewpoint, smoking is substantially a means for gratifying the soul-spirit (*nahe'itamən* [Mistassini], *milowe'ltamən* [Lake St. John], "to satisfy" (see discussion on p. 42), as we learn from the testimony of the hunters. Its results, namely, the dizziness experienced by inhalation, the narcotic effects in general, are to them the proofs of its influence upon the heart, the Great Man, or soul-spirit, as will be recalled from an earlier chapter. During the intervals given to meditation concerning the problems of gaining material subsistence, the hunter indulges in smoking his stone pipe. For, despite the almost universal adoption of the wooden pipes sold them by the traders, some of the more conservative individuals possess the native-made stone pipes which to them represent the proper means for inducing the sensations from smoking that they associate with spiritualism. Frequently, they refuse to part with specimens of the fine stone pipes, keeping them as treasures to be employed in their silent communion with self. The bead-woven strips usually seen attached to the stem and bowl of the pipes made by the northern bands are further indications of their sacrosanctity. In the same category fall the carved bone pipe cleaners (pl. xi) and the multiform tobacco bags (tc'stemawu'c) so extensively used by hunters in every part of the territory. As part of the spiritual hunting equipment the smokers' articles are all helps in the pursuit and securing of game. Their use, also, is regarded as a stimulation to the hunters' mental faculties, or as the individual would explain it when asked pointedly about them, they help secure "good luck." The idea of fumes as incense does not seem in any sense to apply in this region. Their influence rather is felt to be retroactive upon the smoker.

Another observation is called for: that apart from its psychic aspects smoking has become a common habit, a profanity indeed, among the northern Indians of all ages and both sexes. It is chiefly in connection with the stone pipes that the practice holds to its religious function.

String Figures from Seven Islands

The name *pi'cagonia'bi me'towa'gən*, "skin-string game," is given to the string figures which are quite commonly played among both the children and adults at Seven Islands, whose hunting grounds lie at great distances in the interior. They say that they thus amuse themselves in winter in the woods when there is nothing else to do. Others tell how they make these figures to bring good luck in the hunt, this particularly being the case with such patterns as the

"caribou," "throwing the spear," and some other animal representations. From our observation, the men seemed to know more about
the play than the women. With the exception of the "birch tree"
and the "trail," indulged in by the women, it was a game for two
persons. Another interesting observation is that the majority of the
figures, all the complicated ones in fact, were made by one man,
Peta'banu, and the craft seemed unknown to the others; and this
man, who came from Ungava, was often, perhaps in jest, perhaps
in seriousness, called a conjuror.

The ensuing section is the contribution of Dr. Dorothy Kern Hallowell, who, with Mr. W. H. Hauser, gave considerable time to
collecting data on string figures of the Indians at Seven Islands in
1926.

Without desiring to enter unduly into the details of the string
figures, the subjoined notes of Dr. Hallowell's bring out certain points
concerning the distribution of names and forms of the Montagnais-
Naskapi as compared with those of the Eskimo. The table shows
facts of historical significance in the study of interaction between
the two peoples.

"Since limited time did not permit my learning to reproduce these
figures, I was able only to make a collection of the finished products.
It is accordingly not possible yet to make accurate study of distribution of similar patterns among other peoples without knowing the details of the processes. With our prsent information it is only possible
to compare a sketched figure with our figure, sewed to a card. Even
if the final product is the same, the procedure might have been quite
different. Of forty-two figures made by the Naskapi and two trick
plays, fifteen, or about one-third, are found in other tribal groups.
Some of the figures vary slightly, for instance in a different twist, but
the finished pattern is at once recognizable as the same.

"The comparisons are based upon Eskimo string figures studied
and treated in great detail by Jenness.[28] Some references to figures
listed by Mrs. Jayne are also included.[29]

"The distribution is as follows: (The numbers in the Naskapi
column refer to those of the list which follows:)

28. D. Jenness, "Eskimo String Figures," *Report of the Canadian Arctic Expedition, 1913-18*, Vol. XIII, Part B (1924), pp. 1-192.
29. C. F. Jayne, *String Figures* (New York, 1906).

Naskapi Name	Reported by	Location and Names				
No. 4 wolf	Jenness No. 33	Central Alaska — lake fish	Northern Alaska — spirit of lake	Coronation Gulf — fish nibbling hook	Mackenzie Delta — mammoth	Eastern Eskimo — mammoth?
No. 5 rabbit	Jenness No. 24	Central Alaska — caribou	Northern Alaska — rabbit	Mackenzie Delta — caribou	Coronation Gulf — caribou	Eastern Eskimo — caribou
No. 6 wild goose	Jenness No. 139		Northern Alaska — swan	Mackenzie Delta — swan	Coronation Gulf — swan	Eastern Eskimo — swan
No. 10 caribou	Jenness No. 34	Central Alaska — lake fish	Northern Alaska — spirit of lake	Mackenzie Delta — mammoth	Coronation Gulf — fish nibbling hook	Eastern Eskimo — mammoth
No. 11 2 little caribou	Jenness No. 57			Mackenzie Delta — 2 fawns	Coronation Gulf — 2 fawns	
No. 13 2 porcupines	Jenness No. 116			Mackenzie Delta — mice		
No. 19 scissors	Jenness No. 36	Chukchi — whale's head	Central Alaska — shovel	Northern Alaska — upraised arms		Eastern Eskimo — shears
No. 25 Indian leg	Jayne Fig. 810	Nunivak S. (Eskimo) — legs				

Naskapi Name	Reported by	Location and Names				
No. 29 Eskimo feast house	Jenness No. 10			North Alaska — platform		
No. 33 diver	Jayne Fig. 510	Navaho — twin stars	Zuni — lightning			
No. 36 birch tree	Jayne Fig. 825	Tanana — raven's feet	Navaho — tent			
No. 37 birch tree	Jayne Fig. 272	Navaho — 2 hogans (tents)	Cape Bedford — 4 prong spear	Princess Charlotte Bay — speared kangaroo	Ireland Scotland B. E. Africa	
No. 38 trail	Jenness No. 130		Northern Alaska — mountains	Mackenzie Delta — mountains	Coronation Gulf — mountains	
No. 43 seal stomach	Jayne Fig. 775	Batwa Pygmies, Negrito Philippine, Chippewa, Osage, Navaho, Apache, Omaha, Alaska Eskimo, Barrow to Coronation Gulf, Eskimo of Nain Labrador.				
No. 34 birch tree	Jayne Fig. 556	Navaho — hogan (tent)				

"Thus, as far as reported only six out of forty-four possibilities are found in other eastern Eskimo tribes, and only two of these have the same name (goose and shears). There are only fifteen similarities to the string figures of North American Indian tribes, although some of these have a much wider distribution, reaching Africa, Australia and even Europe.

"The following is the list of figures collected from various individuals among the Naskapi in 1924 at the Seven Islands post.

"(1) Dog; (2) wolverine; (3) fox; (4) wolf; (5) hare (rabbit); (6) wild goose; (7) hare, his ears; (8) hare, sitting down; (9) white-headed eagle; (10) caribou; (11) two caribou; (12) white bear; (13) porcupine, head bent out of sight under body; (14) spear for caribou in water; (15) "twisted" in any fashion at all; (16) saw; (17) saw; (18) Indian canoe; (19) scissors; (20) electric lights; (21) door; (22) bed; (23) eye glasses or goggles; (24) canvas tent; (25) foot, leg, thigh or Indian leg; (26) Indian writing; (27) snowshow trail or crisscross; (28) Eskimo house of snow; (29) Eskimo feast house; (30) flower; (31) barren where neither trees nor flowers are; (32) flower species; (33) diver, kingfisher; (34) birch tree (five branches at each end); (35) birch tree (three branches at each end); (36) birch tree (four branches at one end); (37) birch tree (two branches at each end); (38) letter "M," or trail; (39) conjuror's house; (40) white man's house; (41) man sitting down; (42) window; (39-42 were not collected, but Peta'banu was seen making them).

"Several string tricks were observed: (43) seal stomach (chain stitch on fingers); (44) string through hole around neck or finger.

"Figure 7, made by Jos. Gabriel (Michikamau band), figures 15, 24, 38, made by Clara Hestor (Nichikun band), figures 36, 38, made by Ely Fontaine (Ste. Marguerite band), figures 1-14, 16-23, 25-35, 37-44, made by Peta'banu (Ungava band). Figures 37, 38, made by many others.

"I may add, by way of comment, whereas Naskapi string figures show considerable resemblance in form to those of the Eskimo, and there is some reason to think of borrowing from these sources, we do not find the same superstitions associated with the string games among both peoples. The Naskapi have no compunctions against playing them in summer, nor is there the belief in a master spirit of string figures here, as Jenness records of the Eskimo. And especially is the sun-snaring belief of the Eskimo not found among these Indians. If the figures are borrowed from the Eskimo, the Indians have put their own game-snaring intentions into the practice."

MEDICINAL PRACTICES AND
CHARMS FOR HUNTING

Chapter Eight

EDICAL practice has been only weakly developed among the Montagnais-Naskapi. Frequent questioning among various bands shows general knowledge of but a few herbal curative properties. Lists of these obtained from the Lake St. John and Escoumains bands of the southwestern group have been published in previous articles.[1] Even here, in a warmer zone than that occupied by the northern bands, the list of herbal cures is insignificant as compared with that of Algonkian peoples below the St. Lawrence. Commenting upon this situation with the headmen of the Lake St. John and Mistassini bands, I was told that in the North there are fewer sources of plant life upon which to draw. This is the native explanation, but some culture historical factor other than this is evidently at work. It might be thought, as a result of analysis of the character of thought among the northerners, that practical experimentation with botanical properties has languished through the stronger development of magical theory.

Disease arises from neglect of observance of requirements of the soul-spirit; so does death. Also the "arrival" of alien and hostile spirit forces in the body causes ailments and death.

The curing of disease lies within the province of the conjuror, and was so defined a century ago by McKenzie, which is good evidence for the point made here. This idea is consistent with the tenor of native thought. Accordingly, we might expect to discover that magic

---

1.   F. G. Speck, "Medicine Practices of the Northeastern Algonquians," *Proceedings of the Ninth International Congress of Americanists,* Washington, 1915 (Washington, 1917); also G. Tantaquidgeon, "Notes on the Origin and Uses of Plants of the Lake St. John Montagnais, *Journal of American Folk-Lore,* XLV, No.176 (April-June, 1932), pp. 165-67.
     I am aware of the recent intensive monograph of Dr. Forrest E. Clements, *Primitive Concepts of Disease,* University of California Publications, Vol. XXXII (1932), No. 2, whose treatment of disease theories of the North shows significant points.

and symbols are more general among them than pharmacology. This proves to be the case. Preventatives seem more in evidence than cures. Among the un-Christianized groups there is a wealth of material of the magic curative and protective type, of which some illustrations will be given below.

Says Masson, "In his medical capacity, this man administers no other medicine to effect a cure than singing and blowing on the part affected and sucking it, the intention of which is to counteract the machinations of their enemies." [2]

Charms of beadwork and those of leather with painted figures possess protective value. They take a variety of forms, although their function is fairly uniform in regard to disease in being preventative rather than curative for specific ills.

The charm is denoted by the term *wewe'lcipe'lcwagən* (Lake St. John), with cognates in the various dialects. The majority of such objects, being worn about the neck suspended by a thong, are called *tap'cka'gən*, "something hanging from the neck," frequently modified by the term *nanto'ho*, "hunting," placed before it. [3] It is interesting to recall that the necktie of the Europeans which the Indians are fond of acquiring is spoken of with the same term and serves the same magical function in bringing luck to the hunter. And I also have recorded the necktie as a dream symbol, the same as the neck-charm of native make, in a text taken down from a man of the Michikamau band (see p. 182). Not only are beaded charms worn on the neck, but among the bands of the northern peninsula they are employed as magical luck-bringing ornaments fastened to the stock and trigger guard of firearms, worn tied around the legging near the knee like a garter, worn by women as wrist ornaments or bracelet charms, sewed upon the breasts of dresses, fastened in the hat, or in the hair of men. The range of charm-wearing is wide, and reaches a richer development where the natives are less in contact with the whites. A series of these charms from different bands, but chiefly from the Barren Ground people, will serve to place at our disposal the data needed to correlate this interesting topic with other features of religious performance among these tribes (pls. XVIII, XIX).

A neck charm obtained from Charley Metowe'cic, second chief of the Mistassini band, consists of a piece of skin from the throat of

2. Masson, *op. cit.*, pp. 414, 415.
3. The term is also applied to the scapular furnished by the priests, though with the modifier *aia'meo*, "prayer," meaning at the same time Catholic.

a loon, six inches in length, backed with green cloth, trimmed on the edges with the same, and having a length of red braid for suspension. On the upper part is sewed a strip of white and blue ribbon, taken from a medal, apparently. It is called *mwɔ'k tapcka'gɔn*, "loon neck hanger." Having been able to secure more specific information concerning the experience by which the owner of this talisman acquired it than is usually the case, I give a translation of his declaration.

"Eighteen years ago in the fall I dreamed of seeing Loon Woman wearing around her neck a nice collar ornament. [The narrator refers to the black and white pattern on the feathers of the loon's neck, which appear clearly in the specimen figured.] She spoke to me and told me that if I wanted to see her again to wear an ornament like hers around my neck. Knowing that her visitation was a good sign for me, I asked my poor wife to make the neck charm for me the next time I killed a loon. I wanted to see Loon Woman again because I knew she was going to help me. In the following May when the first flight of loons arrived at the lake from the south, I put the charm ornament on my neck and went out to get them. This was the first time that I wore it, and in two days I killed sixty loons. Loon Woman gave me some power over loons. Now I always wear it when hunting loons and always have good luck with them. Sometimes I wear it for hunting bears, too.

"The piece of ribbon stands for man [meaning the artificial realm of man], and the skin part stands for the animal. I only wear it when starting on the hunt."

The diamond-shaped woven bead charms with bead pendants at the corners symbolize animals. Specimens from the Barren Ground band are shown in plate xviii. [4]

To prevent and to cure heart trouble the figure of a heart cut out of colored cloth is worn about the neck (Lake St. John and neighboring bands).

The tonsure haircut, a space shaved clean about an inch across, is occasionally seen among women (Natasquan band, 1925), and upon inquiry proved to be a cure and prevention for headache. Hind also mentions this custom among the Moisie band, but he attributed its origin to imitation of the missionary priests. [5] He evidently did not know that the custom had a wider distribution among the nomads, whence we may assume it to have had an older history. This point of view is substantiated by the record of its occurrence among

4. To the student of northern plains Indian culture it should be interesting to note the existence of a similar charm from the Blackfeet in the National Museum of Canada.
5. Hind, *op. cit.*, II, 103. He says that when the Naskapi descended in 1849 for the first time to the post at Moisie they had long hair, and cut it when they saw the custom in fashion at the coast. One poor creature, he adds, observing the priestly tonsure, procured a friend to cut his hair in the same fashion.

the Naskapi of the Davis Inlet or Barren Ground bands by Waugh in 1921. [6] His notes state that the hair is pulled out from a spot on the crown of the head until it bleeds, then some gunpowder is rubbed in as a cure for headache.

Luck Charms

Animal embryo-like forms.—A source of good luck recognized as a potent charm among the various bands of the area is that peculiar embryo-like formation occasionally found within the belly of a slain animal. The hunters claim that such a discovery is not infrequent, that it is loose in the stomach of the animal host, that it has hair as it should, and occurs in either male or female animal. When found it should be dried in smoke and preserved to bring luck to the hunter so selected by the animal for recognition of virtue toward the disposal of its remains. According to the animal in which the miniature form is found, it is called *pi·″tɔati″ḳʷ*, "second within caribou"; *pi·″tɔwabu'cwan*, "second within hare"; *pi·″tɑwakwa'n*, "second within porcupine"; *pi·″tɔwami'ckʷ*, "second within beaver." [7]

In the narrative of Francis de Crespieul (1671), he records seeing the minute figure of a moose no bigger than a thumb taken from a moose killed by his Indian companions—a reference to this charm. Dr. Cooper [8] has some notes of distribution for this belief showing its diffusion over a wide area in the North.

Bead and paint charms on skins for hunting luck.—A general practice to further insure the capture of game is to put marks of red paint, consisting of one or more bars, on the underside of the skin of an animal after the skin has been tanned. The place for these is usually at the terminations of the legs, where the feet have been cut off, and at the neck and sometimes at the base of the tail of the skin. Many of the skin robes of the Barren Ground band are so marked, the reason being given that it is traditionally proper to do so for the continuance of luck. Among these bands, and also more generally where beads are obtainable, short loops or strings singly or in pairs and yarn tassels or ribbons are found as ornament attach-

6. Notes of the late F. W. Waugh placed at my disposal by Mr. Jenness, National Museum of Canada.
7. The stem *pi·″tɔ* denotes an object fitting within another and becoming a part of it; examples, *pi·″tɔcɔna'n*, "ceremonial shot bag," and *pi·″t mokɔma'n*, "knife scabbard."
8. Correspondence with Dr. J. M. Cooper, Catholic University of America, indicates the presence of this charm among the Têtes de Boule and neighboring bands of Quebec and Ontario. See J. M. Cooper, *Northern Algonkian Magic, International Congress of Americanists* (New York, 1928), XXIII, 513.

ments at the eye-holes; and sometimes at the nose and ears of skins which have the tanned head-skin attached. Also, pieces of red cloth are seen sewed over these orifices. The reason given is the same as that offered by the bands father north who employ red paint for such sacrificial decoration. Waugh mentions the Davis Inlet people fastening strings of beads on the ears of valuable fox skins, and says that they are a sign of rejoicing over the first valuable fur taken by a boy who is becoming a hunter. He adds another reason—the decoration denotes extra value, the greater the more beads—and finally remarks that bead strings put on the ears of fox skins are charms to secure more. That the decorations in this category are charms for hunting luck is evident from my own notes covering all the bands southward from the Michikamau to the Lake St. John bands.

The series of beadwork charms from the Barren Ground band secured through Mr. White are so interesting and complete that it seems proper to describe them in some detail.

Charms for rifle butts consist of woven bead strips (fig. 25 B) with looped fringes, averaging one and one-half inches in width and five in length. Charms to be tied on trigger guard of rifle or

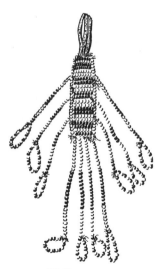

FIGURE 25 B

Beaded charm representing an animal, attached to gun-stock or trigger guard, to add effectiveness to the weapon. (Length, 4 inches; colors, white and purple.)

gun are small, beaded oval-shaped objects, having the symbolical form of an animal with bead loops or lengths representing the animal's legs. They are beaded on both sides.

Neck charms consist of squares of solid woven beadwork averaging two by two inches. A bead fringe falls from the lower edge, and a leather thong is sewed across the top for suspension. The charm is worn outside the garment in front. The diamond-shaped neck charms are made single and double, worn in front when single or both in front and behind when double (pl. xviii). They are of solid woven construction and have several bead strings at the angles, symbols of the legs of the animals. In size they range from two to three and three-quarters inches. The double diamond-shaped neck charms are worn by women. The women also affect the rectangular or square beadwork charm, similar to that worn by men.

Legging and wrist charms of openwork woven beadwork (pl. xviii, lower figures), are worn as garters by men for luck in hunting, and as bracelets by children for protection against sickness. One hunter specified the wearing of the garter charm to secure luck with foxes. The former average from twelve to fifteen inches in length, the latter six inches with a loop pendant.

Round or oval, solid beaded charms are also worn around the neck (pl. xix, lower row). Their function is given as "to bring luck for hunting in general." These, like the diamond-shaped charms, occasionally have the leg symbols of bead strings or fringe.

Neck charms for specific animals.—For hunting the bear and the otter, and perhaps other creatures, a portion of the animal's under-lip with a section of solid woven beadwork fastened below it, and a bead fringe to finish it is worn about the neck. A series of typical examples from the Barren Ground band is illustrated in plate xix, upper row.

Among other bands the bear lip charm is less elaborate, often being simply the dried lip bordered with an edging of beads. Again, the tongue sinew of the animal is dried and preserved in a small leather sack, as among the Lake St. John people. The reason for preserving these emblems of slain bears is to afford satisfaction to the spirit of the beast. It seems, indeed, that a similar spirit of granting recognition to the game is the motive behind the wearing of all the various beadwork ornaments found among the bands in general. The same applies to the woven, beaded hair strings worn by the women. In all such individual creations of art the forms, techniques, and designs are limited to several categories which exhibit their allied functions.

Charm to get good birch bark.—When about to set forth to gather birch bark for making a canoe, the hunter may wear a woodchuck tail in his hat (Lake St. John).

Wind control.—To lower the wind when it is blowing so hard that the hunter dares not venture forth upon the lake, a wood-chuck's scalp is thrown into the water with the wish that the wind will cease (Lake St. John).

Charm for porcupines.—Hind informs us that when wood hisses in the fire words are muttered as a charm to cause porcupines to be killed on the next hunt. [9] He adds, incidentally, that the Lake Superior Ojibwa do the same.

Charm against thunder.—To cause a thunderstorm to break up and pass by, an ax is struck into the ground so that its blade points toward the cloud (Mistassini).

Charm against clouds.—Low-flying clouds sometimes descend upon the ground and they are believed to be poisonous to those who breathe them. To dispel this horrid mist it is shot at (Mistassini).

Medicine practice.—For the relief of swellings and pain, blood-letting is a general practice, as we learn from one end of the region to the other, even as far as the Algonquin on the western borders of the province of Quebec. The Montagnais-Naskapi employ for the purpose split sticks three or four inches long with needles or small splinters of glass set transversely. At Seven Islands I obtained from a Michikamau hunter a caribou bone bloodletter of the same size having a sharpened projection cut out near one end (fig. 26). The point of the instrument is placed over the seat of pain or swelling and the point driven into the flesh by a slight, swift blow from

FIGURE 26

Lancet of caribou bone used by individual for letting blood to relieve pain and swelling, natural size (Michikamau band).

9. Hind, *op. cit.,* I, 186.

some heavier article. Waugh's notes on the Barren Ground band mention that a needle or a sharp instrument was stuck in the flesh until it bled to cure pains in the limbs. At Seven Islands the name *pəck̨we'manabətu'k̨'ʷ* is applied to the bloodletter. There I was instructed to fasten a ligature below the elbow and to stick the point of the instrument into the wrist to relieve pain of apparently every nature.

Taboos

According to the system of protection by which it is believed that calamity in its many forms of bad hunting, bad weather, bad gathering, famine, and disease may be averted, the charm or fetish is the real agent of magic, while the taboo, either positive or negative, is an auxiliary one. Ideas of conduct play their part in regulating the degree of "luck" achieved by the hunter. Both serve a similar purpose in balancing life against misfortune. A few taboos and prescribed actions are given below—gained mostly from observation and experience, since they are rarely obtained by direct inquiry.

In a preceding section of our study the taboos surrounding the contact of the dog with the remains of animals has been covered. It is most essential to recall these restrictions again in connection with the accompanying remarks.

The hunter should not allow a woman, especially during her menses, to step over his legs or his snowshoe tracks. To do so would result in his developing weakness or soreness in the legs (Lake St. John and Mistassini.)[10] It is, however, considered lucky to take wives on hunting trips.

The moon must not be looked at when game is shot.

For some unspecified reason (perhaps because it might call ghosts), the people never indulge in whistling. They are conscious of the difference in habit in this respect between themselves and the whites.

Something should be said of the taboo governing contacts of maidens at the first appearance of menstruation. It is noted by Richard White for the Barren Ground band that they spend three days in the tent in seclusion, the face covered with a veil of caribou skin reaching to level of the mouth, the veil occasionally fringed and painted with lines and angles in red. This serves to ward off harmful influences. Among the southern bands the custom is not observed.

10. A similar restriction for women is recorded for the Athapascan (Dog Ribs) by Caspar Whitney, *On Snow-shoes to the Barren Grounds*, (New York, 1896), p. 88.

AFTERWORD

Chapter Nine

D ELVING into the inner life of uncivilized peoples has an effect upon the curious something like that of adventure. Lure and the unknown seem to be proportionate to indifference and the known. My adventure has been to try to capture the spirit of native religion of the Montagnais-Naskapi. Now the student of material like that I have presented has indeed to broaden his lines of thought in many directions, and some of these I might presume to point out.

To the general reader—and one must always think of him in these days of broadening interest in primitive human history—it is the differences in forms of worship of the uncivilized and the civilized that usually appear phenomenal, while for others more penetrative in judgment the basic resemblances of religious conventions, high and low, evoke surprise. Much of the point of view taken seems to depend upon what each of us understands in respect to the term religion. If, then, the religion of a tribe is thought of only as a system of belief formulating the origin and order of the universe, deism, and teaching something of the destiny of mankind and regulation of his ethical behavior, it embraces only a portion of the religious sphere—its inner realm. The rest is the realm of action in observance of rites and ceremonies. And these group themselves in a parcel with customs.

Fundamentally, religious beliefs—creeds one may liberally term them—are lately being discovered to possess some universal similarities, the more we get information on uncivilized peoples and cultures. Examining these forms we find convergences. Customs, on the other hand, or religious rites and ceremonies excite surprise by their wide differences. Some we may condemn, being advocates of a different discipline of behavior, and some we cannot understand without knowing other customs or habits of the tribes whose outward methods of life are so much at variance with our own. Secular customs vary extensively; so with religious customs. Hence if theism, creation, transformation, ethical precepts and soul-beliefs are almost universally recorded in cultures both advanced and retarded, and if shamanism, masking, iconolatry, exorcism and other spectacular performances are not, the differences are due to the vagaries of custom. Customs or rites may indeed differ widely among those observing the same religious creed, as may be seen in the case of Christianity, with sects ranging from Quakerism to Roman Catholicism and Mormonism to Shakerism.

So the northerners with whom we have been dealing may impress us either by the similarities of beliefs to those of more advanced types or by the strangeness, grotesqueness even, of their observances and superstitions. It depends upon whether we have in mind such beliefs respecting man and the universe, or unusual habits and customs employed in appeal to non-human forces.

Naskapi is a term of disdain in the mouths of the northern natives. It denotes a person so impoverished in property of mind that he has no realization of religion; that is, religion in the sense of a code to live by and through which to communicate with the unseen forces that govern destiny. On the lips of those who use the term, moreover, it means a person who has intelligence so low as to have no inventions, no possessions. All this partly true, but only from the angle of comparison of one whose life is enriched by the acquisitions of trade or by association with a domain of knowledge and teaching outside his own sphere. As a term of reproach it can only be applied by one who has acquired advantages through opportunity which has been denied to the other. It grossly overlooks the fact that the "uneducated" in his struggle to live in a severe environment must possess a greater resourcefulness than he who boasts the protection of more numerous acquired inventions. To be held in disdain is always the lot of those poor in worldly goods through no fault of their own.

The northern "savages" exist under conditions which seem to produce a fluid relationship between economic and social developments. Not necessarily so with their religious scheme. While it is evidently true that the Montagnais-Naskapi Indians are indeed to be ranked among the earth's lowliest, even crudest peoples if judged by economic and social standards, this classification hardly seems to apply with equal plausibility in forming an estimate of their mental condition. Dr. W. Schmidt's eulogy on the depth of native American natural philosophy will no doubt find another instance here in the far northeast, among the ancient mariners of the St. Lawrence and the roamers of the tundra.

The social and economic bisections appear drawn within geographical zones, the Indian bands of the northern treeless barrens deriving subsistence from the caribou herds, hunting as local hordes; those in the forests southward chasing and trapping mixed game as family units, while between the two lie the territories of local hordes which vary the manner of hunting according to season and game conditions. Among the former animal skin serves *prima facie* as work material, among the latter tree skin—birch bark. Material culture and social configuration are largely determined by nature's economy. But not so with religion, the intaglio of tradition. It meets varying conditions with an unchanging profile.

Thought concerning the effect of environment upon culture-imagination may be scientifically outlawed, but in native esteem it calls for consideration. Regions of vastness and desolation weave upon the imagination of all human beings a gossamer web of distraction. The northern Indians are conscious of such influences. Something present there takes hold of the emotions, while the sense of the present, of time in general, becomes dulled. Senses respond equally to passing impressions arising from within or from without and as readily to a passing thought, a fancy, or to the image of a presence which crosses the vision or which vibrates to the ear. Nothing is tested for its reality, for it is all felt as being real.

A great difference separates the outlook of the Montagnais-Naskapi toward the natural world from the viewpoint of the European. The realm of non-human agencies which the European calls the unseen is to the northern aboriginal as often sensed by sight as are the familiar creatures of everyday life that surround the most pragmatic minded. The cannibal giant, the underwater people, the animal owners are to him not questionable beliefs, but realities, proved by personal experience of a nature as satisfactory to him as it would be to have seen a bear or a seal. A superstition becomes as much a fact as a visual or auditory observation.

PLATE XIX

Revelation in dream vision, or in actual sight, bringing luck to hunter; sun-illumination upon landscape. (Sketch by Mr. Albert Stanford).

Prominent among such examples of tribal mind as one may imagine typical of the least materially civilized tribes stand the Naskapi. They move in a heroic panoramic setting tuned, in the vision of the poet or dreamer, to vibrations in deep undertones creating sensations in harmony with the purple of night, the dark green of forests glaring silently against a white background of snow, or in summer against a heavy surf on the shores of some inland rockbound lake. All breeds despair of this world. It stirs a sense of freedom from the disguise of cultural coverings brought by influences arising through contact with other native and more conventionalized civilizations of the continent. Naskapi culture is indeed isolated. Its spirit is as strange to even the Iroquois mind as it is to the European.

Let me illustrate further with a picture seen from the vantage point of distance, whether at sea or on a crag. A veil of fog hangs over the skyline of the horizon mountains—the escarpment of the Labrador peninsula. Glimpses here and there of shining wet faces of cliffs and waterfalls pouring their accumulations from the melting snows of winter over the brink of the plateau to find a way to the broad gulf, reflecting the sun to deceive the eye into thinking them banks of snow or glaciers. But glimpses only here and there. Examine one illuminated space for detail and the haze envelopes it forthwith. Cast the eye upon another illuminated vista and begin again to pick up detail. The bare distant promontories, black-growth in dips of the land appear exposed for an instant, then the cold leaden sky and wind-driven cloud masses close in and the patchwork patterns keep on unfolding and retreating. The observer, trained in our curious world of thought, tries in vain at the moment to integrate the exposures and interpret them into a grand picture. But it is not enough. The fleeting vistas show only the surface in segments of the present. Something phenomenal has been in process here for ages, but its evidence lies beneath the surface. And it seems that no amount of eager search over the surface, among its living men and beasts, will reveal the episodes of their long history. Creatures of the present living in the essentials of a past for which no starting point can be found! A natural history simile of the situation faces us in the study of those shy, vagrant, neo-anthropoid beings whose existence is couched in the sterile milieu of which they are a part, like the quadrupeds, the birds and fish that support their lives and mould their culture. We call our self-imposed research task ethnology! We call the task still needed to deepen its channels archaeology.

A word as to the Indians themselves. We have dealt with them by trying to sound the depths of some of those intangible qualities that we find hard to put down in so many words respecting the character of even our most intimate friends. How much more difficult it is to say half as much concerning those we know only at racial arm's length. Indians of the north have the eyes and mouths of silent men. Their bearing is that of self-centered non-dependent soldiers of chance. Devoid of flippancy, making no exterior exhibition, they do not invite approach. There is, I am aware, nothing in these remarks distinctive of the Montagnais-Naskapi alone in North America. Yet if the peoples of the Southwest have been defined as Apollonian, those of the Plains as Dionysian, we might portray those of the cold forests and barrens as Diogenic, save for the sophisticated attribute of cynicism.

The native attitude is too realistic to foster a sense of frenzied fear of death, fear of superhuman agencies or of ghosts. Reconciliation to events in the cycle of change in life is apparent and striking in its sincerity. Associated with it is a low expression of personality, a minimum of self-exhibition, a balanced desire to live through the life course. And yet self or soul is the physical and spiritual center of life! Cannot egoism—the theory that bases morality upon self-interest—exist without egotism? "From great-grandparents to great-grandchildren we are only knots in a string," expresses the self-esteem of the Naskapi.

Analysis of the northern cultural pattern has, however, only been begun. It will require time and deep and unbiased thought along lines projected in Dr. Benedict's recent studies for its advance. Obstacles to success seem insuperable at present, but they whet one's appetite. We are incited to press on with the help of others toward completing the picture of existing life of the hunter bands before they disappear from their haunts, the picture of a particular culture, expecting that ultimately some tendencies of religious life will reveal themselves with their laws of change to justify still wiser generalizations on the natural history of boreal man set down in "a land as lonely as a star." And so I leave my task for a while.

GLOSSARY

aia'mie'win: practice of prayer, religion.

akwucəmo' pi·'cəm (eastern Naskapi): "concealing sun," solar eclipse.

alambe'gwinosis (Penobscot): "underwater little man," mythological character.

aiamieu' tapcka'gən: "neck ornament," scapular.

ami'ck'ʷ otakəki·'m: "beaver, his leech," the piece of gristle behind the paunch of the beaver

anəmistsu': thunder.

apoaia'miat: "one who does not pray," a "miscreant," native designation of a Protestant.

apci'lni·c (Lake St. John): "little people," dwarfs.

apci·'ni·c (Mistassini and eastern Naskapi): "little people," dwarfs.

acini·'ucpwágən: stone pipe.

acwo'pan: "watching-place."

acəte'atək (Lake St. John): "crossed wood," the crucifix.

Atək·wabe'o (Lake St. John): Caribou Man, master of the caribou.

atə'm: dog.

ati·''k·nakəmə'n: "caribou-song," chants received in dreams from the caribou spirits, and used to obtain good luck in the hunt.

Ati·k·wape'o: Caribou Man.

atik·wədzwa'p: Caribou House, mountain domicile of Caribou Man.

Ati·kwənabe'o (Michikamau): Caribou Man.

ati·kwudzwa'p (Michikamau): a caribou house.

atca'k·ʷ: soul, shadow, image.

atcakwu'c (diminutive): "little soul," star.

atcakwuci'ts (Lake St. John and Mistassini): souls.

Atce'n (Moisie, St. Marguerite, Michikamau): cannibal demon.

Atci'n (Ungava): cannibal demon.

awa'cəts: animals.

awa·tawe's·u (Penobscot): "far-away being," star.

beskwadina'u (Davis Inlet Naskapi, Waugh): "bursting (in the) north," aurora borealis.

elte'ltamən (Lake St. John): "he thinks."

eni· mina'nuts eməlo'tagənts: "songs of rejoicing."

e'pcəmənckweo: "shortest (moon)," February.

epwamia'n nictoti·'k·ʷ: "I dream three caribou."

ətce'n· (Escoumains): a cannibal demon.

ili'twacteo (Escoumains): weather phenomenon.

ilnadju'k̯ (Montagnais): "wise (human-like) seal."

k̯a aia'miat: "one who prays," the Naskapi and Montagnais spiritualist.

k̯ak̯iu'chi·tək̯'ʷ: "our Maker."

k̯ak̯'ʷ ctewə'tc mi·tcəm (Moisie): "black food," circumlocutory name for the bear.

k̯amatcinto'hət: "bad luck or bad hunt."

k̯amələnto'hət (Lake St. John): "making a good hunt."

k̯anaya'pewut (Michikamau): "chicane, clown," term applied to the bear.

k̯antautci·'tuk̯'ʷ: our Creator.

k̯antce·'təpelta'k̯: our great Master or Owner.

k̯aopa'tc mi·tcəmiyu' (Mistassini): "black food," name for the bear.

k̯a'p miuc: cap container.

k̯atəkwa'socəwi·' (Ste. Marguerite): circumlocutory name for the bear.

k̯as·inu' tcetci·'məlopəli·'n: "all forms of good fortune."

k̯awe''kwakwənit: "the one who owns the chin," name for the bear.

k̯ənto·'pwa'men: "he hunt-dreams," the hunting dreams.

k̯eta'nk̯ʷzu. (Penobscot): "ghost" or spirit of a dead person.

k̯eta'nk̯ʷzu audi': "ghost trail," the Milky Way.

k̯e'tce mə'nitu (Cree): Supreme Deity.

k̯e'tci nik̯skam (Penobscot): "great being."

k̯əna'tsi·upi·'cəm: "falling-leaves moon," a term for November.

k̯əcktəwe'ədjiu: "black beast," circumlocutory name for the bear.

k̯iwaytinoshuh (F. W. Waugh) "Man of the North."

k̯oko'c: pig.

k̯tcikwəna'k̯·tc (Wabanaki): "big hard back," the water terrapin.

k̯wakwadjə'c (Eastern Naskapi): "wolverine," a mythical personage.

k̯wəctewa'o mi·'tcem (Escoumains): "black food," circumlocutory name for the bear.

ləgəpeja'gən (Escoumains): "legging," the rainbow.

maguca'n (Naskapi): the ceremony of feast and dance held when a bear has been killed.

mahi'k̯ana'tuk̯'ʷ: "wolf sticks" game.

ma'k̯ocan: a feast.

mani·pi·'cəm: "Mary moon," a name for May.

mante'o: a stranger.

mantu'c (Mistassini): "little spirits, powers," beads or beadwork.

mata'mən məck̯'ʷ: "great bear."

ma'təcənan: cap bag.

məck̯'ʷ: the bear.

məck̯ʷunak̯əmə'n: "bear, his song."

memegwe'djo (Mistassini): mythical creature who inhabits rocky ledges.

meck̯ənu': paths.

me·towa'gən: game, "plaything."

mədətca'n (*mətətsa'n*): sweat lodge.

mənoməntu': good power, spirit, applied to Holy Ghost.

mənto'k̯acun: "zealous; he has spirit for something; he has bravery."

mənto' minu'cits: "spirit berries," beads.

məntoci'ʹwi·n: practice based upon *məntu'*, magical practice, shamanism, conjuring.

məntu': the universe, unknown spirit forces.

məntu' elte'ltak: "spirit-power thinking."

məntume'kuc: smelt, "spirit fish."

məntu'minəsiʹt: *məntu'* berries, beads or beadwork.

məntu'c: snake, worm, insect.

məntu'wian: "*məntu'* skin," cloth.

məsəna'kᵘ (Ste. Marguerite): the moose-fly, master of the fish.

məca'o wətce'gatək: "great star," the North Star.

mətənca'wan: divination.

mətəšte'haman: "he sacrifices to an animal," sacrifice offering.

matone'itcigan (Mistassini): "power of thought."

mətone'ntcigən (Eastern Naskapi): "power of thought."

mətci·məntu': bad power.

miam mətənca'wan ati'ʹkᵘ numeckənu': "good divination, deer hunting path."

mide'win: medicine society.

mi·lowe'ltam: good thought.

mi·lowe'ltamən (Lake St. John): "to satisfy," gratifying the soul-spirit (by smoking).

mi·noto'tak: proper conduct, ethical principles, social usages.

misəna'ʹkᵘ (Naskapi): the moose-fly, the master of the fish.

mišta'peo: "Great Man."

mištə'ʹkᵘ: a peeled fir tree upon which is hung up the bear skull.

mici·ca'kᵘ (Mistassini): "big biter," the moose fly.

micta i'cpamits: "in the heights above," the upper realm.

mictakwe'məgən: "he cried out strong."

micta'mackᵘ: giant beaver.

micta'peo: soul, spirit.

mictəkᵘo'ka'n: peeled pole upon which is hung up the backbone of the big fish.

mictəwətce'gətək: "great star," the evening star.

mictsina'ʹkᵘ (Lake St. John): the moose-fly, master of the fish; (Mistassini) the
terrapin, master of the fish among the Mistassini.

mitsəkwu'n: skinning knives made from leg bone of the bear.

mukᵘca'n (Montagnais): the ceremony of feast and dance held when a bear has
been killed.

mwak tapcka'gən: "loon neck hanger," neck charm.

nahe'itamən (Mistassini): gratifying the soul-spirit (by smoking)

nana'ʹkau ni·kəməna'nuts awe'cicəts (Lake St. John): "different songs for animals."

nackᵘ: cloud.

nembucqutwe'o (pi·'cəm) (Escoumains): "deceiving, false sun," the sun dog,
weather phenomenon.

nemictcu'wəts (Mistassini): "thunder," personified supernatural force.

nenəmickwo' as·i·': "shaking earth," earthquake.

nəkəpeha'gən wiabi·' (Natasquan): "legging-string," the rainbow.

nəkwani·abi·' (Seven Islands): cup-and-ball game.

nəmocu'm: "grandfather," a term applied to the bear.

nəwaye'm: "my friend," circumlocution for the soul.

ni·bo'wo: death.

ni·ma'ban: ceremonial pack string by which the carcass of an animal is dragged to the camp.

ni·čta'yatsuk: "my brother-in-law otter," euphemism used for the otter in divination practices.

ni·təmu'ciatsu'k: "my sweetheart otter," euphemism used for otter in divination practices.

ničtotcima'uts: "three chiefs," Orion's Belt constellation.

ni·člu'ι: spirit, intellect, comprehension, mind.

notcimi·' umi·tcə'm: "forest food," pure food intended for Indians by the Creator.

ntsu'k: the otter.

ntcu'k· nəkəmə'n: otter song.

onicko' pi·'cəm: "goose moon," May.

opətce'sigən ami·ck·ω: "hip-bone beaver," divination by pelvic bone of beaver.

opo'pi·'cəm: "flying-bird moon," August.

ocaka'u pi·'cəm: "(go to) bay moon," September.

ota'meotcəgə'n: "he leaves (*otame'o*) scratching (with his paws)," divination with otter paws.

otə'pmick·ω: "beaver seat."

otipe'litcke'o: "our owner."

otci·ma'u: chief.

papi·makewa'n: "shooting otter" game.

pelckwama'gən: a snap of the fingers on the forehead, a penalty for losing games.

petsi'natcəkwu'c: "falling star," a weather sign.

pəli'ki atca'k·ω (Mistassini): "pure, clean soul."

pəckwe'manabətu'k·ω: the bloodletter.

pi·ji·'u: lynx.

pi·ca'gənwi·abi·: "legging-string," the rainbow.

pi·cagonia'bi· me·towa'gən: "skin-string game," string figures.

pi·'cəm: the sun.

pi·cəmu'c: "little moon," December.

pi·'cəmwiabi·' (Lake St. John): "sun string," the rainbow.

pi·''təati·k·ω: "second within caribou," embryo-like formation used as charm.

pi·''təcəna'n: shot pouch.

pi·''təwabu'cwan: "second within hare," embryo-like formation used as charm.

pi·''təwakwa'n: "second within porcupine," embryo-like formation used as charm.

pi·''təwami'ck·ω: "second within beaver," charm.

pi·'tua'n: to smoke.

pi·tuləkəpeca'gən (Seven Islands): "legging," the rainbow.

pwamo': to dream.

sekωskwecən pi·'cəm (Lake St. John and Mistassini): "sick [?] sun," solar eclipse.

cabətowa'n: long or feast house, literally "through house" [?] by reference to the doors at the opposite ends.

ca'wənəcu' (Mistassini): "south wind," personified supernatural force.

ceta'n pi·'cəm: Ste. Anne moon, July.

cici·kwu'n: disc-like rattle made of skin and wooden hoop.

ci῾ci'p῾pi·'cəm: "duck moon," April.

ckwuteotaba'n: "fire-toboggan," railroad train.

tambe'gwilnu: "underwater man," water dwarf.

tamwini·be'gʷ (Mistassini): "deepest part of the sea," personified supernatural force.

tapi·'gən (*ta'bəgwan*, Moisie; *tapəha'n*, Lake St. John; *ta·'panəgi'*, Barren Ground band): cup-and-ball game.

tapcka'gən: "neck suspended," scapular.

tawa'bətsigən (Michikamau, *tewe'bətsigən*, Lake St. John): buzzer game.

tebiska'u pi·'cəm: "night sun," moon.

təkwa'yəwagən: "short tail," circumlocutory name for the bear.

tipe'ltak (Montagnais, *tɪpe'ntak*, eastern Naskapi): great power "owner."

tsi·'pi pi·'cəm: "dead moon," a name for November.

tsi·təstci·'nau (Mistassini): our world, universe.

tstce' mi·tcəmiyu: "his great food," circumlocutory name for the bear.

tceka'cəko pi·cəma': "spottings of the sun," weather phenomenon.

tce·'məntu: great spirit.

tce'nu (Micmac): cannibal demon.

tce'pi·'cəm: "old moon," January.

tcetciməntu': great power.

Tsəka'bec: mythological hero.

tci·pai meckənu': "ghost trail," Milky Way.

tci·pa'its nimo'wuts (Lake St. John): "spirits of the dead dancing," aurora borealis.

tci·'pi·ətə'k῾: "ghost wood," crucifix.

tci'cəga wətcəkwu'c (Mistassini and Lake St. John): "day star," the evening star.

tci·'cəgwəts (Mistassini): skies, clouds, days, personified supernatural force.

tcitcəwe mi·'tcəm: "great food," circumlocutory name for the bear.

tci·'tc῾stewehidje'o: he prophesies.

tci·we'tən atcəkwu'c (Mistassini and Lake St. John): North Star.

tci·we'tənəc (Mistassini): "west wind," personified supernatural force.

tci·wetənicu' (Mistassini): "north wind," personified supernatural force.

tci·wetinowi·'nu: "Man of the North," personification of the north wind, controller of the universe in this quarter.

tc῾stema'u: tobacco.

tc῾stemawu'c: tobacco bag.

[u]cpwa'gən: pipe.

utabəsi·'gən nəme'c: mandibles of large fish used in divination.

utətci·'gən nəme'c: clavicles of fish used in divination.

utni·'gən meckənu' (*outli'ckan meskinu'*, Montagnais): shoulder-blade path.

utli·'gən (*utəli·gə'n*, St. Francis Abenaki): scapula, shoulder blade.

wabanicu' (Mistassini): "east wind," personified supernatural force.

wa'banu (Mistassini): "day-sky," personified supernatural force.

wabənatca'kwoma'n: "soul seeing," mirror; divination by gazing.

wa'bənatckəwu'c: the morning star.

wabə'ck῾ω (*wampsk*, Penobscot): the white bear.

wabu'c: the hare.

wapəgwu'n: flowers.

wa'pəgwun pi·'cəm: "flower moon," June.
wapuco''kana'n: "hare hunt" game.
wa'cko: heaven, the starry universe.
wactesi·'u pi·'cəm: "leaves change moon," October.
wawa'ctockwao: "(night) lightning illumination," aurora borealis.
wewe'lcipe'lcwagən: the charm.
wətce'kətək: "fisher star," Ursa Major.
wətcə'ck uctəgwa'n me·towagə'n: "muskrat head play," divination game played at Lake St. John.
wi·'nack pi·'cəm: "woodchuck moon," March.
wi'ndigo (Algonkian): cannibal.
wiu'kbecagəniabi·' (Mistassini): "striped legging-string," rainbow.
Wisəke'djak: mythological hero.
wi·ukweabi.' (Mistassini): "vein string," the rainbow.
wi·ya'gən: special form of birch-bark dish.
wuckwi·'lagən: bark dish.
wute'ia·tək·ω (Mistassini): "heart of tree," sap, personified supernatural force.
wutci·'manəc: the Pleiades.

EXPLANATION OF CHARACTERS
EMPLOYED IN RECORDING
NATIVE TERMS

In transcriptions of native terms the following values should be noted for letter-characters (Introduction, *Handbook of American Indian Languages,* Bulletin 40, Part I, Bureau American Ethnology, Washington, D. C., 1911).
Vowels:

  a   medium, as *a* in *father.*
  α   (Greek alpha) short, as *u* in *but.*
  ə   obscure vowel interval like *e* in *flower.*
  i   short as in *pin.*
  i·   long as *ee* in *queen.*
  e   close to *e* in *let.*
  ao, au, eo   glides, no diphthongs.
Semivowels:

  h, w, y.
Consonants:

  p, b, k, g, t, d, as in English (though often intermediate surd-sonant).
  kʷ equals *k* with lip closure and breath.
  p·
  t· } aspirated.

  ts as in *its.*
  tc as *ch* in church.
  c equals *sh* as in shell.
  j equals French *j.*
  m, n, s, l, as in English (*L* occurs as syllable resembling *tl*).
  ' syllable accent (not grammatical).
  · breath after the sound of the aspirate.
  · lengthening of vowel and consonant.
(Values vary with the dialects which are referred to in parentheses.)

INDEX

Acknowledgements, 14.

Andree, R., reference, n., 132.

Animals: sacrifice to spirit of, 124; spiritual nature of, 72 *et seq.*; treatment of bones of, 123.

Anoutchine, V., reference n., 18.

Anthropophagy, *see* cannibalism.

Arrow release, 205.

Ax, magical use of, 66.

Bastian A., n., 133.

Bear: beliefs concerning, 95 *et seq.*; circumlocutions used for, 97, 104, grease of, 187; in art, 107; observances toward 96; smoking over, *see* Tobacco, offering of to slain bear; special method of skinning, 102; treatment of remains, 102, 107, 115; use in material culture, 108; varieties of, 109; *see also* Bone skinning tool and Divination.

—ceremonialism, brief discussion of, 77; extent and distribution of, 95; *see also* 95–109.

—feast: ceremonial features of, 103; observances of taboo at, 104; *see* Taboo; *also* Game feast.

—hunt, 99–100; forms of address used in, 100; sweat-lodge preparation for, 221; *see* nima´ ban.

Beaver: economic importance of, 74; game lord concept, 110–13; place in religious thought, 110–18; power to transform itself, 113; spiritual endowments of, 113–14; treatment of remains, 113, 115, 117; use of in medicine, 117; *see* Divination *and* Dreams.

Benedict, R. F., 245

Birds, as omens, 125 27.

Birket-Smith, K., 6; n., 87.

Birth fables, 44.

Bison, game lord concept in relation to, 85.

Bleek, D. F., n., 38.

Boas, F., quoted, 85.

Bogoras, W., 137.

Bone skinning tool, 224–5.

Burial, 45–46.

Burton, R. F., n., 135.

Buteux, J., n., 17.

Cabot, W. B., 37, 50, 68, n., 15.

Calendar, *see* Lunar divisions.

Campbell, T. J., n., 17.

Cannibal demon, 31, 67–68.

Cannibalism, 36–38, 69–70.

Caribou: color symbolism for, 91; decrease of, 78; economic importance of, 74; master of, 80; *also see* Caribou Man; place in material culture, 89 90, 91; place in religious thought, 79–86; supernatural allotment of to hunters, 83; treatment of remains, 89, 90; *see also* Dreams, Game feast, Games.

—House, 82, 83.

—Man, 80–89, 91.

Chamberlain, B. H., n., 134.

Chance, concept of, 79.

Charms, chap. viii.

Chase: charms for, chap. viii; magical nature of, 5, 73, 80, 192; woman's part in, 73; *see* Taboo.

Christianity, 7 *et seq.*; 15–22.

Clemens, S. L., n., 43.

Clements, F. E., n., 232.

Cod, 77.

Color symbolism, *see* Nīma ban.

Comeau, N. A., quoted, 105.

Comet, 61.

Conjuring, 27, 28, 62, 178; at summer gatherings, 11; individuality of, 8; *see* Drum speech.

Cooper, J. M., n., 31; 128; n., 235.

Cosmology, chap. iv; 10, 30, 52.

Czaplicka, M. A., n., 187.

Dancing, 186.

Davidson, D. S., 89

Decorative art: chap. viii; age distinction in, 194; economic necessity of, 197, 199; magic in, 196–200; native origin of, 197–98; of shot pouches, 222–224; possible Asiatic derivation of, 191; religious motive in, 188–189, 191, 225; sun-ray motif in, 193–94; woman's place in 198–99; *see* Nīma´ ban.

Deer, as dog food, 78; migration of, 74–77.

De Laguna, F., 152.

Densmore, F., n., 186.

Devil, 31.

Divination: chap. vi; by gazing, 164; by tossing fish bones, 168–69; by tossing muskrat skull, 169; by otter paw, 170; by otter tail, 172; importance of, 79; taboo against bear scap-

ula for, 149; use of bear patella in, 107, 167; use of beaver bones in, 117, 165–67, 168; use of fish bones in, 122; *see* Games, Scapulimancy.

Dixon, R. B., 27.

Dogs, caribou bones bad for, 90, 124; disregard of as religious force, 123; marten bones bad for, 125; meat sacrifice to, 79; mortuary use of, 46.

Dreams: as art motive, 190; as omen, 189–90; as preliminary to practice of scapulimancy, 155; as religious process, 187–90; designs used as result of, 107, 116; eating as inducement to, 190; importance of, 35; in connection with bear hunt, 99; with caribou hunt, 91–92; with beaver hunt, 114–16; influence upon ethics, 190; otter in, 125; chap. vii.

Drum: description of, 175–76; use of by women, 182.

—speech, 179.

Dwarfs, belief in, 68.

Eskimo, as good omen, 92; string figures, 231.

Earthquake, 66.

Eel, 77.

Ethics: general precepts, 36; influence of soul-spirit concept on, 43; *see* Dreams.

Family, as social unit, 242.

Fast-vigil, absence of, 40.

Fatalism, 79.

Feng, H. Y., n., 133–34.

Fish: as food, 77; ceremonial treatment of, 120; master of, 118; place in religious thought, 77; *see* Divination.

Fletcher, P., n., 32.

Food preferences, 74–79.

Frog, 44, 60.

Game, sharing of, 89.

—feast, 206 *et seq.*; *see* Bear feast.

—mountain concept, circumpolar distribution of, 52–53; among Labrador

Eskimo, 86.

Games: as magic devices, 200–201; buzzer, 203; caribou hunt, 203–204; cedar-bundle, 205–206; drawing lots, 206; hare-hunt, 204–205; heart-sticking, 206; otter hunt, 205; possible European derivation of, 203; ring-and-pin, 201–203; target shooting, 203; top, 203; *see* String figures.

Ghost, 45, 61, 239, 245.

Goldenweiser, A., 6.

Goyau, G., n., 37.

Gray, C. B., n., 12.

Gregorovius, F., n., 136.

Grenfell, W. T., n., 15.

Grgjic-Bjelokovic, L., n., 136.

Haddon, A. C., n., 7.

Hallowell, A. I., 32, 44, 95, n., 15, 110

—D. K., 201, 228.

Hare, 123; *see* Games.

Harmon, D., 38.

Harrington, M. R., 52.

Hauser, W. H., 228.

Hawkes, E. W., quoted, 86.

Haxthausen, A., 135, n.

Helvetius, n., 43.

Heye, G. G., n., 211.

Hind, H. Y., n., 14.

Holmburg, W., n., 45.

Hrdlicka, A., n., 132.

Hubbard, L., n., 15.

Hyde, W. W., n., 136.

Immortality, belief in, 34–35; *see* Soul.

Infant mortality, 21..

Informants, 13.

Insanity, 69.

James, E. O., n., 45.

Jayne, C. F., 228.

Jenness, D., n., 18, n., 228.

Jesuit Relations:

Albanel, C., 15.

D' Olbeau, J., 22.

Lalemant, C., 22–25.

—H., 15.

Laure, P., 15, 17.

Le Jeune, P., 15, 31.

Ménard, 15.

Nouvel, H., 15.

Sagard, G., 7, 15.

Vimont, 22.

Jochelson, W., n., 139.

Jones, W., n., 27, 73.

Kirkpatrick, C., n., 15.

Krauss, F. S., n., 136.

Kroeber, A. L., n., 134.

Laufer, B., n., 128.

Le Caron, P. J., quoted, 30.

Lenz, O., n., 135.

Low, A. P., n., 15.

Lowenthal, J., n., 15.

Lunar divisions, 66–67.

Malnutrition, 21.

Manitu´ , chap. ii, 8; definition of term, 26.

Marten, 125.

Masks, absence of image, 10.

Masson, C., n., 133.

—L. R., n., 6.

Material culture, general characteristics of, 5.

Mathews, J. J., n., 27.

Matcī'mentu´, *see* Devil.

McKenzie, J., n., 6, 17; quoted, 208.

Medicinal practices, chap. viii; weak development of, 232; *see* Sweat lodge.

Medicine societies, absence of, 10.

Mejo, myth concerning, 98–99.

Memegwe´ djo, 69.

Menstrual seclusion, 239.

Meteors, 61.

Michelson, T., 27, 182.

Mide´ win, 209.

Mirages, 60.

Monotheism, 12.

Moose: absence of development in cult of, 122; economic importance

— 255 —

of, 74; hunt, 80; place in religious
thought, 74–77.
—fly, overlord of fish, 118.
Muskrat, *see* Divination.
Mythology, general discussion, chap.
iv.

Naskapi, meaning of, 241.
Natural forces, personification of, 56–59.
Nelson, R., 152.
Nīma' ban: 210–20; use in handling
bear, 107; beaver, 116–17; hare,
123; otter, 125.

Osgood, C. B., 140.
Otter, religious observances towards,
125; *see* Dreams, Divination, Songs.

Pallas, P. S., n., 132.
Parker, E. H., n., 134.
Pervanoglu, J., n., 135.
Pinkerton, J., n., 132.
Plants: 79; spiritual nature of, 200.
Plath, J. H., n., 133.
Porpoise, 77, 78.
Prayer, lack of importance of, 56; *see*
Manitu.'
Pregnancy, absence of intercourse ta-
boo, 39.
Prshewalski, N. von, n., 132.

Radin, P. n., 12.
Radloff, W., n., 133.
Rainbow, 60.
Rattle, 177, 182.
Reincarnation, of animals, 73, 84, 85,
113; of men, 39, 44.
Revelation, belief in sunbeams as, 192–
196.
Rochette, E., n., 16.
Rockhill, W. W., n., 134.
Rose, H. J., n., 15.
Rudwin, M. J., n., 18.

Sacrifice, of meat, 79; *see* Tobacco.
Salmon, 77.

Salt: hunger for, n., 78; taboo in cook-
ing caribou meat, 78; bear meat, 102.
Scapulimancy: chap. vi; false prophecy,
156; geographical distribution, 129
et seq., 163, 164; rules for interpreta-
tion of cracks, 142 *et seq.*
Schmidt, P. W., n., 15, 242.
Seal: economic importance of, 77; food
taboo against, 78; lack of magical
importance, 77; songs addressed to,
122.
Sexual hospitality, vestige of, 92.
Shaman, 27, 70, 178.
Shea, J. D. G., n., 30.
Shklovsky, I. W., n., 139.
Shot pouches, 221–24; origin of, 222;
see Decorative art.
Skinner, A. B., 27; n., 38.
Solar eclipse, 65, 66.
Songs: bear, 185; caribou, 184–85;
dream origin of, 185; inheritance of,
185; otter, 184.
Soul: general discussion, chap. iii; clas-
sical conceptions of, 34; communica-
tions with, 187; effect of wish-power
on, 191–92; mathematical concep-
tion of, 34; migration of, 39–40;
native term for, 33, 34; star-soul
theory, 44–45; stimulation of, 43, 92,
178, 189, 200; by smoking, 226; and
art, 223–24.
—salvation, absence of, 74.
Speck, F. G., references, 5, 11, 19, 26,
31, 48, 172, 206, 211, 232.
Sprengling, M., n., 132.
Star, North, origin tale of, 62.
—, Morning, 62.
—, Evening, 62.
—, Ursa Major, origin tale of, 62–65.
String figures, 201, 227–31.
Strong, W. D., n., 31; 81, quoted, 87.
Sun, *see* Decorative Art and Revelation
—dance, 52, 85.
—dogs, 60.
Swanton, J. R., 31, n.
Sweat lodge: 220; as preparation for

— 256 —

divining, 155; explanatory myth for, 98.

Taboos: 239; on unclean food, 78; regarding the bones of animals, 123, 124; the bear, 104, 107; *see* Salt.
Tambe´ gwilnu, 68.
Tantaquidgeon, G., n., 173, 232.
Thompson, D., 18.
Thunder, 66; charm against, 238.
Tobacco: bags, 227; offering of to slain bear, 101; smoking, 225, 226; stone —pipes, 225, 226.
Toboggan, magical beliefs in connection with, 51.
Townsend, C. W., n., 14.
Transformation, 49–50.

Tsaka´ bec, as transformer, 10, 47–48.
Tuberculosis, 21.
Turner, L. M., n., 5; quoted, 207, 208.

Wallace, D., n., 15, 86.
Waugh, F. W., 50, 69; quoted, 102.
Whale, 78, 239.
White, R., Jr., 14, 219, 236, 239.
Whitney, C., n., 140.
Wi´ ndigo, 36, 37, 67–70, 149.
Wish power, 40, 191–92.
Wiske´ djak, 125, 126.
Wissler, C., 85.
Wives, 239.
Wolf, belief in giant, 83.

Zingerle, J. von, n., 136.